The Arts in Children's Lives

Context, Culture, and Curriculum

Edited by

Liora Bresler

University of Illinois at Urbana-Champaign, U.S.A.

and

Christine Marmé Thompson

The Pennsylvania State University, U.S.A.

KLUWER ACADEMIC PUBLISHERS
DORDRECHT / BOSTON / LONDON

A C.I.P. Catalogue record for this book is available from the Library of Congress.

ISBN 1-4020-0471-0 (HB)
ISBN 1-4020-0554-7 (PB)

Published by Kluwer Academic Publishers,
P.O. Box 17, 3300 AA Dordrecht, The Netherlands.

Sold and distributed in North, Central and South America
by Kluwer Academic Publishers,
101 Philip Drive, Norwell, MA 02061, U.S.A.

In all other countries, sold and distributed
by Kluwer Academic Publishers,
P.O. Box 322, 3300 AH Dordrecht, The Netherlands.

Printed on acid-free paper

Printed in the Netherlands.

TABLE OF CONTENTS

THE ARTS IN CHILDREN'S LIVES

FOREWORD

Long before children acquire a "proper" vocabulary for the arts, they know something of choreographed movement, orchestrated events, staged activities and the difference between music and incidental sound. As children sing, dance, draw, tell or dramatize stories they are engaged in mindful learning. Although it is easy to say, "The arts are caught more than taught," that assertion overlooks the countless forms of arts education that children receive from unexpected and often unnoticed sources. This anthology invites readers to think again about the purposes and origins of early childhood education in the arts. The arts under consideration include the visual, literary, and performing arts of music, drama and dance, along with television, a hybrid presence in the lives of many children. The authors examine the special experiences afforded in each of the arts as well as synergistic relationships among them

Co-editors, Liora Bresler, Christine Marme' Thompson and others who have contributed to this volume, share a passion for understanding what and how young children learn from age three to about eight. In their collaboration, the editors have selected studies that meet the analytical demands of scholarship, capture the wisdom of teaching experience and disclose a deep knowledge of particular arts. As thoughtful teachers, the authors have a deep understanding of early childhood experience as lived in-the-moment and as the source of affinities that may be elaborated over a lifetime. As artists, they also know that the arts are carriers of tradition as much as they are vehicles for creativity and imagination. As scholars, their work is informed by dialogue with children, study of their activities in varied settings and reflection on the many conundrums involved in deciding what to teach children, when and how.

A major premise of this volume is that culture and context matter at every turn in the nurture of artistic learning. This premise calls for reflection on the artistic sensibilities that parents, teachers and others may honor (or suppress) as children move from the less formal settings of home and community into more structured environments in schools. It calls for attention to the pervasive influence of artfully contrived images and products designed just for children, from *Teletubbies,* television for one and two year olds (with a line of ancillary products from Itsy Bitsy Entertainment Company) to *Sesame Street* for preschoolers, the latter from Children's Television Workshop the license-holder for over 5000 products. In remote regions of the world, children imitate dances seen on MTV, beamed in by satellite. In consumer-oriented cultures, infants as young as two and three months recognize branded toys.

No less important are the lessons embedded in the allocations of curriculum time and resources to arts education in schools and the character of the arts taught, or neglected, under its institutional authority. Children learn from the specialized "school arts" they see, hear, create, perform and are asked to respond to. Many of these arts reflect the decorative tastes of teachers and traditions of child-oriented dances, songs, poems, stories, plays and crafts. "Masterpieces" by "famous" artists are sometimes present along with the latest in popular culture. The genres are often mixed, ungoverned by any obvious educational or artistic criteria.

Further, some of the most important influences on artistic development are not routinely labeled as "art," or clearly recognized as educational in purpose. For example, I grew up in a household where drawing, painting, crafts, model making, interior redesign and architectural drafting were not unusual activities. Of these "home" arts, my teachers knew little, inquired not at all. What I learned outside of school was not seen as relevant to in-school activities or to events in a larger world of art. That is personal history, but it highlights how the artistic culture in a home and the context of family-pleasing activities can mediate the significance children attach to particular arts.

Shared contexts for learning do not, of course, ensure a shared experience. Consider, for example, my third grade classroom, by definition a communal context for learning. Even with the passage of six decades, some images remain indelible. Our classroom was graced with a three-octave pump organ for musical instruction. What remains vivid is not the music I was taught with the aid of this instrument, but that marvelous piece of furniture. It was assembled from delicate and beautifully crafted moving parts. The frame and cabinet were fashioned from wood having a fine grain resembling fluid patterns in water. I remember too, the contoured legs of the stand and bench, these ending at the floor with carved lion-like paws. In grade three, my attraction to the visual, tactile, kinetic and structural qualities of that antique surpassed my interest in learning to play it or listening to the music it made. What children register and cherish in memory can be at odds with the best intentions of their teachers.

Contributors to this anthology are attentive to subtleties in learning like these because details bring into sharp focus the networks of associative meaning that children construct as they respond to the arts and perform in the manner of artists. The studies in this book are driven by a quest for enlarged understanding of artistic learning more than a desire to prove theories. Evident here are the struggles of conscience that mark contemporary scholarship and thoughtful teaching in the arts. These artists-teachers-scholars understand that there is no mythical and universal child, developmentally programmed, who, with the "correct interventions" at the perfect moment, will unfold as an artist and appreciator of art. Their writing captures the uncertainties, ambiguities and puzzles in teaching and learning. Their recommendations comport with an ethic of "best guess at the moment," not indisputable truths. They write with uncommon clarity, empathy for children and teachers, and with a narrative flow that makes reading a pleasure.

This book reveals the surprising complexity and wonderful subtlety of early learning in the arts. It reminds us that children themselves have more savvy about the "magic" and "mystery" of the arts than adults may realize. It demonstrates the interdependence of apprehending and creating in the arts as well as the significance of aesthetic ambiences—in homes, schools and the larger culture—as these affect tastes and criteria for judging what counts as "art." It offers compelling and uncommon observations on the dilemmas and delights of teaching the arts.

If we look for metaphors to describe the process of learning in the arts, we might think of ripples from a stone dropped in water, or a seed taking root, or a network of filaments seeking connections with others. Where any given childhood arts activity begins does not predict how it may end in terms of educational significance. Whatever the metaphor, arts learning is never just about learning to make pretty pictures, cute projects, singing nice songs, doing fun dances and so on. Indeed, these bland and uninspired adjectives—pretty, cute, nice, fun—almost always reflect a poverty of thought, perception and judgment about the arts.

Within the larger enterprise of education, the arts, well taught, bring into the process of learning a host of associative possibilities that do, literally and figuratively, "make sense" to children. The challenge is to look again at the arts, not only as explicit content for study in schools, but also as paths for understanding the difference between the world as "given" and possibilities for re-envisioning and re-inventing it. I hope this anthology will inspire teachers and caregivers to examine how their affinities for the arts were nurtured by the informal and formal lessons made available to them. I hope it stimulates personal reflection and collegial dialogue about missed opportunities for learning, the clichés and stereotypes that surround the arts, and how these are perpetuated. Even more do I hope that this book inspires readers to practice artful teaching of the arts.

Finally, the studies in this volume position research itself as a creative enterprise and thus properly informed by the researcher's ideational fluency, sensitivity to nuanced flows of meaning, and skill in conveying those meanings to others. For scholars interested in qualitative research, this anthology captures the vitality of arts-centered paradigms for inquiry and their potential for enriching studies beyond the arts.

Laura H. Chapman
Cincinnati, Ohio

PRELUDE

For generations, most North American children spent their preschool years at home, particularly if those homes were middle class and graced with two parents, only one of whom worked outside the home. Preschools were of two varieties—compensatory programs for the children of the poor, or enrichment experiences for children of the privileged. In the great majority of cases, children simply stayed at home until it was time to enter kindergarten, playing with siblings or the children down the block, and relying almost exclusively on family and neighborhood to mediate between them and the culture. The music children listened and danced to, the poems and stories they learned, the images they saw on walls or in books or moving across video screens, the materials and toys available for their use, all the elements that contribute to children's artistic experiences, were selected and introduced—and, at least tacitly, endorsed—by parents. No matter how insular this situation might seem, however, it is impossible to keep all external influences at bay. As parents of children who spent their early days with Mom, Dad, Aunt, or Uncle, we remember our surprise when they began to use phrases whose source we could not readily trace or attribute. The world rushes in quickly.

The tremendous increase in children's participation in preschool education—a necessity for many families in which one or both parents are employed outside the home, a condition of contemporary life in the United States and much of the world—has expanded the life worlds of preschool children exponentially. Not only do the great majority of young children spend their days in education or care settings outside the home or in the company of paid caregivers; they spend their days increasingly in the company of other children, in a culture of their peers, absorbing rhythms and routines far different from those their parents may recall. The social changes in adult lives that have brought about these corollary changes in the lives of children have effects we have scarcely begun to recognize. As Joe Kinchloe (1998) puts it, " In the context of childhood education the post-modern experience of being a kid represents a cultural earthquake" (p. 172).

Advocates for the arts have contributed significantly to the philosophy and practice of early childhood education throughout its history. Yet the nature, value, and purpose of arts experiences in the lives of young children seem to remain puzzling and problematic to those most directly involved in teaching the very young. Conversations between scholars and teacher educators in the arts and in early childhood education occurs all too infrequently. It seems, in fact, that each group can and sometimes does forget that the other exists for generations at a time.

With the emergence of more inclusive sociocultural perspectives in education and psychology has come a recognition that young children are capable of far more than previously supposed and that the developmental process itself is far more idiosyncratic, culturally specific, and malleable, than we had thought. Recent attempts to define developmentally, or educationally, appropriate practice in early childhood education acknowledge the possibility of actively teaching young children while preserving the element of individual exploration which has been the hallmark of excellent practice in Western early childhood education throughout much of the century just past. Many early childhood theorists and practitioners continue to perceive visual arts experiences as an inviolate realm of self–expression which should be immune to adult intervention or influence, or as a temporary expedient, a developmental phenomenon that children are destined to outgrow and discard as they develop greater facility with written languages, or as purely illustrative or descriptive in function, having more to do with science that with art.

At the same time, art educators, still relatively unaccustomed to teaching preschool and kindergarten children, frequently misjudge the terms of relationship between art and children's lives, focusing on elements of form to the exclusion of issues of meaning, and forsaking opportunities to build upon children's interests as the basis for early artistic learning. Recent developments and discussions in the fields of early childhood and art education indicate that these two groups, who between them bear primary responsibility for interpreting children's artistic experiences to the culture at large, maintain divergent, even conflicting attitudes about art and children. Despite considerable activity and interest in the arts and children in both fields, we frequently find ourselves speaking at cross-purposes.

We are in a period that is particularly promising, and at the same time perilous, for the arts in early childhood education. New perspectives on children have emerged, revealing hitherto unsuspected degrees of competence and immersion in the social world. Many early childhood educators influenced by the ideas of Bruner (1990), Vygotsky (1962, 1978), Gardner (1980, 1991), and others, have been persuaded that the arts can function as symbolic languages and, as such, can be considered central to the process of early learning. When the arts are viewed as intellectual and interpretive activities, and thus more closely related to the central aims of schooling (Bresler, 1995; Thompson, 1997), substantial possibilities for integrated learning become apparent. Simultaneously, the true complexity and intrinsic virtues of each art form seem to become increasingly well–defined.

The purpose of this anthology is to generate renewed dialogue on the role and the significance of the arts in the education of children from age 3 through age 8, at a time when such dialogue is likely to evoke substantial interest among arts educators and early childhood specialists alike. Sixteen authors whose work represents the best of contemporary research and theory on a constellation of issues concerning the role of the arts in young children's lives and learning contributed to this volume.

Exemplary early childhood programs emerge and prosper in many parts of the world, and interest in learning from the childcare and educational practices of others is high within the field of early childhood education. Many of the most innovative practices, which tend to attract the attention of researchers and teachers worldwide, are the result of a complex interweaving of circumstance, custom, deeply ingrained cultural assumptions and practices. Yet, as the world becomes increasingly accessible to each of us, the possibilities of appropriating and adapting the best of others' practices become increasingly real. The significance of the fact that our ways of parenting, teaching, and understanding of young children are inevitably filtered through a series of personal and cultural lenses cannot be overestimated. The more familiar we become with the ways in which similar incidents can be viewed from different frames of reference, the more fully we understand that even the most basic things that children learn are socially and culturally mediated.

The book is organized in three sections:

1. Context. The settings in which children's earliest experiences with the arts occur inevitably shape those experiences and to a great extent determine what children will learn from them. Chapters describing the cultural contexts of early arts experiences amplify the cultural perspective maintained throughout the book, as authors from several cultures discuss how a particular art form and its practices are transmitted, valued, and perpetuated in the countries and communities which they have studied most extensively. Chapters describe the ways in which children's experience is mediated by the immediate culture of the schools they attend, the micro and meso levels, as well as by the culture at large.
2. Development. The process through which children's abilities to participate in particular art forms evolves has served as the foundation of arts education practice in early childhood years. Contemporary interest in the relationships between development and learning, and in development itself as a socially mediated process, influence interpretations of the nature of development and its centrality to early education. Chapters on development review established knowledge within a particular field, explore recent reconceptualizations of the relationships between development and learning, and offer promising directions for research and teaching.
3. Curriculum. The identification of arts experiences that are both artistically authentic and developmentally appropriate is a primary concern for early arts education. The tendency to sacrifice one goal for the sake of the other has been responsible for much mutual discontent between early childhood educators and arts specialists. These chapters describe exemplary approaches to conceiving and presenting art experiences that resonate with the "human sense" (Donaldson, 1978) that young children require and enhance their abilities to participate in the arts as creators, participants, and beholders.

Historically attempts to subsume all the arts in discussions of their educational integrity and prospects were motivated more strongly by political expediency than by philosophical conviction. In the United States, "arts" projects tended to attract federal funding more readily than similar undertakings, which involved only one art form. A few pedagogical texts which appeared in the 'sixties and early 'seventies (Dimondstein, 1974, e.g.) presented a search for deeper similarities of intention or structure, or presented experiences in the arts as exemplars of experiential learning. For the most part, however, the legitimacy of the notion that the arts can be grouped for educational purposes has remained largely unexamined.

Recently formulated National Standards for Arts Education (Consortium of National Arts Education Associations, 1994) recognize that the ties that bind the arts are deep and fundamental, having to do with the broad purposes and functions of creation, performance, and reception of art forms. But in the schools and beyond, each field has its distinctive concerns, its own ways and means. The four art forms typically recognized in such discussions—dance, music, drama, and visual arts—have unique histories, purposes, and pedagogies in schools and preschools throughout the world. Interactions among arts educators are rare, often short–lived, initiated and pursued at the local level. This volume is an opportunity for arts educators to learn from one another, and an occasion in which similarities among the concerns and convictions that preoccupy educators in each art discipline may be considered for their relevance to others' situations. The inclusion of literature as a fifth art form which children encounter in schools provides an additional opportunity to compare and contrast methodologies and meanings, and perhaps to discover new possibilities for thought and practice that can be adapted for use in other disciplines.

REFERENCES

Bresler, L. (1995). The case of the Easter bunny: In C. M. Thompson (Ed.) *The visual arts and early childhood learning* (pp. –). Reston, VA: National Art Education Association.

Bruner, J. S. (1990). *Acts of meaning*. Cambridge, MA: Harvard University Press. Consortium of National Arts Education Associations (1994). *National standards for arts education*. Reston, VA: Music Educators National Conference.

Dimondstein, G. (1974). *Exploring the arts with children*. New York: Macmillan.

Donaldson, M. (1978). *Children's minds*. New York: W. W. Norton.

Gardner, H. (1980). *Artful scribbles*. New York: Basic Books.

Gardner, H. (1991). *The unschooled mind: How children think and how schools should teach*. New York: Basic Books.

Kincheloe, J. L. (1998). The new childhood: Home alone as a way of life. In H. Jenkins (ed.), *The children's culture reader* (pp. 159–177). New York: New York University Press.

Thompson, C. M. (1997). Teaching art in elementary schools: Shared responsibilities and distinctive roles. *Arts Education Policy Review*, 99(2), 15–21.

Vygotsky, L. S. (1962). *Thought and language* (E. Hanfmann & G. Vakar, trans. & ed.). Cambridge, MA: M. I. T. Press.

Vygotsky, L. S. (1978). *Mind in society*. Cambridge, MA: Harvard University Press.

Context Interlude

As Martin Buber (1965) wisely observed, *everything* educates: Everything children encounter—"nature and the social context, the house and the street, language and custom, the world of history and the world of daily news in the form of rumour, of broadcast and newspaper, music and technical science, play and dream—everything together" (p. 106)—makes an impression that gives form to their experience. The teacher is "only one element amidst the fullness of life" (p. 106), but distinguished from all others by the **intention** to influence children through her teaching, and by the **consciousness** of the special relationship which allows her to do so, more directly, thoughtfully, and systematically than the remorselessly streaming education by all things.

In the years since Buber wrote his classic essays on education, we have become increasingly sensitive to the many influences that operate even early in children's lives, and the undeniable impact that family, community, media, and culture exert even in the nursery school.

Donaldson, Grieve and Pratt (1983) acknowledge that the early childhood years have always been a critical period in children's construction of social selves, with significant consequence for self–concept:

> It is during this time that children enter the social world beyond the family and establish themselves, more or less easily and successfully, as members of a community of their peers. . . .By the time this period is over, children will have formed conceptions of themselves as social beings, as thinkers, and as language–users, and they will have reached certain important decisions about their own ability and their own worth. This places a very special responsibility on those involved in the teaching of young children during this period, either at preschool or at school. (p. 1)

The meaning of any form of art or arts instruction is inseparable from the contexts and conditions under which it is generated and experienced (Bresler, 1998). Contexts affect both *what* is taught and *how* it is taught, shaping explicit and implicit messages and values. This section focuses on the macro contexts, including the larger culture, its customs and cherishing, out of school with their distinct structures and opportunities. In trying to highlight some of the compelling aspects of various cultures, we include dance and music in Namibia's indigenous culture, the all–pervasive Japanese manga, as well as Native American, and Iranian musics.

The contexts in which children now encounter the arts, in which they begin to acquire the symbolic languages used by their culture to embody, explore and communicate meanings, tend to be social and school–like in many respects. Teachers who work with children in these settings cannot help but be aware that their students, even at age 3, come to them with lives already in progress, with histories, experiences, preferences, opinions based upon songs learned from favorite television shows or older relatives, dance moves perfected in sessions with preadolescent siblings or babysitters, theatrical performances improvised in bedrooms and backyards, and a visual aesthetic honed on illustrations in children's books and parental decisions about home decor.

L. Bresler and C.M. Thompson (eds.), The Arts in Children's Lives, 9–13.
© 2002 *Kluwer Academic Publishers. Printed in the Netherlands.*

These experiences and the preferences they foster may be liberal or conservative. In either case, they provide a context in which teaching, conscious and willed, begins and proceeds.

The authors in this section come from different disciplines and orientations, but together they define a basic task for teachers and researchers in recognizing the validity and acknowledging the appeal of art forms and practices that originate in cultural contexts beyond the school. As Daniel Walsh and Liora Bresler suggest, we must maintain a critical stance toward "arts for children"—arts created especially for the consumption of children—just as we must remain wary of the elitism that can result from an insistence that only exemplars of "high art" are worthy of children's time and attention. Other authors pose related and equally significant questions: In what ways are children's experiences expanded, modified, shaped, constrained or directed by the number and nature of artistic cultures with which they are familiar? What is the teacher's role in formal and informal settings mediating between the child and the cultures and subcultures which insinuate lessons of their own? How should we respond to the inevitable variety and the inexorable change that is part of human experience as we teach young children?

The question of influence, as Lark–Horovitz, Lewis, and Luca (1973) imply in their brief but potent description of four types of child art, is not whether adults influence children's artistic activity, but rather how much and in what way, and with what impact on the authenticity of the child's experience (Beittel, 1973).

The "school art style" has been discussed frequently in the literature of art education since Arthur Efland named the phenomenon in his landmark article of 1973 (see, for example, Anderson & Milbrandt, 1998; Bresler, 1994, 1999; Greenberg, 1996; Pariser, 1981; Smith, 1995). Karen Hamblen enters that dialogue as she considers the multiple ways that contemporary children and adults encounter and experience the visual arts in various art contexts. She observes the clear discrepancies that exist between the knowledge, values, and attitudes promoted in each context. The professional community, in which artists create and exhibit their work, and participate with others in ongoing critical dialogues, presents a version of art that is very different from the one represented in school art classes. In their everyday lives outside of school, children know still another kind of art, the more informal type of "local art" that thrives in the spontaneous work of children and of adults who have not been educated in professional art schools nor initiated into prevailing professional practices and theories.

Hamblen's focus in this chapter is fixed on the nature of school art and the problems it presents. She is especially concerned, as were Efland (1973) and Bresler (1994), that what is taught and learned in the name of art is so frequently unrelated to the more enduring forms of art practiced in nonschool settings. Hamblen's analysis of this situation is provocative and challenging, illuminating problems unique to art education as well as those which beleaguer all school subjects. She suggests that the type of informal learning that is characteristic of local contexts and traditional cultures—learning that is exploratory, concrete, experiential, and specific to individuals and situations—is honored in many preschool and kindergarten settings as young children's natural way of coming to know the world. The challenge she presents to art educators at all levels is to preserve the unified approach to art making that is practiced in the best of early childhood education. She urges us to recognize, honor, and incorporate the forms of art learning that characterize professional and, especially, local art contexts, to value what children can do and already do in their spontaneous art making, in order to facilitate their passage from one artistic context to the next.

Bruno Nettl expands this conversation, by introducing a perspective from the discipline of ethnomusicology. Ethnomusicologists as a professional group, writes Nettl, are interested in discovering the ways music is taught in the world's cultures, and in learning how musical systems are taught and transmitted through the generations. Ethnomusicologists based in the west are usually also, naturally, interested in the way the world's musics are taught in American and European systems of primary and secondary education. Nettl's chapter discusses the ways these two areas of endeavor can inform one another.

One important issue in Nettl's chapter is the politics of representation. School music focuses mostly on "classical music," and "music for children" (Bresler, 1998). What effect, asks Nettl, does this taken–for–granted structuring have on our presentation of world music? In his discussions with musicians in Iran about how they would wish to be represented in American music education, there was no question: by the classical repertory and performance practice. Folk music of the villages is of interest largely because it nurtured the classical—a viewpoint similar to that held by many European musicians a few decades ago. It was the classical music that integrated and also distinguished Persian culture. No one ever mentioned popular music; it was the music that least conformed to the Islamic traditions about music, that mixed the musics of the world with those of Iran in undesirable ways. Still, people clearly loved the popular music. Nettl's chapter highlights the paradox stemming from the notion that the world of music is a group of musics, or that music is a universal language, to a recognition that it's all more complex.

If Nettl addresses the tension between the classical, folk and the popular and their representation in schooling, Brent Wilson focuses on the pervasive influence of visual media and popular culture on children's drawings. This is done through a study of the graphic models available to Japanese children through *manga*, the visual narratives in comic book form that permeate Japanese culture. The *manga* style and format have been adopted in a wide variety of Japanese publications, from educational materials to advertisements to news reports to pornography. Wilson describes unique, *manga*–derived characteristics of Japanese children's drawings and reflects on the ways in which the graphic models children select and emulate shape and mirror their perceptions of self and society. He probes the collusion between commercial interests and children as consumers in the construction of national identity. As an outsider considering the extent to which voluntary drawings by contemporary Japanese children differ from what teachers and researchers in the West have come to regard as typical of children's work, Wilson provides a focused case study of the process of learning to draw within a culture where appealing and attainable graphic models abound. The phenomenon that Wilson considers is peculiarly Japanese, but at the same time it is symptomatic of a process of emulation in which all children particpate as they acquire facility with the tools and symbol systems that constitute the basic vocabularies of the arts in their own time and place.

In the next chapter, Minette Mans examines the context of indigenous dance and music in informal educational settings, exploring how young Namibian children engage with dance and music. What and when do children perform and play? How are they educated in the performing arts? Mans portrays informal, community–based arts education in Namibia. She then examines the principles on which arts education in schools are based, focusing on dance and music. In a discussion of context, it is important to remember that the "same" terms can have different meanings in different cultures. The term music, for example, must be understood in an African framework where dance and music tend to be holistically integrated and often inclusive of costume, ritual, and stories framed within a particular cosmology.

The context and its relationship with musical materials together create the fundamental cognitive and affective structure of musical learning, a complex structure which can be called the child's musical world. Music is something children do and it is always informed by the social context or culture from which the child emerges. Music and dance involve the reciprocal influence of the child and his/her social context. The construction of 'musical world' of a particular culture takes place over a period of time and is embedded in their cosmology. Therefore this musical world reflects existing cultural values and beliefs, while also allowing for the active (re–)construction and change of peoples' values, beliefs and thereby their cultures. Children quickly learn that there is music for everyday and for special occasions. They discover there is music for children, adults, elderly, males, females, commoners, specialists and royalty. Thus groups of people have constructed their musical world or models according to their ways of life, systems of production, values and beliefs—they have enculturated their social system. A musical world includes a background or field of all the music of their culture (songs and their structures, instrumental pieces, instruments used, dances and their structures), as well as all the rules (play frame) guiding the practice of the music.

Patricia Campbell's discussion of the interplay between formal and informal learning in children's acquisition of musical cultures continues this theme. Campbell suggests that children must be recognized as an encompassing folk group, a "super–culture" in the words of Mark Slobin (1993), who share and perpetuate common traditions in language, values, and behavioral patterns. Each member of the culture of childhood is also, as Campbell reminds us, affiliated with other, more exclusive subcultures, defined by age, stage of development, type of schooling, national origin, family group, similarity of experience and so on. Each of these subcultures has its own, constantly evolving, musical traditions, preferences, and practices. Thus, even the youngest child approaches formal music education with expectations and habits born of the process of musical enculturation which has been in progress from earliest infancy.

Describing the functions music serves for young children, and the various ways in which the cultures to which children belong contribute to children's intuitive understanding of music and its uses in their lives, Campbell addresses the terms of the relationship between enculturation and education. Recognizing that school music, like school art, is shaped and constrained by the structures of schooling, by state mandates, and by teachers' professional cultures, Campbell concedes that musical education provides learning that is more narrow than the learning that occurs through the process of enculturation. If it is more narrow, however, school music may also be more focused and selective, less diffuse, and easier to grasp. Campbell argues that both music educators and classroom teachers have essential contributions to make to music education, for it is teachers who consciously and intentionally select what aspects of music will be presented to children, at what time, and in what context. She urges teachers to regard children's experiences with musical cultures outside of school—the experiences children acquire living in a particular time, place, and situation—as the foundation upon which early music education should be constructed.

The decisive impact of the various contexts in which children develop and learn, the influence of family, neighborhood, school, community and culture on the experiences children have and the meanings they construct, is the focus of the five chapters that follow. Each author addresses the issue of context in terms of its relevance to learning in a particular art form—the visual arts for Karen Hamblen and Brent Wilson, music for Bruno Nettl and Patricia Campbell, dance/music for Minette Mans. Yet, as different as the perspectives and traditions of each field may sometimes seem, these chapters remind us of the deep resonance that exists among art educators concerned with young children, the shared concerns and the common problems which are addressed in distinctive ways, sometimes in ways unheard of in other disciplines. Writing of issues unique to their particular fields, these authors remind us of how much we can learn from one another.

REFERENCES

Anderson, T. & Milbrandt, M. (1998). Authentic instruction in art: Why and how to dump the school art style. *Visual Arts Research, 24*(2), 13–20.

Beittel, K. R. (1973). *Alternatives for art education research: Inquiry into the making of art.* Dubuque, IA: Wm. C. Brown.

Bresler, L. (1994). Imitative, complementary, and expansive: Three roles of visual arts curricula. *Studies in Art Education, 35*(2), 90–104.

Bresler, L. (1998). The genre of school music, its shaping by meso, micro and macro contexts. *Research Studies in Music Education,* 11, 2–18.

Bresler, L. (1999).The hybridization and homogenization of school art: Institutional contexts for elementary art students. *Visual Arts Research, 25*(2), 25-37.

Buber, M. (1965). *Between man and man.* New York: Macmillan.

Donaldson, M., Grieve, R. & Pratt, C. (Eds.) (1983). *Early childhood development and education (Readings in psychology).* Oxford: Basil Blackwell.

Efland, A. (1973). The school art style: A functional analysis. *Studies in Art Education, 17*(2), 37–44

Greenberg, P. (1996). Time, money, and the new art education versus art and irrelevance. *Studies in Art Education,* 37(2), 115–116.

Lark–Horovitz, B., Lewis, H. & Luca, M. (1973). *Understanding children's art for better teaching* (2nd ed.). Columbus, OH: Charles E. Merrill.

Pariser, D. (1981). Linear lessons in a centrifugal environment: Sketch of an art teaching experience. *Review of Research in Visual Arts Education, 13,* 81–90.

Slobin, M. (1993). *Subcultural sounds: Micromusics of the west.* Hanover: University of New England for Wesleyan University Press.

Smith, P. (1995). Commentary: Art and irrelevance. *Studies in Art Education, 36*(2), 123–125.

KAREN A. HAMBLEN

1. CHILDREN'S CONTEXTUAL ART KNOWLEDGE: LOCAL ART AND SCHOOL ART CONTEXT COMPARISONS

After a series of classroom lessons on linear perspective, a student is unable to render this type of perspective in drawings done in the natural environment. A graduate student prepares an exhibition of art work for review, but she does not include drawings that she works on during her spare time. A natural history museum exhibition of fishing equipment and related art forms draws record crowds of people from a wide range of occupational backgrounds; an exhibition of abstract art at an art museum is attended primarily by art professionals and students.

These familiar occurrences illustrate discrepancies among differing art contexts, each of which relies upon and perpetuates specific types of art knowledge, skills, behaviors, and attitudes. For example, there are various knowledge bases and assumptions from which classroom art instruction can proceed. Left to their own devices, young children commonly copy sophisticated artistic conventions of cartoon characters but in school settings, they produce work that conforms to the expectations of child art developmental levels (Wilson, 1974, 1985; Wilson & Wilson, 1977). In the history of art education, one can identify child psychology, the aesthetics of fine art culture, modern industrial principles, and formalistic art values as contributing toward some of our art education theories and practices (Logan, 1955). These and other constellations of meaning and value have constituted formalized, school art.

School art is often discussed as differing from other subject areas in that studio art lessons involve the concrete manipulation of materials and the direct experience of visual qualities. It seems that art instruction does not deal with abstract concepts and rules to the extent most school subjects do. In a relative sense, this might be so. However, when *art* contexts are compared, school art can be seen as rulebound and as offering few occasions for transfer to the interactions of individuals in other art contexts. In this chapter I propose that a great deal of formal art instruction in grades K–12 may consist of highly specific, if not false, models of art learning that ill–prepare children for participation in either professional art worlds or informal, local art experiences.

To provide the rationale for rethinking school art practices in terms of differing art contexts and of children's nonschool art expressions, I will discuss the following: (a) assumptions of transfer in general education and art education; (b) characteristics of school art, local art, and professional art contexts; (c) models of institutional and informal learning contexts; (d) research on local knowledge; and (e) areas of nontransfer between school art and the local art of children.

L. Bresler and C.M. Thompson (eds.), The Arts in Children's Lives, 15–27.
© 2002 *Kluwer Academic Publishers. Printed in the Netherlands.*

PERSPECTIVES ON CONTEXTS OF KNOWLEDGE

Knowledge, attitudes, and behaviors, as they are appropriate to specific learning contexts, have been variously discussed as school culture, child culture, situational learning, situated knowledge, contextual knowledge, local knowledge, everyday knowledge, subcultures of learning, formal and informal learning, school subject domains, and so on. For research in general education, as reviewed by Perkins and Salomon (1989), context is most often limited to school domains or what is more commonly known as school subjects, wherein the concern is with the character of school instructional contexts and with whether there is any transfer *among* school domains. In particular, Perkins and Salomon (1989) explored the research and theoretical basis for teaching generalized cognitive skills as opposed to teaching domain–specific cognitive skills.

In most research, the question of whether cognitive skills transfer to other contexts is limited to whether transfer occurs *within* formal school learning contexts. For example, problem solving and analysis as general cognitive skills are often taught with the belief that they will be utilized in math, science, and other classes. However, the case can be made that problem solving and analysis can differ in kind from one subject domain to another–and even differ within a domain. For example, after nonart majors had completed a series of successful drawings from live models, it was found that these students were unable to incorporate learned drawing skills to other models and other drawing lessons (Wilson, 1974; Wilson & Wilson, 1977). This lead Wilson to suggest that for students not talented in art there may be limited transfer even among highly similar activities within the school art curriculum and that students may learn to draw *particular* subjects or objects rather than learn drawing skills per se.

Issues of transfer, domain–specific cognition, and general cognition have become embroiled in the wide–ranging and often media–oriented debate involving the merits of teaching cognitive processes as opposed to teaching the content of subject domains along with their domain–specific cognitive skills (Eisner, 1997, 1998; Hamblen, 1993b). Colleges of education and programs for teacher preparation have come under attack for focusing on methods of teaching to the detriment of subject content (Holmes Group Executive Board, 1986). Proponents of cultural literacy identify the knowledge of Western traditions as constituting a particular, desired content for curricula (Bloom, 1987; Hirsch, 1987). While head of the National Endowment for the Humanities, Cheney (1987) faulted education for teaching thinking skills without attention to information on literature, historic events, philosophies, etc. Cheney suggested that teaching thinking processes is specious unless there is substantive content about which to think. The back–to–basics thrust of current reform poses questions not only about whether there is transfer across subject domains but even whether cognitive processes should be the core of emphasis in any subject domain.

OCCASIONS FOR TRANSFER

In studio–based and child–centered art instruction, art educators have been particularly fond of emphasizing the benefits of process over product and the many possibilities of cognitive and attitude transfer. Some art educators have claimed that art study involves the general thinking skills and behaviors of creativity, problem identification, problem solving, tolerance for conceptual ambiguity, etc. (see Eisner in Getty, 1985), and that these will transfer and translate into an increase in mathematics test scores, a rise in reading levels, job–related skills, and a generalized creative attitude toward life (The Arts, Education and American Panel, 1977; Boston, 1996). According to Eisner (1997, 1998), many of these claims have their basis in the desire to secure art's place in the core curriculum. Unfortunately, these claims also tend to obscure or call into question the actual, research–validated benefits of art study (also see Hamblen, 1993b; Winner & Hetland, 2000).

Since the turn of the twentieth century, there have also been various claims that art instruction will result in moral behavior, psychological well–being, and life–enhancing insights unavailable from other types of study. Although such optimistic claims have a tenuous basis in research (Hamblen, 1993b; Lanier, 1970, 1975; Winner & Hetland, 2000), they do indicate that the issue of transfer goes well beyond the school contexts that have been the usual concern in general education (Perkins & Salomon, 1989)

Transfer has been discussed in terms of specific skills, knowledge, strategies, attitudes, and values. Broudy (1982) studied the everyday uses of schooling in terms of replication (recall), association, application, and interpretation. Relevant to this paper, there are four occasions for transfer: (a) within a particular school domain; (b) among school domains; (c) between a school domain and everyday contexts in general; and (d) between a school domain and the local, everyday context of that domain.

Relatively little research has been devoted to how school–based knowledge and skills translate into nonschool settings or vice versa. For example, children's developmental levels are often discussed as something to overcome or as deficiencies, e.g., a child is described as unable to draw objects perpendicular to a baseline, a child seems unaware that human figures have jointed limbs (Hamblen, 1993 a). Art education research has tended to focus on school learning as preferable, with nonschool art knowledge and responses considered "unschooled"; i.e., criteria for success is set up in terms of school art learning (Hardiman, 1971). In a tautology of school learning and school success, student assessments are based on how well students perform on tasks learned in school and utilized in the school context. Except for correlating occupational success with school learning, there is little follow–up research on how specific school–learning "items" are utilized outside the school context (Rogoff & Lave, 1984) and more specifically, how domain–specific learning, such as art, transfers to other art contexts. Some studies of everyday, out–of– school cognition suggest that not only is much learning and application context–specific but that transfer of some skills and knowledge from school (a) does not occur or (b) is not considered useful for any of the events that occur in nonschool settings (Rogoff & Lave, 1984). Employers note the absence of basic work skills among entry–level employees, and school–aged children have long protested the irrelevance of what they are required to learn in school.

The concern in this paper is not with business and industry's complaints that schools should provide on–the–job training in both basic and job–specific skills. Such complaints are based more on seeing the schools as conduits for business and industry, and on students not learning basic reading, writing, and computational skills. (For a highly publicized and widely distributed polemic on how art learning may support business and industry–related job requirements, see the Getty Education Institute for the Arts' publication, *Education for the Workplace through the Arts* [Boston, 1996]). Rather, the concern in this paper is that what is *actually learned* in formal institutions may not transfer to or have relevance in other *domain– related* contexts. Students entering professional art training are often asked to unlearn or ignore what they have acquired in their K– 12 art training; art students in K– 12 art classes must often censor images from the popular arts and their fantasies (Michael, 1983; Smith, 1989; Wilson, 1974; Wilson & Wilson, 1977). In describing traditional studio–based art instruction, Efland (1976) bluntly stated that such art "doesn't exist anywhere else except in schools" (p. 38). Unless such school art incorporates *principles* applicable to other art contexts, children may be losing contact with their own art worlds as well as access to the art of professionals.

THREE ART CONTEXTS

Ultimately, all of education is concerned with how well students will be able to apply what is learned in school to everyday living and to the skills required in particular professions or vocations. In this sense, there are three basic learning settings: (a) professional communities, (b) school contexts, and (c) the local context of everyday life experiences. Art that is made and/or responded to in these three contexts will be referred to in this paper as *professional art, school art* and *local art*. Although reference will be made to disjunctures among the three contexts, the focus will be on differences between school art contexts and the local art contexts of children.

Professional art is the art of galleries, museums, academic settings, and commercial art businesses in which socially designated art experts exercise the behaviors, skills, and attitudes of institutional art knowledge. *School art* is formalized art instruction that occurs in K–12 classrooms. The training of artists at professional art schools and at universities is not being included in this discussion; such formal learning contexts have more kinship with professional art contexts than with the school art of grades K–12. *Local art* is the art of everyday experiences, wherein art responses and production are learned through informal processes. This is the art one meets as one goes about the business of life. Popular, commercial, environmental, etc., arts may be produced as part of professional contexts but experienced as local art. Domestic art, folk art, child art, the hidden stream art of the homeless, and other similar types are created in and may always, remain in the context of local, everyday experiences.

The three art contexts identified have fluid boundaries and are themselves composed of many subcontexts (Becker, 1982). For example, local, everyday art consists of popular, commercial, folk, environment, and child art as well as communal and individual expressions and responses to art. These art forms can also be found within professional contexts of experience, but they would probably be understood and responded to differently there.

CONTEXT MODELS

Brown (1989) and Feldman (1980) developed theoretical models of how societies develop different learning contexts and how individuals create, experience, and give meaning to those contexts. Brown examined three cultures of learning which are highly similar to the three art contexts discussed in this paper. According to Brown, learning occurs in the cultures of (a) experts, (b) students, and (c) "just plain folks". Each of these learning cultures has different goals, focuses of action, and cognitive processes. The culture of experts is goal focused, and action is based on (more–or–less) professionally agreed–upon values and assumptions. The culture of students is characterized by individual cognition, an emphasis on abstract thought, abstract symbol manipulation, explicit rules, and context–free abstractions and generalities. These are the learning characteristics of modem industrialized societies that are based on patriarchal, hierarchical systems of organization. In contrast, learning in the local contexts of "just plain folks" tends to be collaborative, involve the manipulation of concrete materials, and be experiential and situation–specific. These are characteristic of the actions of pre–K children and youngsters before they internalize the demands of school contexts. These are also the learning characteristics often attributed to nonindustrialized, traditional cultures based on matriarchal systems of organization.

In much the way individuals learn varying forms of etiquette for different social settings, individuals experience and learn socially sanctioned forms of knowledge in different learning contexts–and responses vary accordingly. How a particular phenomenon, such as art, is experienced and understood in highly divergent but co–existing contexts is suggested by Feldman's (1980) developmental model of subject domains. According to Feldman, development does not occur within the cognition of the individual. Rather, development exists within the way a particular domain is experienced in different contexts. In other words, development is socially situated, which may explain why children exhibit different developmental levels within school from what they seem to be capable of doing outside the school context. At times, learning may involve figuring out what is appropriate, not what one is literally capable of doing.

Feldman proposed a continuum of five contexts for domain development: the universal, the cultural, the disciplinary, the idiosyncratic, and the unique. These contexts extend from what humans universally experience, such as the acquisition of a verbal language, to what is considered professionally unique, such as the creation of a new form of poetic verse.

Applied to art, Feldman's model accounts for the universal production of graphic symbols by children and for the universal presence of art throughout time and space. From the universal, art expression and response move to the learned experiences of art in cultural context. Everyday art experiences and visual forms of communication constitute particular, culturally sanctioned forms of art. Specific study of art in the formal contexts of school results in understanding art as a *discipline* or body of knowledge and skills. The development of an individual artistic system is *idiosyncratic* to the discipline. Innovations which might change the discipline, and, perhaps, eventually become everyday cultural experiences of art, are considered *unique* to the subject domain. For example, Pollock's abstract expressionist style would qualify as a unique contribution which has had a great impact on the idiosyncratic behaviors of other artists and on the disciplinary knowledge of art However, abstract expressionism remains alien to the everyday cultural experiences of most citizens. Proponents of a Western–based cultural literacy would move a disciplinary knowledge of art to the status of a cultural norm, so that, for example, abstract expressionism and the rest of Pollock's work would be understood and appreciated as part of ongoing, broad–based cultural experiences.

Of course, not all citizens experience everyday culture in a similar manner. Some individuals do have an everyday, cultural appreciation of abstract expressionism. Educational background, personal interests, and class distinctions become evident in the distribution of different types of knowledge and different aesthetics. In this sense, each of Feldman's contexts is composed of subcontexts. It is beyond the scope of this paper to discuss the manner in which art knowledge within and between contexts is given social legitimation as well as how it is often distributed along class lines. However, it may be significant that fine art traditions within the discipline of art are often considered essential to the education of gifted children and children in private schools. The preference given to professional art contexts, the sometimes inconsequential outcomes of school art contexts, and the ignoring of local art contexts constitutes a continuum that ranges from social legitimation to benign neglect to delegitimation.

RESEARCH ON LOCAL COGNITION

Some studies suggest that types of learning are specific to their context because differing contexts require different problem–solving strategies (Perkins & Salomon, 1989). Lave, Murtaugh, and de la Rocha (1984) discuss learning strategies in terms of "closing the gap" between problem and solution. Applications within the school context or transfer of school learning to nonschool contexts involve the recognition of problems in relationship to similar, appropriate rule–bound strategies.

Ways in which mathematical portions are calculated in everyday contexts suggest that the formalized inversions and multiplications of fractions may be specific to school instruction. Local contexts allow for opportunistic solutions, as indicated by the often–cited example of the person in a Weight Watchers Program who needed to calculate 3/4 of 2/3 cup of cottage cheese. Given 2/3 of a cup of cottage cheese this individual merely patted the cottage cheese into a circle, divided the circle into quarters, and eliminated one of the quarters, thereby having 3/4 cup remaining (Lave, Murtaugh, & de la Rocha, 1984). In much the same way, young children in art will use concrete and opportunistic manipulations to solve visual problems, e.g., drawings that incorporate multiple perspectives, that utilize x–ray views, and that show action over time—if a complete picture is desired

A study of grocery shopping strategies to calculate price comparisons suggested that ways to "close the gap" between problems and solution are specific to this everyday activity (Lave, Murtaugh, & de la Rocha, 1984). In selecting the least costly products during grocery shopping, mathematical computations were carried out with 98% accuracy. In similar school test examples, responses were 59% accurate. Accuracy in grocery shopping was unrelated to years of schooling, although accuracy on the pencil–and–paper test was related to educational background. This research relates to the folklore of the absent–minded professor, of the student who excels at being a student, of the single–minded expert, and other instances in which "book learning" remains relevant only within the world of academia or a narrow range of professional expertise.

School contexts provide the learning of rules and deductive strategies, whereas everyday problem–solving is context–specific and opportunistic. According to Lave, Murtaugh, and de la Rocha (1984), problem solving in everyday, local contexts is practical and concrete, with efficiency the primary criterion for a selected strategy. Everyday instances of "closing the gap" between mathematical problems and solutions involve estimating, rounding numbers up or down, and using whatever conceptual or physical tools the context provides, such as counting on one's fingers or verbal counting. Contextualized mnemonic devices and talking to one's self or fellow shoppers were strategies used by the grocery shoppers–strategies that would be inappropriate in school settings. In early child art, the schematic stage in drawing is characterized by a baseline and a line of sky across the top of the paper (which I fondly call the "sandwich stage"); this stage provides one of the most efficient formats for conveying visual information. Houses, families, pets, flowers–and the ubiquitous sun–can be filled in between sky and earth, and if there is no more room, the child may merely verbally describe other objects and actions that are part of the scene. These are pictorial problem–solving strategies that are discouraged within sequenced programs of art study or are considered something to be overcome through instruction.

The above examples suggest that strategies to infer meaning or to solve problems can differ in nonschool and school contexts. Other studies suggest that learning remains specific to context because what is learned in one context is without meaning or application in another (Rogoff & Lave, 1984). It is not that what is learned in one context becomes nonsense in another, but rather that it may make "no–sense" to utilize it. One might suggest that many school art lessons, such as the construction of color wheels, value charts, dried–pea mosaics, and fish mobiles, have limited application to local experiences of art. This may, in part, be due to the limited school experience students have with particular art concepts and a lack of practice in making linkages to art content in other contexts. Reform in art education in the 1990s focused on between and within grade sequential learning of art knowledge and techniques (Greer, 1984, 1993). However, this type of logical, internal linkage has often resulted in textbook curricula that emphasize the formal qualities of art (McReynolds, 1990) and that give limited options for exploring any one type of concept. Color wheels, for example, from grade 1 through grade 6, are most often presented in the triadic system without information indicating that this is but one way in which to study pigment mixing relationships (Burton, 1984; Chapman, 1994). In this paper it is proposed that transfer between school art contexts and local art contexts may be limited both because each has differing problem–solving strategies and there is little possibility of transfer between contexts.

School Art Characteristics

Although there are in actuality many school art contexts and even more local art contexts, researchers have noted basic characteristics of each. According to Efland (1976), "school art is an institutional art style in its own right" (p. 38). It is "conventional, ritualistic, and rule– governed" (p. 38). Media, themes and products are predictable; art products have a look that is recognizable and appropriate for bulletin board display and exhibition at parent night gatherings. The school art style is individualized, irregular, and visually pleasing; it involves "filling the space, using clean colors, spontaneous brush strokes, looseness as opposed to tightness" (Efland, 1976, p. 523). Such rule–bound school art emanates from a child–centered philosophy of instruction wherein individualism, creativity, and free expression are ostensibly valued.

School art activities are no less predictable in the classroom in which technical skills and art content consisting of formal qualities are emphasized, i.e., in classrooms which follow a subject–centered philosophy of instruction. Exercises dealing with color wheels, value charts, repeat designs, shading techniques, ways to show perspective, skill in various media techniques, etc., can result in technically impressive art products. Assumptions that the content of art resides in its material substance and formal qualities have a long and embedded history in formalist art theory and modernist values, and many published curricula are structured along formalist principles (Chapman, 1994; McReynolds, 1990). Although Bruner's (1960) idea that curriculum should be structured according to the activities of professionals has appeared in much art education literature, many art activities are idealizations that are a far cry from how professional artists organize their time, complete art work, and develop new ideas. In the art classroom, creativity must be expressed in specific time increments (1 hour or less), noise must be kept to a minimum, work produced must not be messy, the clean–up of used materials must be accomplished in approximately five minutes, work spaces are depersonalized, and the products produced must be easily stored.

Local Art Characteristics

Wilson (1974, 1985) has documented the themes and artistic strategies of children drawing in nonschool settings. Sexual fantasies, scatological images, and cartoon figures are common in children's nonschool art. Duncum (1989) has also recorded the depiction of violence and "gross" subjects which, needless to say, are usually forbidden in school art contexts. Much school art is taught to *overcome* art learning from other contexts and, in particular, the local contexts of the popular culture and of personally based learning. In local contexts, children will draw on lined paper, scrap paper, their own bodies, and, of course, on walls and on the sides of buildings. They use ball–point pens, rulers, and erasers; they copy, trace, and use stencils. These are materials, tools, and techniques discouraged in school art.

Children readily copy from one another and from the imagery of the popular media (Duncum, 1984, 2001). They incorporate, via copying or tracing, sophisticated artistic conventions that do not appear in their school art (Wilson, 1974; Wilson & Wilson,

1977). Many of the artistic conventions that are laboriously taught over time in the art curriculum appear spontaneously in students' nonschool drawings and may appear well ahead of the expectations of developmental stage theories. In a study of 35 children (who later became artists) born between 1724 and 1900, Duncum (1984) found they learned primarily through copying. In other words, various types of copying occur on local and professional levels, but copying carries a negative connotation in school art contexts where positive values are placed on competition and individualism.

In the commonly designated, but perhaps erroneously characterized, *child–centered* classroom, students quickly learn not to copy, and they learn to be individually responsible for their own work. Children appear to learn on a tacit level what techniques and subjects are appropriate in school art. They also seem to be able to move from the expectations of the school context to the nonschool context and vice versa, without confusing the two (Wilson, 1974; Wilson & Wilson, 1977). Like professional artists who often have a public art and a private art, children may hide their nonschool art or only share it with out–of–school contacts,

Unable to find major collections of child art predating the last century, Wilson (1985) has located children's drawings in the margins of old textbooks, diaries, and journals. He discerned both distinctive characteristics of spontaneous child art as well as changes over time that can be best described as stylistic changes, such as we have assumed only occurred in adult art. Likewise, graffiti art, which occurs both outside the school art context and the sanctions of professional art institutions, shows strong stylistic changes and styles particular to individual youthful artists.

Local art expressions can be considered merely inappropriate to school art contexts, or they can be seen as distinctly anti–school and antithetical to the spirit of school art and to the school administration. Duncum's (1989) study of children's images of violence indicates that teachers are often uncomfortable with such depictions and consider them to be pathological in nature. In local contexts, children produce art that is personal, autobiographical, and fanciful–and sometimes socially irreverent. Their art is not necessarily created to be publicly displayed or publicly critiqued.

CONTEXT DISTINCTIONS AND INCONSISTENCIES

School art lessons are believed to be exemplars that, in addition to being valuable in themselves, will transfer to art appreciation for the lay person or art skills for the art professional. However, since school art not only differs from local art but also does not seem to provide a great deal of preparation for professional art study or appreciation of institutionally validated art, the question arises as to why school art has the characteristics discussed above. Efland (1976) believes that child–centered, studio–based art curricula serve a compensatory function within the total school system. Other school subjects are taught with prespecified outcomes that conform to the timetable of published textbooks and the dictates of exit testing. Within this scheme of educational regimentation, art in the school curriculum appears to be sensitive to individual potential and to freedom of expression, and it appears to be concrete and contextually rich with meaning. School art gives the patina of humanistic values. Art teachers often cite how art learning personally benefits students in terms of confidence, motivation, and self–esteem.

According to Efland (1976), art instruction has been treated as an educational public relations frill that offers visual niceties in the form of decorations for the principal's office and attractive bulletin boards–and, of course, since the 1870s, art classes have been described as providing students respite from the demands of *academic* (sic) subjects. Although creativity and art have been equated in much of our thinking about art, it is a polite rendition of creativity that is allowed in the school art context. Controversial subject matter, experimental art, and innocuous, but messy, art do not fit the requirements of the school context. The school art described by Efland (1976) has little or no counterpart in professional contexts or in the context of everyday and personal experiences of art. It is, however, supportive of the value system and institutional character of the school context and, as such, supports and perpetuates school culture values, attitudes, and behaviors.

Within discipline–based art education (DBAE), it has been proposed that art should be taught as a discipline that, in addition to studio production, encompasses art criticism, art history, and aesthetics (Greer, 1984). Through the support of national art professional organizations and the J. Paul Getty Trust (1985), discipline–based art education (DBAE) moves art instruction closer to, if not into, the core curriculum of the school (Wilson, 1997). If traditional studio–based curriculum resulted in a specific school–art style, it might be anticipated that a discipline–based curriculum would be even more removed from local contexts and more aligned with traditional school learning characteristics, although transfer to professional contexts would probably be enhanced.

Feldman's model has found application in DBAE curricula in that the novice or naive child in the disciplinary context is to move toward the ideal of professional idiosyncratic knowledge and behaviors (Clark & Zimmerman, 1978, 1986). Art study is justified on the basis that it differs from what can be learned about art outside the school setting, and children are not assumed to have substantive art knowledge or experiences prior to entering the art classroom. Feldman's cultural context—i.e., local art context—is considered something to overcome. Art criticism instruction is structured so that students will overcome personal associations, and they will anchor their analysis in the perceptual qualities of the object (Feinstein, 1984; Greer, 1984, 1993; Hamblen, 1984). Likewise, aesthetic stage theory places a premium on a formalistic, decontextualized appreciation of art as the desirable outcome of development (Parsons, 1987). One might also note that such a developmental scheme is biased toward modernist interpretations. In other words, our models for appropriate or desirable art behaviors support the traditional characteristics of the school context.

Local art has most often appeared in school art under the rubric of "relevance," with the goal of moving students from initial local art experiences to an understanding and appreciation of school art and ultimately fine art (Lanier, 1970). Local, nonschool art experiences have not been considered as having merits in their own rights. Some of this, however, is changing within DBAE circles (Greer, 1993; Hamblen, 1997). Proceeding from the rationales of critical theory, populist interpretations of art, educational pragmatism, and ethnographic studies of school and nonschool learning, a number of art educators have proposed various reasons and various ways for attending to the art of local, everyday experiences and the even broader scope of all visual culture (see Blandy & Congdon, 1991; Congdon, 1986; Duncum, 2001).

For art criticism instruction, Congdon (1986) has provided rationales for giving educational validity to local art speech and informal analyses of art. Statements made by children, lay persons, and folk artists indicate that highly complex art concepts are already discussed in local speech (Hamblen & Galanes, 1997). Such naturalistic speech, however, has usually been dismissed as uneducated or inconsequential. As indicated earlier, school–aged children continue to produce nonschool art, but it is done with unsanctioned materials and techniques. After conducting research on differences between children's behaviors in school art and local art contexts, Wilson, Hurwitz, and Wilson (1987) published a program of art study that uses copying as the integrating and overarching concept for a series of drawing lessons.

CONCLUSION

I am suggesting that local art contexts may provide clues to significant art learning and the experience of "real time" art tasks, for both young children and for adults. The specific skills used in local art production and response need to be identified, not merely for purposes of providing motivation for school art learning, but as valid in–and–of–themselves. This would require a rethinking of art curriculum content. Art contexts and transfer among these contexts need to be identified and researched in relationship to attitudes, knowledge, and skills. Specifically, studies need to be done on adult knowledge and attitudes toward art in terms of their K– 1 2 art experiences. Continued disappointing results from the National Assessment for Educational Progress in the Arts (Chapman, 1982; Stankiewicz; 2000, Wilson, 1997)) cannot be attributed only to weak art requirements inasmuch as test items reflect or relate to typical art lessons. It is highly possible that low test results are also due in part to the perception that school learning has negligible value.

Considering that art has a tenuous place in the school curriculum there is a certain dangerous irony involved in suggesting that art curriculum content needs to be rethought in terms of local art. The irony of such a proposal is compounded by the fact that selected aspects of school art, even in its current state, are seen as worthy of emulation in broad–based educational reform, e.g. the studio model of instruction, portfolio assessments, formative evaluations, hands on learning. However, the perceived desirability of some art education practices may be more a function of the problems in the rest of education than they are a function of art education successes. It is not being suggested that school art, whether child–centered or discipline–based, is devoid of value, let alone that it should be replaced with local art experiences. It is proposed that opportunities need to be provided for children within local, school, and professional contexts for the purpose of their experiencing the learning and underlying value systems of these contexts and for the more pragmatic purpose of revealing how local art might be incorporated, legitimated, and developed in the school curriculum to enrich children's art learning.

REFERENCES

The Arts, Education and Americans Panel. (1977). *Coming to our senses: The significance of the arts for American education.* New York: McGraw–Hill.

Becker, H. S. (1982). *Art worlds.* Berkeley, CA: University of California Press.

Blandy, D., & Congdon, K. (1991). *Pluralistic approaches to art criticism.* Bowling Green, OH: Bowling Green State University Popular Press.

Bloom, A. (1987). *The closing of the American* mind. New York: Simon and Schuster.

Boston, B. 0. (1996, October 28). Educating for the workplace through the arts. *Business Week*, pp. 1–16.

Broudy, H. S. (1982). *Report on case studies on uses of knowledge* . Chicago: Spencer Foundation,

Brown, J. S. (1989, April). *Situated cognition and the cultures of learning.* Paper presented at the American Educational Research Association Annual Conference. San Francisco.

Bruner, J. S. (1960). *The process of education.* New York: Vintage.

Burton, D. (1984). Applying color. *Art Education. 37(l),* 40–43

Chapman, L. H. (1982). *Instant art, instant culture: The unspoken policy in American schools.* New York: Teachers College Press.

Chapman, L. H. (1994). *Adventures* in art. Worcester, MA: Davis.

Cheney, L. V. (1987). *American memory.* Washington, D.C.: National Endowment for the Humanities.

Clark, G., & Zimmerman, E. (1978). Walk in the right direction: A model for visual arts education. *Studies in Art Education, 12(2),* 34–39.

Clark, G., & Zimmerman, E. (1986). A framework for educating artistically talented students based on Feldman's and Clark and Zimmerman's models. *Studies in Art Education 27(3),* 115–122

Congdon, K. (1986). The meaning and use of folk art speech in art criticism. *Studies in Art Education, 27(3),* 140–148.

Duncum, P. (1984). How 35 children born between 1724 and 1900 learned to draw. *Studies in Art Education, 26(2),* 93–102.

Duncum, P. (1989). Children's unsolicited drawings of violence as a site of social contradiction. *Studies in Art Education, 20(4),* 249–256.

Duncum, P. (2001). Visual culture: Developments, definitions, and directions for art education. *Studies in Art Education, 42, (2),* 101–112.

Efland, A. (1976). The school art style: A functional analysis. *Studies in Art Education 7(2),* 37–44.

Eisner, E. W. (1997). Cognition and representation: A way to pursue the American dream? *Phi Delta Kappan, 78,* 348–353.

Eisner, E. W. (1998). Does experience in the arts boost academic achievement? *Art Education, 51(1),* 7–15.

Feinstein, H. (1984). The metaphoric interpretations of paintings: Effects of the clustering strategy and relaxed attention exercises. *Studies in Art Education, 25(2),* 77–83

Feldman, D. H. (1980). *Beyond universals in cognitive development.* Norwood, NJ: Ablex.

The J. Paul Getty Trust. (1985). *Beyond creating: The place for art in America's schools,* Los Angeles, CA: Author.

Greer, W. D. (1984). A discipline–based view of art education. *Studies in Art Education, 25(4),* 212–218

Greer, W. D. (1993). Developments in discipline–based art education (DBAE): From art education toward arts education. *Studies in Art Education 14(2),* 91–101.

Hamblen, K. A. (1984). The culture of aesthetic discourse (CAD): Origins, implications, and consequences. The *Bulletin of the Caucus on Social Theory and Art Education, 4,* 22–34. Hamblen, K. A. (1993a). Developmental models of artistic expression and aesthetic response: The reproduction of formal schooling and modernity. *The Journal of Social Theory Art Education, 13,* 37–56.

Hamblen, K. A. (1993b). Theories and research that support art instruction for instrumental outcomes. *Theory Into Research, 32(4),* 191–198.

Hamblen, K. A. (1997). Second generation DBAE. *Visual Arts Research, 23(2),* 98–106.

Hamblen, K. A., & Galanes, C. (1997). Instructional options for aesthetics: Exploring the possibilities. *Art Education, 50(l),* 74–84,

Hardiman, G. W. (1971). *Identification and evaluation of trained and untrained observers' affective responses to art object* . Washington, DC: Office of Education Bureau of Research.

Hirsch, E. D., Jr. (1987). *Cultural literacy: What every American needs to know.* Boston: Houghton Mifflin.

Holmes Group Executive Board. (1986). *Tomorrow's teachers: A report of the Holmes Group,* East Lansing, MI: Holmes Group.

Lanier, V. (1970). *Essays in art education: The development of one point of view.* New York: MSS Educational Publishing.

Lanier, V. (1975). Objectives of art education: The impact of time. *Peabody Journal of Educatio , 52(3),* 180–186

Lave, R., Murtaugh, M., & de la Rocha, 0. (1984). The dialectic of arithmetic in grocery shopping. In B. Rogoff & R. Lave (Eds.), *Everyday cognition: Development in social context* (pp. 67–94). Cambridge, MA: Harvard University Press,

Logan, F. (1955). *The growth of art in American schools.* New York: Harper and Brothers.

McReynolds, T. (1990). *An examination of discipline–based art education materials using criteria establishsed from discipline–based art education theory.* Unpublished master's thesis, Louisiana State University, Baton Rouge.

Michael, J. A. (1983). *Art and adolescence: Teaching art at the secondary level.* New York: Teachers College Press.

Parsons, M. J. (1987). *How we understand art: A cognitive developmental account of aesthetic experience.* Cambridge: Cambridge University Press.

Perkins, D. N., & Salomon, G. (1989). Are cognitive skills context–bound? *Educational Research,* 18(1), 16–25.

Rogoff, B., & Lave, J. (Eds) (1984). *Everyday cognition: Its development in social context.* Cambridge, MA: Harvard University Press.

Smith, P. (1989). A desert landscape: Art education's inattention to secondary education. *Studies in Art Education, 30(3),* 188–189.

Stankiewicz, M. A. (2000). Discipline and the future of art education. *Studies in Art Education, 41* (4), 301–313.

Wilson, B. (I 974). The superheroes of J. C. Holz: Plus an outline of a theory of child art. *Art Education, 27(8),* 2–9.

Wilson, B. (1985). History of children's styles of art: Possibilities and prospects. In B. Wilson & H. Hoffa (Eds.), *The history of art education: Proceedings from the Penn State Conference* (pp. 177–184). Reston, VA: National Art Education Association.

Wilson, B. (1997). *The quiet evolution.* Los Angeles: The J. Paul Getty Trust.

Wilson, B., Hurwitz, A., & Wilson, M. (1987). *Teaching drawing from art.* Worchester, MA: Davis.

Wilson, B., & Wilson, M. (1977). *Art iconoclastic view of the imagery sources in the drawings of young people.* An Education, 30(1), 412.

Winner, E., & Hetland, L. (eds.). (2000). *The Journal of Aesthetic Education, 34* (3/4).

An early version of this chapter was published in *Visual Arts Research, 25* (2), 1999, pp. 4–13.

BRUNO NETTL

2. WHAT'S TO BE LEARNED? COMMENTS ON TEACHING MUSIC IN THE WORLD AND TEACHING WORLD MUSIC AT HOME

Ethnomusicologists as a   professional group are interested in discovering the ways music is taught in the world's cultures, and in learning how musical systems are taught – transmitted – through the generations. They are usually also, naturally, interested in the way the world's music are taught in American and European systems of primary and secondary education. Less attention has been paid to the ways these two areas of endeavor can inform each other. This essay provides some comments, largely from my own experience as an ethnomusicologist and a parent.

NATIVE AMERICAN MUSIC IN FIRST GRADE, 1999

In December of last year, I carried out an annual ritual which I've always found satisfying but for which I always prepare with several days of stage fright. I visit the first–grade class of my daughter, an elementary school teacher, to teach for an hour and a half about Native American music. Of course it was fun for me to see my daughter, whom I still see as a little girl, now the experienced educator very much in charge; and fun for the children to imagine their (they think) middle–aged teacher having a dad who knew her when she was small.

But what to teach? I know that a number of texts in music education provide material and sophisticated relevant discussion, but the purpose was for me to bring my own experience and background. I could play recordings, but the children's attention span wouldn't be long; I could teach some songs, but in the end they wouldn't sound the least bit like Native American singing; I could try to explain some rudimentary things about musical style, but that's a lot to ask of first graders. We could imitate some activities, learn a gambling game or a Peyote song, have a miniature powwow. These activities would show something about the musical styles and a bit, too, about music as it contributed to culture. We could maybe learn to do a Stomp Dance

Actually, I tried them all, none with great success, none total failures. Surprisingly to me (but broadly described by Campbell, 1998), the children quickly picked up simple songs, bits of typical dance steps, and at least some comprehended the difference between the cascading melodic contour of Plains music and the undulations of a Navajo song. But I wondered whether they would, the next week, be able to recall anything — identify contours, tell what a Stomp Dance is like, know that songs are important in worship, say that drums and rattles and flutes are the principle instruments.

L. Bresler and C.M. Thompson (eds.), The Arts in Children's Lives, 29–41.
© 2002 *Kluwer Academic Publishers. Printed in the Netherlands.*

Probably not, my daughter thought, but rather, twelve years from now, in college, in a world music course, one or two of them might say to themselves, "Oh yes, I remember this from first grade." So, I'm not sure how worthwhile my attempt was, but throughout I kept wondering about my mission — not the cultural, but the explicitly musical one. Should I be trying to show that this music is really like "ours," whatever "ours" is, easy to understand and internalize; in that case, would these songs have been integrated more, given English words and piano accompaniment? Or should I stress that this music is really very different, very strange, show how we can't really make our voices sing it without a lot of practice, that they really employ a different language, if you will? Should I say to the kids, "This is really like the other kinds of music you know," and compare the Stomp Dance to some call–and–response games they knew, and the Peyote syllables to tra–la–la or ee–yi–ee–yi–yo? Or should I keep pointing out how the songs always go with other activities — ritual, recreation? How could I bring up, at a first–grade level, concepts such as ethnicity, questions such as "whose music is this," and the validity of comparison? Most important, should I put forward or guard against the implication that this music is only interesting because it is associated with Native Americans, while the great music by Mr. Bach and Mr. Mozart — the kids had heard of them — is always interesting to everyone? Well, in the end, these energetic first–graders didn't think this music strange, didn't question whether it sounded like music, took for granted that this was indeed the music of Native Americans, different from their own, but that one could listen to it and sing it.

The questions raised in my experience are also the ones that I always faced as a college teacher of world music, who must decide whether the basic assumption in his courses is that all of the world's music is basically one system that can be comprehended by all of our students with modest effort, or that the world of music is a group of discrete musical languages each of which can be learned only with great effort and never completely, whose role in culture cannot be fully comprehended by outsiders. And the approach to my daughter's pupils that I should have followed, had I had time and expertise, results from the following assertion: In any society, the way in which music is taught and transmitted is an integral part of the musical culture. And so, in thinking of how to teach something essential to my first–grade friends, I should have tried to do it in the way the Native Americans, whose music I was presenting, taught their children.

HOW DO YOU GET TO CARNEGIE HALL?

Not an easy task; but we as educators should probably pay more attention to the learning processes – and the purposes of learning – that lead to the music, or to any domain of culture, that we ourselves are imparting. To ethnomusicologists, discovering the way a society teaches its music – well, more broadly, the way a musical system "teaches itself" or "transmits itself" — should be a major endeavor.

"How do you get to Carnegie Hall?" asks the newcomer to New York, trying to find his way to a concert. "Practice, practice, practice," replies the Broadway wag. But there are actually many ways in which one arrives at the Carnegie Halls of world music and, like "practicing" as a concept, "learning music" means many things. One may learn pieces, or a way of performing, or the abstract fundamental principles of a musical system. Perhaps one learns how to listen and appreciate music; perhaps one learns exercises such as scales, or short and easy pieces composed for learning. Each of these, or any combination, amounts to learning a musical system, and this in any case consists of many (and sometimes various types of) discrete units that a musician – composer, performer, improviser, even informed listener – learns to manipulate. In one way or another the method of teaching breaks a system down into these basic units. In Western academic or classical music they may be pieces or compositions, or smaller ones such as chords, characteristic sequences of chords, or tones in a melody. The way the members of a society teach the music of their culture tells us what is important about the music; but also, learning how the music works teaches us about the values and guiding principles of its culture.

In many societies, including in particular some of those of the South Seas, children and young people learn the important elements and values of their own culture through musical experience, and adults continue to undergo this process into old age (Ramseyer, 1970, pp. 28–31). Among the people of Yirkalla, South Australia, only old men knew the entire ceremonial musical repertory (R. Waterman, 1956, p. 49), and the men in some North American Plains Indian tribes moved every few years into a new warrior society, learning each time new ritual and cosmological materials, education continuing well past middle age. Perhaps music has something of this enculturative function everywhere, but if we have recognized the importance of music in the learning of culture, we have not paid much attention to the way in which people learn music, and surely not to the ways in which the elements and values of a culture affect the learning of music. If we are to take cognizance of all the music of a culture, we must be concerned with the way it is learned and even with the materials that are used to teach it.

In the general Western academic conception of music, learning plays a major role. Study and teaching at all levels come up in many American conversations about music. A large proportion of musicians make their living by teaching, and much of the population spends time and energy in formal learning of music, though in most cases not with the aim of professional musicianship. A large percentage of published music is didactic in nature. We care greatly with whom one studies music and how one goes about learning. If one could monitor all musical sound produced in this society, perhaps the majority would turn out to be for the purpose of learning, in some sense of that word. One reads general statements to the effect that in non–Western cultures, and certainly in nonliterate cultures, learning is "by rote," and there are of course writings about the nature of oral tradition. Often we know little more, even where other components of musical culture are admirably documented. Merriam (1964, pp. 145–64) was one of the first to look at the problem as a whole.

There are a number of issues for us to be concerned with; let us look at a few. Most important among them, perhaps: When music is transmitted, what is actually learned? While we assume that a musical system in written or oral tradition is transmitted more or less as a unified whole, there are probably certain things which people learn about a musical system that are most important, and which must be handed down, while others are left more or less to be picked up by chance without special attention or instruction. Another area of interest in this sphere of learning is how people practice, in what activities they actually engage when they are teaching themselves music, when they are carrying out the instructions of a teacher, mediating between the points of instruction and performance. Also related is the use and nature of special materials whose purpose is to help people learn – exercises, etudes, texts on the principles of musicianship. Then there is the identity of teachers and their role in society and in music. And we should know, in an intercultural context, how people in infancy acquire music, and the way in which a musical system, first heard by small children before they are in a position to reproduce it, is perceived by them. There are many other matters that might be of interest, but these issues are sufficient to illustrate a general point that I am trying to make, that a musical system, its style, its main characteristics, its structure, are all very closely associated with the particular way in which it is taught, as a whole and in its individual components.

Western academic musical culture is surely one of the most specialized, in the sense that a musician is primarily involved in one aspect of the "music delivery" process – composing, performing, teaching, etc. It is further specialized in rather rigorously separating various kinds of musicians from each other. Singers in the United States are not even members of the musicians' union. Solo violinists rarely play in orchestras. A pianist is regarded mainly as a soloist, or accompanist, or jazz ensemble musician. Yet the course of musical education is very much the same for all. One normally begins with an instrument (even if one ends up as a singer), and almost everyone at some point learns to play piano. Piano lessons normally begin with exercises, and the terror of serious beginning students is the requirement that, before all else, they must master the scales in all of the keys and always begin practice with them, with the knowledge that even if they become virtuosos, the need for practicing these scales will not abate. After becoming somewhat proficient on an instrument, one is likely to take up the study of music theory, a subject that is theoretical not in the general sense of the word but rather in that one learns material which does not apply directly to the making of musical sounds but is generalizable to all aspects of musical activity. Until recently, music theory concentrated almost exclusively on harmony and began with types of chords, its basic units.

In both cases, instrumental and theoretical, one first learns things that do not normally constitute music but that must be manipulated and extended in order to be recognized as components of music. Few serious pieces merely use scales or use chord sequences precisely in the way they are learned at the beginning of music theory classes. In Western academic music, then, much of the musical system is learned in the abstract. What the teacher first teaches is largely theoretical concepts and gymnastic exercises rather than units of a higher order, i.e., actual compositions.

In most of the world's cultures these compositions are imparted directly by the teacher to the student. Not so in Western academic music – or at least one does not learn the teacher's special approach. Piano students usually do not learn Beethoven sonatas *from* their teacher, with the latter first playing the piece for them, asking them to interpret as they have heard. Rather, the teacher usually confines herself more to general observations, to the instruction of technique and of the materials that make possible the learning of technique, and beyond that asks the students to imbibe

Beethoven from the written page, learning, as it were, from the composer. I see our system of teaching as a combination of theoretical and practical materials, with the teacher playing a much larger role in the former.

TEACHING AND LEARNING THE BUILDING BLOCKS

In the classical music of South India the situation is somewhat similar. While the Western musician learns the basic system through piano and theory classes, the Indian is likely to learn it by exposure to vocal music, even if he turns out an instrumentalist. At the knee of the teacher he studies a long series of exercises that exhibit the characteristics of *raga* and *tala*, melody and rhythm, and juxtapose the two in various combinations. These exercises and some simple introductory pieces constitute or include fundamental units such as rhythmic and melodic motifs that are later used in learned compositions and, more important, in the improvisation which forms much of the core of musical performance. The emphasis is upon memorizing materials that will make it possible for one to improvise. Indian composers who, in contrast to improvising, create songs such as the extended South Indian *kriti*, whose structure has common features with improvisations, evidently undergo training similar to that of the performer. In the Western classical system, by contrast, performer and composer in part at least have rather different kinds of learning experience.

Western and Indian musicianship have in common the concept of discipline, the need to practice the building blocks of music for many hours at a time, directing one's effort only indirectly to what will happen in a performance. A pianist spends much time on scales and exercises, even with a Chopin recital coming up. South Indian singers do not spend their time only trying out various combinations of material and improvising, as they will have to do in public, but also devote hours every day to exercises, from the simple to the very difficult. Indeed, Indian musicians are evaluated by each other only in part in accordance with their musicianship as exhibited in performance or with their knowledge of repertory and in large measure by their reputation for disciplined practice and study, called *riaz* by North Indians (Neuman, 1980, pp. 32–43). "If a musician wants to celebrate the genius of another musician, he will do so. . .in terms of practice habits" (Neuman, 1980, p. 31).

To these two cultures, Persian classical music provides a contrast. The musician of Iran studies the *radif,* memorizing it precisely from his teacher's version, which may be similar but not identical to that of other teachers. The teacher is concerned only with the student's ability to reproduce what he sings or plays for him with utmost exactness. He does not explain the minutiae of the structure of the *radif,* although the student needs to learn these in order to engage in improvisation, the central activity in true performance. The student must deduce from the *radif,* with its many examples of variation, melodic sequence, extension and contraction of motifs, that its very structure is the guide to improvisatory procedure. Once the *radif* is memorized, the student is considered ready to perform without further instruction. He has learned a theoretical construct and must now suddenly move to improvisation. The Indian musician studies building blocks of varying degrees of complexity, units that gradually become increasingly like real music. The Iranian musician leaps directly from study at only one level of conceptualization into true performance.

By contrast with these three high cultures, we have much less detailed information about teaching and learning from those without musical literacy or articulated theory. The Blackfoot believed that humans learned music in two interconnected ways, from supernatural powers such as guardian spirits in visions and from other humans. The ideal is learning songs from the supernatural, and the concepts of learning and creating music are therefore close. The way in which songs are thought to be learned in visions, normally in a single hearing, influences the concepts that people have about learning music in an entirely human context. In the culture of the Blackfoot, once presumably means four times through, so some repetition is there, but the concept that the guardian spirit teaches you a song by simply *singing* it to you is important, and human teachers worked similarly. Thus a medicine bundle, with its attendant songs, was transferred from one person to another by a single performance of the ceremony, during which the new owner was expected to learn the songs. Today, when people learn songs from each other and recognize the process as such, they indicate that quick learning is desirable and certainly possible, though often violated by the ever–present cassette recorder. The standardization of form and the possibility of roughly predicting the course of a song from its initial phrase as teaching devices are also cases in point.

The varying emphases on various kinds of units and different aspects of the musical system given by a teacher help to identify the building blocks of the music. It is obvious that in northern Plains music the head motifs are the most important things, actually identifying the songs, which frequently do not have names. On the other hand, when I studied the *radif* with an Iranian musician, I was told that parts of it were important, and while these are stressed to some extent in the performances, the fact that they are singled out as important particularly in the teaching of the *radif* may well reflect ideas extremely important to the culture. Those parts of a *dastgah* that tended to depart from the norm were often stressed by my teacher as being important, and in other respects, in Iranian culture, events or actions that departed from a norm were sometimes particularly valued. By a similar token, the fact that the Western music student learns a theoretical system based largely on a particular part of his repertory, that of the period between 1720 and 1900, indicates rather forcefully what we consider most important in our musical experience and contrasts interestingly with our tendency to prize innovation. While we are surely cognizant of the fact that melody and rhythm are of major importance to our own music–making, the fact that music theory has always stressed harmony indicates that perhaps of all the things that make our music properly an art, the system of harmony is one of the most important.

PRACTICE, PRACTICE, PRACTICE

Not only what is taught, but also the activities involved in learning, can tell us what is valued in a music. A few almost random examples: Western practitioners of art music have many techniques of practicing. For one thing, the repetition of a great deal of didactic material – scales, exercises, and etudes – is standard. Many musicians are unwilling to practice "real" music without first going through theoretical material of the above–mentioned sort. Just what the function of this theoretical material is may not be quite clear, but surely the concept of warming up mentally or physically is rather important. In India musicians have a similar approach to practicing, the daily repetition of exercises being an almost religious necessity, and the function of theoretical materials as building blocks for improvisation is clearer. Elsewhere again, among the Shona people of Zimbabwe, where virtuosity certainly also exists, the idea of warming up is combined with the introductory section of a formal performance.

In a second aspect of practicing, Western academic musicians try to memorize things that might not really have to be memorized, mainly in order to show ability to absorb musical materials. One might have thought that the development of notation could lead specifically to the opposite effect. Third, the habit of singling out short bits of music in order to repeat them indicates the great stress on technical proficiency we have developed in Western music. Indeed, a Western concert is to a large extent an exercise in mental and dexterous ability. The idea of doing something very difficult, of music as a craft, is highly developed. Such a view is also found in India, but to a much smaller extent than in Iran, for the tradition of learning the Persian *radif* was that one had to learn slowly because of the music's essential philosophical and mystical significance. The introduction of Western notation into Iranian music has always been controversial, partly because it made possible the learning of the *radif* very efficiently and very quickly, violating the belief that the music was in itself something to be contemplated. Nour–Ali Khan, for example, wished to teach only a very small amount of it to me every week, saying that it was important for me to play it frequently, to look at it from all sides, listen to it, examine it, contemplate it. Perhaps contemplation acts as a stimulus for students to learn to understand the way the structure of the *radif* teaches the techniques and concepts of improvisation.

What do we know about the way in which Native North Americans traditionally practiced? There is evidence that those cultures in which the precise rendering of music for validation of religious ritual was very important also had systematic musical competition, practicing, and rehearsing. We are told this about the Navajo and the north Pacific Coast peoples (Herzog, 1938, p. 4, 1949, pp. 106–7; McAllester, 1954, pp. 76–77). Rehearsing was essential, mistakes were punished, rituals in which mistakes were found would have to be repeated entirely or in part in order to be valid. The northern Plains Indians took a somewhat less formal attitude. Having been learned largely from visions for the use of one person, music was more closely associated with the individual and private rituals, and therefore the control of the community over musical performance was less highly developed. Evidently a man who learned a song in a vision would use his walk or ride back to camp as an opportunity to rehearse or work it out. No doubt, actual composition took place along this walk; the inspiration from the white heat of the vision would be rationally worked out. Practicing took place at this point, and the song would be readied for presentation to the other members of the tribe. But since music was primarily a personal and individualistic activity and experience, practicing was not done systematically to any large extent and not much heed was paid to the accuracy of performance. Just as composing and learning are related concepts, composing and practicing overlap.

The introduction of Western notation to many non–Western cultures accompanied and perhaps caused changes in practicing. The various types of notation long used in Asian societies (Kaufmann, 1967) have hardly been used for reading while performing, but have functioned as references and perhaps, even more as aids to scholarly discussion of music (Hickmann, 1970, pp. 45–47). Along with Western music, mainly in the nineteenth and twentieth centuries, came the idea of learning music visually rather than aurally. In Iran and India musicians critical of notation realized that it was more than a mechanical convenience, and that fundamental changes in the music system would result from its use.

GURUS, SPIRITS, AND THE RECORD DEPARTMENT OF "BEST BUY"

One might expect notation to become so thoroughly developed that from it a student could learn an entire musical system without hearing it, and without human intervention. We haven't yet arrived at that point, and, indeed, the learning of music is almost everywhere an experience of intense relationship between student and teacher. The identity, social role, and approach of the music teacher is an important component of a socio–musical system, and ethnomusicologists have in recent times come to describe some instances very thoroughly. (See the following publications for examples: Berliner, 1978; Daniélou, 1973; Nettl, 1974; Neuman, 1980; Tracey, 1948; and in a very unusual way Mitchell, 1978, in which a Native American singer describes his own learning in detail.)

It is interesting that in many cultures, including those used to illustrate this chapter, there is some difference between practicing musician and master teacher. To be sure, ordinary musicians do teach, but great teachers are often people who know material well but are not necessarily best at rendering it. The concept of the specialist music teacher actually exists in a large number of societies. In Western music we have, of course, a large group of professionals who do little beyond teaching. They are often people who are not highly respected and may be denigrated by performers and composers as people who have not made it in the practical field and are therefore relegated to teaching. Actually, society does not treat them all that badly. It is interesting to see that most performers are paid worse than teachers, that teachers develop certain kinds of job security not shared by performers and composers, all of which may be related to the low evaluation of music and the somewhat higher value of the concept of education. Interpreting much more broadly, it may be that in our culture the handing on of the tradition is regarded as more important than its expansion.

In India as well, great teachers are not necessarily great performers, but they are renowned for their *riaz*. For a performer it is important, even more than elsewhere, to be associated with a highly qualified teacher. The genealogy of student–teacher relationships is typically recited in introducing Indian concerts, and a performer is praised for carrying on the tradition of his teacher's gharana. It is therefore interesting to see that in the most recent period of Western culture the Indian concept of guru has come to symbolize the idea of devoted study and teaching. In fact, two terms are widely used in India, "guru" (originally associated with Hinduism) and "ustad" (of Muslim origin). The two concepts are no longer limited to religious or ethnic groups and are more or less interchangeable in actual use. But they represent two approaches to the concept of teaching (Neuman, 1980, pp. 44–45), with both terms applied to the same person. The ustad, best translated as "master" or even "professor," symbolizes the technical expertise of the teacher, his musical ability and knowledge. The term "guru" symbolizes the teacher's role in molding not only the student's musical learning but also his adoption of an appropriate lifestyle, his absorption of music as a part of culture.

In the classical tradition of India one was expected to become a particular kind of person in order to be recognized as a musician. As modern and Western approaches to music teaching came to be used in the twentieth century, there developed a bifurcation between those who studied in the traditional way, with guru–ustad, and those who went to music schools, spending three years in a conservatory atmosphere taking courses with various professors and emerging with a B.A. The latter might be given credit for excellent knowledge and technique, but they were accorded little respect by those more traditionally schooled. It would seem that they lacked the close personal association, comprising much more than simply music, with the figure of authority.

Normally, music teachers are human, but some, like certain figures in Indian music history, have become mythological figures, the subjects of stories of incredible accomplishment. Ustad Allauddin Khan, father of modern development of North Indian classical music, is said to have mastered eighty instruments. Another musician was said to have practiced daily for sixteen hours without interruption. Of course there are also many legends about the ability of master musicians to affect the course of nature and history through their control over ragas. Stories about the power of music are almost universal, and familiar from the figures of Orpheus and Tamino, but in India the powers of the great teacher seem to be particularly stressed. In yet other cultures we find the music teacher to be a directly supernatural figure. Native Americans of the Plains learned their songs from beings who appear in dreams, and the concept, though not the process, of teaching songs appears very prominently in folklore and mythology. But in modern Blackfoot culture there is also a sharp distinction between individuals who, in guru–like fashion, know the older traditions but do not perform in public, and others who sing for social dances. A mixed system of supernatural and human teachers is described by Berliner (1978, pp. 136–45) for mbira players of the Shona of Zimbabwe. The spirits are thought to encourage students and players in dreams, and also to teach the instrument and its repertory. The human teachers of the Shona use a number of ways of approaching their task. Some (Berliner, 1978, pp. 140–41) break down the music into component phrases, teaching them one at a time. Others teach the part of each plucking thumb separately, then combine the two. Berliner stresses the lack of a common method, which goes no further than an insistence that there be a proper approach (whatever that may be in the individual case), and on developing a good memory. This diversity of method must be related to the highly individualistic approach that Shona musicians have to their instruments and their repertory. Again, the musical system results from, but also determines, the way of teaching.

In connection with the techniques and technicalities of studying to be a musician, we must also consider the fact that individuals learn the fundamentals of their own music very early in life, somewhat as they learn language. They learn to recognize music as a category separate from other types of sounds and, it seems likely, to distinguish new sounds that belong to a particular music from those that do not. They learn "their own" culture, "their" music, and distinguish it from those of "others." At least that's our conventional wisdom.

But in the last couple of decades — give or take a few years —the notion of "ours" and "we," when it comes to music, has changed. We (in Western–style ethnomusicology) continue to recognize that "a" society or "a" culture has its own music, that the world of music consists of a group of musics. These, we used to think, were like languages, each with its distinct style characteristics and repertory. Overlaps in style and repertory, sure; but languages influence each other in phonology and there are loan words, too. And I guess a great many of the world's societies also see their music as something *musically* distinct. I suspect we don't know nearly as much about this as we ought, as one society's conception of what constitutes its own music may have primarily stylistic criteria, while in another they may involve association with events, cultural concepts and contexts, or persons. Thus, when in Iran, I found urban musicians talking about Persian music that was the music of the *radif* and the twelve *dastgahs*, and about international music — in Western style — composed by Iranians. On the other hand, I've been told that in Chinese culture today, Chinese music means music composed by Chinese, whatever the style. That's just a quick illustration. Let me use it as a jumping–off point for a bit more on Native Americans.

If you visit the "Native American" subdivision of the International section of large record stores or Best Buy, you are now confronted by a quantity of disks, a few of them recordings made by ethnomusicologists in the 1960s and issued by Smithsonian–Folkways, and sounding — I haven't figured out a good term — traditional, and non–Western. You may find some recordings of powwow music, not explicitly identified by tribe, sounding traditional but with words in English. Probably most of the recordings are by Native American musicians, with words that deal with issues significant to Native Americans, but in musical styles indistinguishable from those of mainstream popular music in USA. I haven't quizzed Native American associates about this music, but there are questions I'd like to ask: 1) Which of these recordings are the ones with which you most associate yourself as a Native American? 2) Which of them do you think we, teachers of music, should be using the tell our students, college age and first–grade, about American Indian music? 3) Am I being naive in thinking that the popular music really doesn't have a distinctive Indian sound? 4) Is there a distinctive Indian, or Blackfoot, or Navajo music? Where does the following example belong? Sung by Jim Pepper and his band ca. 1968. And I'll add to it a piece by Thomas Mapfumo: To some people in Zimbabwe, it's their central music; to others it might be a sellout to Western–style instrumentation, harmony, musical commodification.

FIFTH–GRADE CHORUS AND THE POLITICS OF REPRESENTATION

That December seems to have been my month for excursions to the public schools of my home town, because I also had the opportunity of hearing my grand–daughter's 5th-grade chorus perform a concert. An unmitigated success: The children were enthusiastic and had clearly worked hard to learn a good many songs, with a teacher obviously both slave driver and angel. Technically, the children had achieved a lot. Intonation, rhythm, ensemble were good. With me they got high grades on "standards," on aspects of musicianship. But the program was billed as "music from many lands," and of the twelve songs, one was described as South African, one Israeli, one Caribbean, one old English, one Mexican. There was also a song titled "Hello from the World," with greetings in a number of languages worked in. The melodies were largely tunes composed especially for music teaching in schools. I asked myself in what ways this repertory was teaching world music, in what sense it was multicultural. The South African and Caribbean tunes departed a bit from mainstream American school melodic patterns, but they were accompanied by piano and one rarely even heard a minor triad. The children weren't learning that different cultures have very different musical sounds. The words were, naturally, in English. Mainly, it seems to me, they were learning that different cultures have their musics, maybe not very different from each other, and that all of this music deserves respect and, in fact, sounds the same. Social goals were being met, and musical goals too in the sense that the children were learning Western music and performing for their parents. I don't know how typical such an event is in America, but I'm struck by a parallel to what we have recently been teaching in classes in "world music," in contrast to the courses of earlier times.

Ethnomusicologists are accustomed to use the present — sometimes called the ethnographic present — in their rhetoric. Describing a ritual she observed two years back, my student says that "they do this," "they play this," not, "I heard that," with opposing implications: a) that we make no claims about the past, which can't be recovered; and b) that the societies we study are static and consistent — or perhaps that in characterizing a culture we concentrate on those elements that are constant. This is true despite the frequently stated belief among other academics that we are interested in the ancient. We observe the present and analyze processes and changes as they occur. This would suggest that the repertory on which we should concentrate in presenting Native American music should be the popular music, the music of Carlos Nakai, Jim Pepper, Xit, and perhaps the intertribal repertory of powwow songs.

But do Native Americans wish to be represented in this way? Some surely. Others again may wish us outsiders to know that there are large repertories of older music, some known only to a few, which ought to be preserved. But does preservation suggest knowledge by a privileged few, or a scattering in the American and maybe world population as a whole? Do we give our students the sense that the old ritual music, that's the REAL Native American music, and the recent popular music, only a subterfuge? Or again, should we suggest that Native Americans, earlier on, had simple, unharmonized, vocal music but escaped from it as soon as they were exposed to the superior Western music, creating then their own version of Western music? Just what conception should we be encouraging? The International Society for Music Education has made valiant efforts to approach this and related questions, but we are not very far along. (See Lundquist and Szego, 1998, for analysis and bibliography from intercultural and multicultural perspectives.)

The norm of Western music in our system of education is classical music. Yes, often, it appears in our school curricula, in simplified versions and pieces, and sometimes with a nod in the direction of rock and jazz, but underneath, let's not kid ourselves, it's the classical repertory of the common practice period that is the center. I just wish to ask what effect this structuring has on our presentation of world music.

So, when I conversed with musicians in Iran about how they would wish to be represented in American music education, there was no question: by the classical repertory and performance practice. Folk music of the villages — yes, but it is interesting largely because it nurtured the classical, a viewpoint similar to that of many European musicians a few decades ago. I don't know whether this idea came to Iran from Europe, but actually I doubt it. Rather, it was the way in which the classical music had come, actually as part of the cultural politics of the Pahlavi dynasty, to be regarded as an explicitly national product and emblem. Folk music, called "mahalli" or "regional" music, characterized the various districts. It was the classical music that integrated and also distinguished Persian culture. But no one ever mentioned popular music; it was the music that least conformed to the Islamic traditions about music, that mixed the musics of the world with those of Iran in undesirable ways. Still, people clearly loved the popular music.

What a complicated situation we've come to ! From elementary school teaching that was determinedly unimusical to conflicts on the nature of the world and of multiculturalism; to competition between multiculturalism and standards K to 12; from world music as marginal in the college curriculum to a position of centrality. From the notion that the world of music is a group of musics, or that music is a universal language, to a recognition that it's all more complex. It has been a half century of trial and error, at all levels of musical education.

The point is — and I guess this is how I should conclude these meandering remarks — that we have been trying to have it both ways, in elementary schools and in universities. We want our students to be conscious of a multifarious world of music, want them to wonder at the otherness, the foreignness of most of the world's music; but we also want them to think, "I can sing that African song with the musical equipment I have," or "I can learn to play on that gamelan in a couple of half–hour sessions." And also, a bit more contemplating: "Long ago, when recordings were first made, much of the world's music sounded strange, but now most of the world's music has a familiar sound to us, uses something like our diatonic scale, slips into the mold of functional harmony and of accompanied melody." We are faced — in first grade and in the university — with the question of which end to emphasize.

I have to admit to ignorance of the record of research in education and what answers it might propose. But for me, in the end, it has been the "otherness," the degree of difference from familiar sound, of difference from the social contexts and concepts I once considered as normal, that have driven my interest in the world's musics. So, when I visited my daughter's first–graders, I felt more comfortable saying to them, "Wow, doesn't this sound different from anything you've heard? Isn't that interesting?" instead of saying "Here's a native American song; you can sing it easily." We want our students, above all, at all levels, to know a great deal about – well — everything; to be able to locate themselves in a wide cultural, historical, and musical space. To marvel at the incredible diversity of the world's ideas about music, and of the world's musical sounds. That, it seems to me, is a worthwhile attitude for us as teachers – teachers of children, and of the child in everyone.

REFERENCE

Berliner, P. (1978). *The Sopul of Mbira.* Berkeley: University of California Press.

Campbell, P. S. (1998). *Songs in their heads: Music and its meaning in children's lives.* New York: Oxford University Press.

Danielou, A. (1973). *Die Musik Asiens zwischen Misachtung und Wertschätzung.* Wilhelmshaven: Heinrichshofen.

Herzog, G. (1938). Music in the thinking of the American Indian, *Peabody Bulletin,* May 1938, 1–5.

Hertzog, G. (1949). Salish Music. In M.W. Smith (Ed), *Indians of the urban Northwest* (pp. 93–109). New York: Columbia University Press.

Hickmann, H. (1970). Die Musik des Islamisch–Arabischen Bereichs. In *Handbuch der Orientalistik* 1. Abteilung, Ergänzungsband IV. Leiden: Brill.

Kaufmann, W. (1967). *Musical notations of the Orient.* Bloomington: Indiana University Press.

Lundquist, B. & Szego, C. K. (Eds) (1998). *Music of the world's cultures: A source book for music educators.* Reading, U.K.: International Society for Music Education.

McAllester, D. P. (1954). *Enemy way music.* Cambridge, MA.: Peabody Museum Papers, *41,* 3.

Merriam, A. P. (1964). *The anthropology of music.* Evanston: Northwestern University Press.

Mitchell, F. (1978). *Navajo Blessingway Singer* (Charlotte J. Frisbie & David P. McAllester, Eds), Tuscon: University of Arizona Press.

Nettl, B. (1974). Nour–Ali Boroumand, a twentieth–century master of Persian music, *Studium Instrumentarum Musicae Popularis, 3,* 167–71.

Neuman, D. M. (1980). *The life of music in North India.* Detroit: Wayne State University Press.

Ramseyer, U. (1970). *Soziale Bezüge des Musizierens in Naturvolkkulturen.* Bern: Francke.

Tracey, H. (1948). *Chopi musicians.* London: Oxford University Press.

Waterman, R. A. (1856). Music in Australian aboriginal culture – Some sociological and psychological implications, *Music Therapy, 5,* 40–50.

This chapter is based on and uses material from "How to get to Carnegie Hall," in *The Study of Ethnomusicology* (pp. 323-332), 1983, University of Illinois Press.

BRENT WILSON

3. BECOMING JAPANESE:
MANGA, CHILDREN'S DRAWINGS, AND THE CONSTRUCTION OF NATIONAL CHARACTER

INTRODUCTION: CULTURAL INFLUENCES IN CHILDREN'S DRAWINGS

We now have considerable evidence that children in various parts of the world draw humans, animals, and objects differently (Aronsson & Anderson, 1996; Wilson, 1987; Wilson & Litgvoet, 1992; Wilson & Wilson, 1979, 1981, 1984). Although cultural graphic influences on the style of children's drawings have been documented, the consequences of these influences on children's lives have not been studied. If one culture provides graphic models that are radically different from those of another, and if children use those models, do they affect the way children see themselves, influence the way they conceive of their society, determine the way they construct their views of the world, and perhaps even govern how they live their lives? If we are to understand the role that art making plays in the lives of children, we need to pose questions such as these and search for answers.

One of the predominant cultural graphic influences on the style of young people's drawings is that of the popular media; there may be no country where the influence is more pronounced than in Japan (Wilson, 1997). As I will show, when Japanese children enter kindergarten, some of their drawings already reflect one or more of several distinct styles of *manga* (the comic books read by the Japanese from infancy into adulthood). The influence becomes ubiquitous as Japanese children grow older. The strong *manga* influence present in Japanese children's drawings provides an opportunity to study the role of media in providing models through which children understand themselves and their society. The use of *manga* by Japanese children also provides an opportunity to study the "collusion" between commercial forces and children in shaping conceptions of national identity.

A GRAPHIC NARRATION TASK:
CLASSIFICATIONS OF CHARACTERS AND STYLES

I am currently conducting two related inquiries of Japanese children's graphic narratives. One study involves an analysis of thematic content and narrative structure of these *manga*–influenced graphic narratives. The second more basic study, reported here, is an analysis of *manga* types and characters. As a researcher, however, I find myself torn between modern and postmodern desires. On the one hand I feel a

L. Bresler and C.M. Thompson (eds.), The Arts in Children's Lives, 43–55.
© 2002 *Kluwer Academic Publishers. Printed in the Netherlands.*

compulsion to study cognition, to present classifications, and to point to a table of statistics relating to the types of characters Japanese children depict in their graphic narratives. On the other hand, what I really wish to do is to read the graphic narrative characters as signs that will inform us about children, art, and culture. I'll try to have it both ways.

Children's sequential narrative drawings have been studied for two decades (Wilson & Wilson, 1983, 1987). In 1988, as part of an ongoing cross–cultural study of children's story drawings, I visited various regions of Japan to collect samples of young peoples' drawings. In schools in and around Joyetsu, Monbetsu, Nagasaki, Osaka, and Utsinomya, 1151 students in kindergarten, second, fourth, and sixth grades were given sheets of 12 x 16 1/2 inch paper on which six 4 1/4 x 4 3/4 inch frames were printed. Instructions were to draw a story by creating characters, placing them in settings, showing what happens, what happens next, and how things finally turn out. In short, students were asked to respond to a task to produce graphic narratives much like those that they were accustomed to seeing in *manga*.

The Classifications

Preliminary analyses of Japanese children's graphic narratives revealed that the popular media, especially *manga* and *anima* (animated cartoons) strongly influenced their drawings. In fact, Japanese children's drawings so closely resembled *manga* and *anima* that it was possible to develop a classification system based on specific types of *manga* characters. The method of classification, in effect, consisted of asking, "What are the sources of the characters children put in their drawings and are those human, animal, and other characters drawn using the shapes and configurations for bodies, heads, eyes, hair, limbs, etc. that are found in commercially produced *manga* and *anima*?"

Figure 1 illustrates the major classifications used. They include: (a) doll–like characters—the contemporary paradigmatic *manga* female type's heart–shaped face (although some are drawn with a flattened chin), saucer–shaped eyes, and razor–cut hair (the bodies range from elongated Barbie–like bodies to diminutive Cupie–doll types); (b) animals and birds—the most common is an anthropomorphic rabbit with enormous stylized ears and simple facial and body features (including other animals such as cats, bears, foxes, birds, and turtles—fish were not included in this classification); (c) cyborgs and superheroes—the classification includes robotic types and humans with extraordinary powers; the most common cyborgs are an atomic–powered cat named Doraemon, superhuman samurai warriors, and robotic types; (d) monsters are limited to a few Godzilla types usually depicted as no larger than household pets; (e) comic characters include a variety of types, nearly all of which invite derision because of their peculiar features and abnormalities; (f) other *manga* types consist primarily of humans, mostly males, with a variety of stylized features such as large eyes and shaggy hair, and vegetables and flowers often depicted with human characteristics; (g) mixed types contain hints of some of the features from one or more of the foregoing *manga* types combined with features associated with Japanese child art; and (h) non–*manga* drawings—humans and animals (of the types children either borrow from one another, learn to draw from their observations of photographs and non–*manga* illustrations, or sometimes learn to draw by themselves). The non–*manga* classification also includes things such as architectural structures, automobiles, space ships, etc. containing features that are sometimes found in *manga* but which are difficult to attribute to specific *manga* styles. Some non–*manga* drawings are clearly associated with child art, others are stick figures, while a sizable number depict sports figures such as baseball players (often similar to the life–like figures found in *manga* sports stories but with insufficient characteristics to identify them specifically with *manga*). Finally, in the case of the youngest children, the classification included scribbles, and geometric and amorphous shapes.

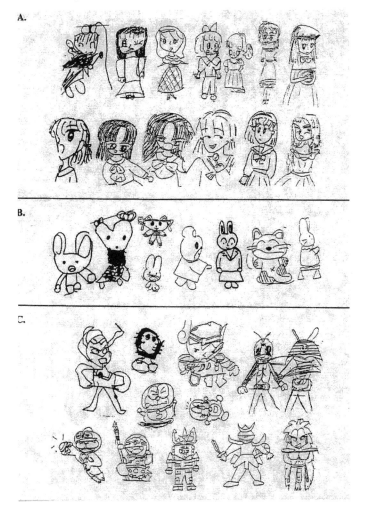

Figure 1. (A) Manga "Dolls Types," (B) Animals, and (C) Cyborgs

Most of the narrative sequences consisted of six frames, but some children used as few as three and others as many as 16 frames. In the analysis process all the frames were reviewed to determine whether one or more *manga*–type characters were present in the sequence. (1) If one or more *manga*–type characters were present, the one most dominant or the most characteristically *manga* character was classified. (2) When there was no clear indication of one or more *manga*–like types in the narratives, a determination was made regarding the presence of features that were influenced by *manga*, but did not follow a paradigmatic *manga* style. These characters were classified as "mixed types." (3) When characters, other objects, and things appeared not to have been influenced by *manga* they were placed in the non–*manga* classification.

The Presence of Manga and Non–manga Types in Japanese Children's Graphic Narratives

Table 1 shows a variety of different patterns in the use of *manga* characters by Japanese children. Only two–percent of kindergarten children produce the paradigmatic "doll" figure. By sixth grade, however, 19 percent of the drawings contain this "doll" figure as the dominant type. Twelve percent of the kindergartners produce a prototypical animal character, and by second grade, 18 percent of the children's narratives are built around these cuddly creatures. It is notable, however, that the incidence of cuddly creatures declines between second and sixth grade. Seven percent of the narratives, from kindergarten through sixth grade, are based on a cyborg character and there is little difference in usage among the grades. It is interesting that monsters are hardly used by any group. The presence of comic types is rare in kindergarten and second grade drawings, while fourth and sixth grade students employ comic types in their drawings between four and five percent of the time. The use of other *manga* types increases steadily from one percent in kindergarten to 25 percent in sixth grade. The classification "mixed types" reveals that a third of the kindergarten children may have tried to draw *manga* characters, but didn't quite succeed. From second through sixth grade the presence of mixed types declines—perhaps indicating a growing mastery of *manga* features and types. Finally there is a decline in the presence of non–*manga* types after kindergarten (46 percent). Approximately one third of the drawings of second through sixth grade depict non–*manga* styles and types.

*Table 1. **Percentages of Manga and Non–manga Types among Japanese Children***

Grade	Doll	Animal Bird	Cyborg	Monster	Comic Type	Other Manga	Mixed Types	Non–Manga
Kinder –garten (94)	02	12	05	00	01	01	33	46
Second (351)	12	18	09	03	01	04	18	34
Fourth (409)	14	14	08	02	04	11	16	30
Sixth (297)	19	06	05	01	05	25	14	34
Total (1151)	11	13	07	02	03	10	20	34

When the types are combined for all four groups, 46 percent of Japanese children's drawings in the sample show the direct influence of *manga*. When this figure is combined with the mixed types, two thirds of the Japanese drawings are influenced by *manga*. The influence of *manga* is probably even higher than the data reveal. Some of the realistically drawn sports characters and things such as automobiles, space ships, and architectural structures found in *manga,* but not easily identifiable as *manga* styles, must surely have affected the children's drawings. Moreover, many of the children who chose not to draw *manga*–type characters in their stories, probably could have—if they had been invited to.

In short, the influence of *manga* on the characters and features of Japanese children's narrative drawings is enormous. What are the consequences of Japanese children's use of *manga* models? What do these findings tell us about Japanese children and Japanese society?

THE SEMIOTIC ANALYSIS OF JAPANESE CHILDREN'S NARRATIVE DRAWINGS: PRETEXTS AND TEXTS

The entire Japanese *manga* industry can be seen as an enormous sign that contains a collection of other signs that when read, tell things about the Japanese people. When Japanese children create their own versions of *manga,* their modeling of adult *manga* may also be viewed as a sign composed of other signs. Every individual *manga* sequence drawn by a Japanese child becomes a sign that contains a collection of other signs. Therefore, Japanese children and their drawings can be understood by reading them as signs in relationship to larger signs and their constituent signs. That is to say, any individual drawing by a child can be read as a text that tells: (1) something about the child and his or her interests, values, purposes, etc.; (2) about art including child art—its types, features, and functions; (3) about society and culture—the range of beliefs that individuals living together hold about themselves, about values, and about goals they either share or disagree about; and (4) when the children's works are interpreted, those interpretations also tell us something about their interpreters. The signs found within and around the drawings of children provide connections to what has been called "absent items"—the things for which the signs stand (Bal, 1991, p. 215). Just as in the interpretation of adult art, the meaning of the art of the child becomes possible only through a tension created among: (1) the pre–texts (Pollock, 1993, p. 530)—to both the dimensions of reality to which the child refers and the artistic traditions that affect the child's work; (2) the texts—the child's art works themselves; and (3) the post–text—the interests, values, and assumptions of the interpreters of child art (including both children and adults). In other words, when we study children's art, we must look not only at what the child has represented, but at its antecedents; and we must also look at ourselves and others in the act of studying child art.

Pretext: The Manga Industry

We have no graphic equivalent to Japan's *manga* industry in the West. In the United States, a sizable number of young people read comic books at some time in their lives. In Japan nearly every child reads *manga* every week. Almost forty–percent of all books and magazines sold in Japan are *manga* (Schodt, 1996, p. 20). *Manga* are published for pre–school and early school–age children. During the middle–school years *manga* take a decidedly gender–oriented turn; separate books are published for pre–teen and teenage girls and boys. A single weekly of around 400 to 450 pages (some monthlies have over 900 pages) might contain 20 or more serialized stories—romance, seduction, pets, tennis, horseback riding, and adventure for girls, and for boys, Judo, historical fantasy, basketball, gag/slapstick, science fiction, soccer, police, comedy, baseball, and psycho–chic/occult. A steady reader of a single *manga* will devour over 1,600 pages each month, and it is worth noting that young people often purchase several different *manga* which they can "read" at great speed—four hundred pages in about half–an–hour.

The industry has created consumers with voracious appetites for the various *manga* genres. To publish *manga* is to engage in a highly competitive business. What encourages such passionate "reading"? Publishing a successful magazine means gaining the profits that come from selling more than six million copies of a single magazine each week. To attract and keep this kind of readership, *manga* artists and their publishers must keep readers "hooked" by maintaining their current stable of characters in a perpetual state of romantic and adventurous uncertainty. At the same time they must create new characters, which, if appealing enough, will gain a vast new readership and new profits. There are literally thousands of *manga* characters, and new *manga* characters are continually being created to replace less successful ones. In giving birth to new characters, however, *manga* artists and publishers walk a narrow line between convention and innovation. New creations must look like the *manga* characters which have already seduced readers; at the same time they must appear more attractive (or unattractive, as the case may be), possess greater powers, and do more marvelous things than the existing characters their creators hope they will replace. Once having developed the voracious appetite for narratives and characters, *manga* artists and publishers must feed it with endless variations on familiar themes.

It is the Japanese young people themselves who, rather than remaining mere passive readers and consumers of *manga*, consort with the forces of artistic capitalism. They organize *manga* clubs; it is estimated that there are as many as 50,000 *manga* clubs or circles in Japan (Schodt, 1996, p. 37). Young people create their own *manga* characters, draw stories, and share them with others. The means they use to share their work is fascinating and tremendously important. Young people mimic the commercial aspects of *manga* by publishing *dōjinshi*—their own *manga* magazines or "fanzines." Then at *manga* or comic book markets they rent booths in order to sell their creations. These markets, some large and some small, are held throughout Japan. The summer 1999 Tokyo Comic Market called "Comike" contained approximately 22,000 booths and perhaps as many as 100,000 different *manga* publications created by young people. Clubs with names like "Active Boys," "Cry Wolf," and "Honey Dip" compete for prizes, advertise, and sell their publications—primarily to other young people. Japanese children have recreated for themselves the very conditions that fuel the adult *manga* industry. Their motives, however, are probably more for fun than for profit.

The Texts

Should we be surprised that so many of the characters in the children's story drawings have *manga* types as their source? Certainly the magnitude of the relationship between popular art and child art is unprecedented anywhere in the world. What does it mean when an entire nation of *manga* creators and consumers, adults and children alike, decides that these are the characters through which it will play out its fantasies? Because the appropriation of *manga* characters is perpetuated on such a massive scale, if we understood the phenomenon, then would we gain insights into Japanese people through their youngest members? This is the central question I wish to address. In offering my initial interpretations of the meaning of the *manga* character types appropriated by children I am somewhat confident of my ability to understand children's drawings and graphic narratives and much less confident about commenting on the character of an entire nation. My readings are tentative at best. Nevertheless, I take pleasure in providing a multiplicity of readings, and even in giving contradictory interpretations.

Female Dolls with Saucer–shaped Eyes. What is it that fascinates us Westerners about the Japanese face? It is the eye. Barthes (1982) connected the Japanese eyelid to calligraphy. Likening an eye to forming an ideographic character, he wrote, it is this same tracing of a pressure which we rediscover in the Japanese eye. As if the anatomist–calligrapher set his full brush on the inner corner of the eye and, turning it slightly, with a single line, as it must be in painting *a la prima*, opens the face with an elliptical slit which he closes toward the temple with a rapid turn of his hand; the stroke is perfect because simple, immediate, instantaneous, and yet ripe as those circles which it takes a lifetime to learn to make in a single sovereign gesture. (p. 99)

And how very different the contemporary *manga* eye is from the elegant narrow line of Barthes' description and also how different from women's eyes in the woodcuts of Hokusai (the original *manga*). Today's *manga* faces come with enormous circular eyes. Indeed, with their blond hair, the faces of these Barbie Doll–like females have the appearance of "the other." It is almost as if the entire nation has conspired to change its face from Asian to Caucasian.

Manga artists draw these non–Japanese humans with eyes that sometimes fill a third of the face, and their eager young apprentices do them one better—sometimes filling half the facial area with eyes the size of headlights. In their narrative drawings many young Japanese children demonstrate that they have mastered the *manga* eye; eyes sparkle with huge highlights, star bursts, and pearl–like strings of secondary highlights. The children have mastered even more than the expressive eyes. When coupled with mouth shapes, hand gestures, and body language they clearly signal an amazing array of emotions and states of being: eagerness, apprehension, seductiveness, distress, wonder, innocence, evil. (These expressive features are seldom found in children's drawings which have not been influenced by *manga*.) Although the graphic models had their origin with the work of adult *manga* artists, now young people circulate their creations through *dôjinshi*. Models for drawing *manga* characters travel from child to child through *dôjinshi* clubs and market catalogues. Influences travel from top to bottom, laterally, and if we were to examine them closely perhaps influences might even be found to travel from gifted younger children to older ones. We might even look to see if adult *manga* artists are influenced by their younger counterparts. This speculation notwithstanding, *manga* models are there to follow, and follow them children do—with astonishing skill.

But why are the models there in the first place? Why is it that over 90 percent of the female figures found in young peoples' *manga* convention catalogues have eyes that contradict the anatomical Japanese eye? Schodt (1983) claims that it is evidence of a "revolution in the way Japanese people view—or wish to view themselves" (p. 92). I agree, and I also think that there are both simpler and more complicated reasons. Any creator of cheesecake art knows that humans are attracted to large eyes. "Make the eyes like saucers and you can get away with anything," that's what my Detroit landlord and airbrush school owner, J. Zeller Allen, taught me in 1957. But we also need to look further. The Japanese are attracted to foreign physiognomies, especially Nordic types. "An aesthetic fascination for the West is . . . evident in modern Japan. Fashion magazines use blondes from Sweden and California to show Japanese designed clothes; Caucasian dummies stand stiffly in Japanese shop windows; students decorate their dormitory walls with *Playboy* magazine pinups" (Buruma, 1984, p. 51).

I think that the doll–like figures represent "the Japanese" and "the other" simultaneously. The doll–like figures provide a way for Japanese people to construct, for example, the "wide–eyed" features that they see in and admire about themselves, but they also reveal a longing for more of that feature—to look more as "the other" looks. Is it also possible that by drawing these doll–like figures, Japanese children think of themselves as possessing these idealized features while at the same time, unconsciously, expressing a dissatisfaction with themselves?

Animals: Mostly Rabbits. In Japan *chojugiga,* ink scrolls showing humorous pictures of birds and animals engaging in human activities, were painted as early as the twelfth century (Schodt, 1983, p. 30). In the famous *chojugiga* in the Kozanji Buddhist temple near Kyoto, rabbits, foxes, monkeys, and frogs converse, read, and gesture. Indeed, the *chojugiga* are the forerunners of *manga.* Contemporary *manga,* especially those created for preschool age children, are filled with animal characters—especially rabbits.

When animals are depicted as humans, we may assume that different animal species provide ways to examine particular human traits of character and behavior. Monkeys, as the young Chinese artist Yani (Wai–Ching Ho, 1989) shows, provide ways to explore deviousness, playfulness, and mischief. But what is the meaning of the placid huggable rabbit with large ears, found in *manga* produced for very young people and reproduced by young children?

My reading is this: the rabbit is a cipher, albeit a cute one. Although visually appealing, the rabbit's most notable characteristic is a blankness that when reproduced time and time again results in the very epitome of sameness. Is the rabbit a sign of conformity and of the complacency desired especially in little girls? Does the rabbit character provide the opportunity to practice staying in line, being satisfied with following rules, doing ordinary things? Is it a sign that one should be like everyone else—not to stand out within the group? Is it the ultimate sign of cohesion where individual interests and desires are subordinated to those of the group? At the very least, when young children borrow animal characters such as the rabbit from *manga,* personality is reduced nearly to the point of disappearance.

It is fascinating that adult publishers present these cute animals in magazines directed to the youngest children and it is the youngest children who employ the figures in their own drawings. (Twice as many are found in the drawings of kindergartners as sixth graders.) Adults give children what they assume children want and children reciprocate by reading the magazines and drawing their own versions of the cute little animals whose occupation is to play it safe, follow the rules, and passively engage in the most ordinary of everyday activities. The cute animals who present the orderly and mannered side of Japanese behavior, however, have their counterparts in cyborgs and superheroes.

Cyborgs. As in the West, *manga* has its share of characters who possess extraordinary mental and physical powers. Superheroes of the sorts that Japanese children produce may have their roots in *samurai* traditions, they may come from muscular robots with mechanical prowess (patterned after characters such as Mazinger Z who is controlled by a young man from a cockpit inside its head), or they may be taken directly from types who are tiny but quick–witted. Indeed, no *manga* character appropriated by young children is more clever than Doraemon, the diminutive atomic–powered cat who "suddenly materialized from the top drawer of [his] young [friend] Nobita's desk one day... The desk–drawer was a gateway to the Fourth Dimension, and so was Doraemon's kangaroo–like pouch, which could produce almost anything Nobita wanted" (Schodt, 1983, 14). Doraemon fulfills wishes by taking his friend on adventure filled journeys, cleverly solving problems, and serving as Nobita's protector. If a threat or a need arises Doraemon can obtain from his pouch the gadget or the means that will overcome any difficulty or obtain any desired thing.

Doraemon is much like the children who eagerly draw him in their own stories. He is tiny, cute, and clever, and he has control over his world in ways that the young child can only wish. The places he goes may represent the unknown—journeys into the future. When Doraemon gets into difficulty, he possesses the "inner resources" needed to solve the problem—in his pouch. When children draw the cyborg Doraemon stories, they symbolically rehearse ways to overcome difficulties.

From the standpoint of the nation, symbolically overcoming difficulties and solving endless problems is good practice for kids in a small country whose survival depends upon the development of the one natural resource it has in abundance—the minds of its young people. Japan's future rests with its children who must eventually make their contributions to its continuing prosperity by creating the next in a never–ending series of technological miracles. Doraemon and other cyborgs represent power, intellect, ingenuity—not bad qualities to possess—and to practice possessing.

The contrast between the passive cute animals and the cyborgs, one of whom is himself a cute animal, illustrate the complexities—even the contradictions—in the character models presented to and used by Japanese children. At the same time that children must follow rules and lead ordinary lives they must also practice ingenuity and imagination. In *manga* they find models for both types of behavior.

Comic Characters. The comic category consists of a clutter of characters—many of whom are ugly, undesirable, and funny. For example, there are short ugly males with buck teeth, squinty eyes, glasses, and runny noses, and characters with undesirable physical features such as obesity. Whereas the doll–like characters are signs of the selves–we–see and the "others" we wish to be, most of the "assorted others" are the selves–we–wish–not–to–be and the selves–we–are–afraid–others–might–see. In they main they are characters that invite derision and disgust. And what purposes might they serve? The child who draws one of these characters can feel superior to the poor and pitied creatures. Indeed, they provide the opportunity to discriminate, to belittle, to revile, to look down upon "the other" who is so different from the ideal self. Is it also possible, however, that within this derision, there is the subtle hint of insecurity—the quiet raising of the personal question, "Is this me?" and the social question, "Is this us?" Do these characters represent the "us we are afraid others might think we are?" or even "the people we sometimes, deep down, think we actually are?" Are these "assorted others" signs of individual or national insecurity? At the very least, when children draw comic characters they have the opportunity to feel superior to others.

Others Manga Types Including Monsters. This final classification is like a broom closet into which I placed all the rest of the *manga*–type characters. There are the ideal male characters with razor–cut hair and large eyes—but not as large as those of the female doll characters. There are cute little humanoid characters that have the blank cipher quality of the rabbit characters described above, but without the ears. There are characters formed from vegetables, fruit, and flowers. There are the monsters, many looking like a cross between miniature dinosaurs and dragons. And there are turd characters and piles of shit that take on odorous lives of their own. Because the classification is so broad, it is not possible to make a single generalization regarding the roles that these characters might play. Nevertheless, in some respects, the classification reinforces the notion that the characters are related to the variety of roles that individuals might play in Japanese society. The characters provide the means to act as–if one had certain attributes, potentials, or handicaps. They provide ways to experience symbolically what it is like to be handsome, dim–witted, desirable, offensive, different, or nearly anonymous through one's featurelessness. This classification contains almost the same range of features and characters found in the individual types discussed above.

The Non–Manga Types. To me, the non–*manga* types appear bland, especially when compared to the distinctive characters children model after *manga*. Most of the non–*manga* possess ordinary looks, ordinary powers, and in the main, they do ordinary things. They simply don't appear to have as much fun as their *manga* counterparts. The realistically drawn sports heroes are the exception: they do show lots of action; they do not, however, display much emotion. They may show a range of human actions, but these characters lack the personality and the capacity for human feeling and emotion displayed by the *manga* characters. I wonder if the *manga* characters and fabulous variety of potentials, when activated through appropriation, don't make ordinary ways of being seem somewhat dull.

SOME TENTATIVE CONCLUSIONS

In the *manga*–like characters found in Japanese children's graphic narratives we see what happens when the youngest members of a society make use of a pervasive elaborate system of shared images that carry meaning, beliefs, values, and understanding. Curiously, it is possible to attribute to the children's process of appropriation precisely what Bruner attributes to education—the complex process of fitting a culture to the needs of its individual members while permitting children simultaneously to explore ways of knowing appropriate to the needs of the culture (Bruner, 1996).

The one large sign, *manga* (and for the purposes of this study, *manga* characters), signifies how the Japanese people see themselves, how they want to see themselves, and how they are both attracted to and repelled by "the other." Through *manga* Japanese children are presented with characters that are ready to fulfill the potentials of their types. Individually they show desirable and undesirable traits of character—the traits that must be cultivated or discounted. Nevertheless, the *manga* characters must be understood collectively, not just individually. Collectively the *manga* character types provide the opportunity for acting out social roles—the opportunity to explore what is it like to be beautiful, ugly, cute, plain, ordinary, extraordinary, brilliant, stupid, clever, powerful, stigmatized, revered. The facets of the "Japanese character" revealed by adult–created *manga* and child–appropriated *manga* are filled with contradictions—some blatant and some subtle.

Manga characters appropriated by children reveal the complexity of learning what it means to be Japanese, and Japanese children's drawings reveal how quickly and how thoroughly children model the complexities of being a Japanese person in Japanese society. The children's drawings also reveal the complexity of the task of maintaining collective images of "ourselves" while at the same time coping with change and rehearsing roles of individual and collective innovation in both the national and international realms. I think *manga* drawings offer advantages to Japanese children which many children in other countries do not have. They provide a marvelous means through which to experiment. At the same time the character models, through which Japanese children plot their individual and collective futures, are frequently shallow, stereotypical, and multidimensional in problematic ways. At the same time that *manga* characters provide possibilities for innovative behavior, they may also perpetuate stereotypical thinking and ways of behaving.

Nevertheless, I must express the awe I feel in the presence of children's *manga*–appropriating process. Because of *manga* models, Japanese children draw differently from children in other cultures—and far more skillfully than most. (They also draw differently because of the highly structured school program, but their *manga* drawings bear little resemblance to the contour–like drawings they make during art classes. Japanese children, in effect, speak two graphic languages, one belonging to the school and one belonging to the popular arts [Wilson, 1997].) Because of *manga* Japanese children take fuller advantage of the graphic/symbolic system—use it more effectively as a tool for human understanding—than any group of young people I have observed anywhere on the globe. Rather than being inhibited by the character models served up by *manga*, Japanese children improvise upon the possibilities provided by the character models. Through the appropriation and creation of their own *manga* characters they grasp dimensions of human cognition and emotion, pay collective, albeit largely unconscious, attention to the ways Japanese people might be and behave, and grasp (also unconsciously) the significance of what it means to act as an individual within a conforming society. For these reasons, and more, I think drawing after *manga* characters liberates more than it constrains Japanese children.

My reading of and writing about the *manga* industry pretext, children's *manga* character texts, and some possible post–textual consequences relating to Japanese children and the Japanese people now becomes a text that awaits reading by others. Readings that contradict mine are welcome.

REFERENCES

Aronsson, K. & Andersson, S. (1996). Social scaling in children's drawings of classroom life: A cultural comparative analysis of social scaling in Africa and Sweden. *British Journal of Developmental Psychology, 14*, 301–314.

Bal, M. (1991). *Reading "Rembrandt": Beyond the word–image opposition.* Cambridge: Cambridge University Press.

Barthes, R. (1982). *Empire of signs.* New York: Hill and Wang.

Bruner, J. (1996). *The culture of education.* Cambridge: Harvard University Press.

Buruma, I. (1984). *Behind the mask.* New York: Pantheon Books.

Pollock, G. (1993). Review of Mieke Bal, *Reading "Rembrandt": Beyond the word–image opposition, The Art Bulletin, LXXV*(3), 529–535.

Schodt, F. L. (1996). *Dreamland Japan: Writings on modern manga.* Berkeley: Stone Bridge press.

Schodt, F. L. (1983). *Manga, manga!: The world of Japanese comics.* Tokyo, New York, and San Francisco: Kodansha International.

Wai–Ching Ho.(1989). *Yani: The brush of innocence.* New York: Hudson Hills Press.

Wilson, B. (1997). Types of child art and alternative developmental accounts: Interpreting the interpreters. *Human Development, 40*(3), 155–168.

Wilson, B., (1987), Histories of children's styles of art: Possibilities and prospects. In B. Wilson & H. Hoffa (Eds.),*The history of art education: Proceedings from the Penn State conference* (pp.177–184). Reston, VA: The National Art Education Association.

Wilson, B. & Ligtvoet, J. (1992). Across time and cultures: Stylistic changes in the drawings of Dutch children. In D. Thistlewood (Ed.), *Drawing: Research and development* (pp.75–88). Harlow, Essex, England: Longman.

Wilson, B. & Wilson, M. (1979). Figure structure, figure action and framing in drawings of American and Egyptian children. *Studies in Art Education, 21*(1), 33–43.

Wilson, B. & Wilson, M. (1981). The case of the disappearing two–eyed profile: Or how little children influence the drawings of little children. *Review of Research in Visual Arts Education*, (15), 1–18.

Wilson, B. & Wilson, M. (1983). Themes and structures in the graphic narratives of American, Australian, Egyptian, and Finnish children: Tales from four cultures. *The Journal of Multi–Cultural and Cross–Cultural Research in Art Education, 1*(1), 63–76.

Wilson, B. & Wilson, M. (1984) Children's drawings in Egypt: Cultural style acquisition as graphic development. *Visual Arts Research, 10*(1), 13–26.

Wilson, B., & Wilson, M. (1987) Pictorial composition and narrative structure: Themes and the creation of meaning in the drawings of Egyptian and Japanese children *Visual Arts Research, 13*(2), 10–21.

An early version of this chapter was published in *Visual Arts Research, 25* (2), 1999, pp. 48-60.

PATRICIA SHEHAN CAMPBELL

4. THE MUSICAL CULTURES OF CHILDREN

Music is important to children, and there are few who do not revel in it. They welcome opportunities to think and act musically, and they do so with exuberance. The music is in them, too, manifesting itself both audibly and visibly in the pitches and rhythms of their play, in the songs they sing, and in the ways that they step, sway, bounce, and "groove" to it. Children express and entertain themselves, and communicate and socialize through the musical sounds they make or that surround them in their homes, neighborhoods, and schools. They are drawn to music, for as they explore, experiment with, and respond to it, music is the refuge in which they find fulfillment and safe harbor away from the worries of their young lives. While all the arts provide children with outlets for expression, the power of music as both aural phenomenon and a stimulus of kinesthetic activity functions for them—on request—as much as a veil of protection from, as well as a bridge for interactions with, others. As they take in other performances or make their own musical sounds, children are often transformed by the density and intensity of patterns that are logically ordered and expressed from the heart (and soul). For children, music is a natural inclination, and it often appears to be as essential to their well–being as it is for them to be warm, fed, and well–rested.

School is one of the places in which children acquire music. They learn songs and gain other musical knowledge from their music teachers, their classroom teachers, and from other children. These songs sometimes enhance their learning of language, or mathematical concepts, or appropriate social behaviors, and they may be accompanied by "action," be it signifying gestures, dance, or games. Music is accessible to children beyond the classroom, too, so that many learn music as it is provided to them by their parents, siblings, and extended family members and by the social and religious communities of their family's involvement. It is also mediated to them in a large variety of ways: radio, TV, recordings, videotapes and films, CD–Roms, and other late–breaking technological avenues. Thus the acquisition of musical repertoire and a set of techniques for making and responding to this music are available to children formally and informally, both in school and "on the outside."

The purpose of these pages is to consider the roles which music plays in children's lives, and the manner by which the various folkways, technologies, and institutional settings help them to perpetuate and preserve particular musical expressions and experiences. Children's membership in various social and cultural units will be explored, and the inevitable influences which those units have upon children's musical ideas, values, and behaviors will likewise be considered. An understanding of the content and processes of children's play (and in particular their musical play) will give rise to a discussion of the use and function of music in their lives, and will bring focus to some of the salient musical and textual features of their playful musical "lore." How

L. Bresler and C.M. Thompson (eds.), The Arts in Children's Lives, 57–69.
© 2002 *Kluwer Academic Publishers. Printed in the Netherlands.*

children are musically enculturated and formally educated in and through music will comprise the greater extent of this chapter, which will close with the interface of their formal and informal experiences in coming to know music.

CHILDREN'S SOCIAL UNITS AND CULTURAL GROUPINGS

Children's societies are a blend of progressive and conservative patterns of behavior, fantasy and innovation, and routine and ritual. At times they invent expressive behavior all their own in clever and original ways, while at other times they embrace behaviors they have heard or seen before through mimicry (if not outright mockery) of their perceptions of it. They dress up like their heroes of the media, shoot toy laser guns like space warriors, and lip–sync to the songs of their favorite recording stars. More often than not, children are likely to settle for the center of the spectrum, developing variants on language, stories, games, and songs that they have already experienced. They "tamper" with what they have witnessed but also adhere to its essence, ascertaining that it remains substantially the same as they had first perceived it. They create parodies of songs and new "editions" of stories, and are known for their ability to shape language to a dialect and vocabulary all their own. Children are prone to playing with the components of music in order to make them fit their expressive needs, yet they are also anchored to the values and practices of the adults who raise them.

Children constitute their own over–arching, all–encompassing folk group (Dundes, 1965; Sutton–Smith, 1995), in that they share common traditions in language, values, and behavioral patterns. They are thus a "big" culture, united by experiences of their brief lives and the knowledge they have acquired and stored within them. In their early phases of learning, as children's acquisition of conceptual knowledge is rapidly developing, this knowledge is still in various formative stages. Their world view is not the same as that of adults or adolescents who have had longer life experiences, and while their perceptions are colored by their sociocultural surroundings, children share with each other similar extents of knowledge, as well as play preferences and interests that are associated with their similar intellectual and physical development.

But children's culture is large, multifarious, and decidedly pluralistic. Thus, it is possible for children to be members of more than a single folk group, belonging as they do to a family sibling group, a neighborhood, a preschool play group, a class within a school, a soccer team, a girl scout troupe, a youth choir, a gang. Children belong to big and little cultural groups, overlapping one to the next and learning the lore of each.

Among the traits that are most likely to break the larger culture into sub–cultures (or "little" cultures), age and stage of intellectual, social, and emotional growth are prominent. Jean Piaget (1951) divided childhood into four stages of intellectual development from infancy through age twelve, from sensorimotor learning to the immediate application of abstract reasoning to the knowledge they acquire. Likewise, Jerome Bruner noted three age–based phases of learning (1966). Gregory Bateson (1978) discussed the manner in which learners proceed through early, middle, and mature phases of cultural acquisition, and Catherine Ellis (1986) further moved these phases into a framework that is pertinent to the development of children's musical selves: from their musical enculturation, to their conscious commitment to practice, to their musical mastery. Children's culture can also be divided by types of care and schooling provided to them: nursery or daycare, preschool, elementary school (and middle or junior high and high school); they are further distinguished by primary (kindergarten through grade two or three) and intermediate (grades three through six) grades, and even more so by individual grade levels. Distinctive children's groups are also based upon factors such as gender, ethnicity, socioeconomic status, and ability level.

It may thus be difficult to conceive of a single children's culture, and to "lump" children as one musical culture. Like snowflakes, each one is unique and not easily homogenized into a single entity. Perhaps, as Mark Slobin (1993) suggested, big music cultures (like "children's culture") are best conceived in smaller units (p. 11). His claim that people live at the interaction of three cultures suits children well. They can be conceived of as members of the "super–culture" (the large and overarching category, "children"), several "sub–cultures" (embedded units, e.g., preschoolers or fourth–graders, girls or boys, African American or Chicano children), and "intercultures" (unities resulting from shared experiences and widespread influences that cut across the sub–cultures, such as players of various ball games, collectors of dolls and action figures, or listeners of mass–mediated popular music) (p. 12). To this can be added each child's idioculture, or culture of the self, to which Charles Keil has given considerable thought (1994). Children have their idiosyncratic thoughts and behaviors, and can take their place as members of multiple cultures, each with its own musical affiliations.

All children start out in the nuclear culture of their family, and then graduate to others (Slobin, 1993, p. 55). Their musical knowledge spins out from this primary source in ever–widening concentric circles first within and then beyond the family. These circles are the result of developmental changes, so that with increasing age they graduate from one progressive layer of age–culture to the next. Children's first live musical experiences are often lullabies sung to them by their parents, particularly their mothers, during infancy and throughout their first year as "lap babies" (Whiting & Edwards, 1988, p. 5). While these lullabies may vary in pitch and rhythmic information from one family to the next, their soft and slow dynamic qualities nonetheless are universally intended to lull little ones to sleep. Remarkably, some of this early music is remembered and recalled even into adulthood, so integrated is it within the young and impressionable minds of infants.

With toddlerhood comes the play songs of the "knee children," which continue to be sung through their later preschool years as "yard children" (Whiting & Edwards, 1988, p. 198). These songs are sung as children play in yards and parks, on swings and in sandboxes (and certainly indoors as well). Play songs and rhythmic chants are not always consciously rendered, but nonetheless trickle out of children in seemingly spontaneous ways as they playfully engage themselves with toys, other objects, and other children. Their musical content is taken from songs they have heard, some of it beamed out to them from their TVs and car radios. Yard children rarely play in silence, but talk, make sounds, and often sing to themselves and others with whom they play.

A shift to the next age–based musical culture occurs as children enter school. At five, six, and beyond, they may still hear lullabies at bedtime, and they will probably continue to semi–consciously sing as they play or work on their projects. Yet when they graduate to the level of "school children," they enter into the realm of singing games, clapping chants, and regular and purposeful rhythms. These musical genres depend upon the interaction of children with other children, in patterns of socialization that were previously unimportant to them. In partners, clusters, and circles and line formations, with or without props (jumpropes, balls, scarves, and sticks), most girls and more than a few boys learn and preserve traditional and contemporary melodies, rhythms, and choreographed forms given them by other children. As in the cases of lap babies and the knee and the yard children, the particulars of music and text may vary from one cultural subset (i.e., neighborhood, religious or ethnic group) to the next, but the engagement of children in these musical genres is a natural result of their entry into this age–based culture.

A particularly intriguing facet of children's cultures is the manner in which their songs can be distinguished by the ethnicity of their singers. Carol Merrill–Mirsky (1988) observed that Euro–American and Asian children were likely to sing pitched melodies while at play, while African–American children performed more non–pitched rhythmic chants. She described African–American children's singing games as more numerous, more syncopated, and more likely to make use of formulaic introductions that those of Euro–American, Asian, or Latino children. She found not only musical but also gestural distinctions among the songs belonging to children of the four broad ethnic–cultures. Others have corroborated these findings, including Campbell (1991), Harwood (1987), and Marsh (1995).

Meanwhile, as children become embedded in the living musical cultures of their families, neighborhoods, and schoolyards, the mediated mass music rains on them as well. It blares at them in the background of their favorite TV shows, and through the jingles that advertise the toys, food, and drink they hope to have. It undergirds or outwardly carries the messages and morals of the videos they watch. The mediated popular music appears as ambient sound or as a provocative experience, and neither children nor their families need to produce it (i.e., to perform it) to "have" it within their ears. But while children may readily receive the media's music already packaged for their passive consumption, they also continue to want to actively participate in it as they hear it. From Barney songs to the music of Clint Black or Pearl Jam, children will sing, move, and groove to mediated, commercial music. They are receiving and working through the musical grammar and idiomatic expressions of popular music, the orally–transmitted urban folk music of their time.

Just as popular music constitutes a musical interculture that is widely shared by children across many sub–cultures, so does the phenomenon called "school music" provide them with a common repertoire. The music which teachers select for their lessons and programs varies from teacher to teacher, of course, but there are also standard sources to which teachers refer in planning lessons. There may even be a common *canon* of songs and musical works which teachers embrace, passing this music among themselves at workshops and professional meetings. For over a century, patriotic songs like "America," "America, the Beautiful," and "The Star–Spangled

Banner" have been appearing in school textbooks, programs and assemblies; added to this are favorites like "This Land is Your Land," "This is My Country," and the more contemporary "God Bless the U.S.A.". While Stephen Foster songs are rarely sung anymore, basal series textbooks like *The Music Connection* (Silver Burdett & Ginn, 1995) and *Share the Music* (Macmillan, 1995) offer a varied fare of traditional and composed songs for singing and listening. Under the rubric of "multicultural music" songs like "Sakura" from Japan, "Kye Kye Kule" from Ghana, "Las Mananitas" from Mexico, and "Sorida" from Zimbabwe recently have been added to old standbys like "Clementine," "Shenandoah" and "Swing Low, Sweet Chariot." Recent development in state–mandated policy for cultural pluralism has governed selections that now rest securely under the umbrella of "school music," a repertoire that many children in American schools may share.

Children of all ages constitute the larger superculture—the big culture of children—and are grouped together and said to be recipients and processors of similar musical knowledge through similar experiences. Yet it is absurd for us to conceive of children as a single musical culture extending from infancy through pubescence, all united by the same experiences. The concept of children fitting into multiple cultural units is far more logical. Indeed, the microcultures and micromusics defined by Mark Slobin suit the many musical realities of children, for their musical worlds are indeed many–splendored, a true conglomerate of styles and influences far too complex to pin down or generalize.

HOW CHILDREN USE MUSIC

For young children, musical meaning is deeply related to function. "Good music," we say, should be the stuff of children's experience; "good for what?," they want to know. Children use music in its every guise and function, and find that as they think and do music, they are buoyed by it, comforted in it, reflective through it, and exuberant as a result of their expressions with it. In my own research on children's musical values (Campbell, 1998), their uses of music ranged from the playful to the serious, and from the solitary to the social. These uses or functions fit categories raised by Merriam (1964), Gaston (1968), and Kaemmer (1993); I use Merriam's list as an organizer here. In interesting ways, these functions overlap one another, so that it is entirely possible for a child to find aesthetic fulfillment as he physically responds to music he hears or is making. Importantly, music contributes in positive ways to children's lives, and many recognize—even in their youth and inexperience—that they could not live without it.

Emotional Expression

Music's power to express raw emotions is not lost on children. I learned about this use of music from ten–year–old Alan, who explained that one of his chief reasons for singing atop a tree stump far removed from everyone (and everything) was that it was a means of releasing his emotions, expressing his feelings, and exploring his musical thoughts without interference. With no one within earshot, his wailing may have been as much for the sheer release of tension as for the opportunity to hear himself at full volume. Much younger children are likewise drawn to music's expressive powers: Five–year–old Darryl confessed that "I sing when I'm happy," and seven–year–old Lisa acknowledged that she "saved it up inside" herself to release when she was safely at home with her family. Children like Alan use music as a means for venting emotions, a means that is civil and thus acceptable by members of their society.

Aesthetic Enjoyment

Contrary to popular belief, the deep emotional and intellectual enjoyment of music is not an exclusive "adults–only" experience. Children are drawn to music for its power to bring fuller enjoyment to their lives. Newborn babies respond well to the musical stimulation parents provide in their "parentese" (that unique genre of musically inflected speech which parents develop while communicating to their wee ones); these infants may even participate in this pressure–free, joyful sociomusical interaction through their own attempts at vocalizing and moving to the features of musical speech (Papousek, 1996). For many years past infancy (prior to the social inhibitions that develop in pre–adolescence), children demonstrate their aesthetic enjoyment through the movements and gestures they make while listening to music —the way they bounce and bob, tap rhythms, and pretend to play imaginary instruments to match the music they hear. Their enjoyment is visible, while the depth of their aesthetic experience may well lie below the surface of the physical manifestations.

Entertainment

Children might not call music "entertaining" to them, but on many occasions that is precisely how it functions. In observations of children as well as conversations with them, I found that children continue to be entertained by their tapes and CDs, by radio music, and by the music on TV, films, and their favorite videos. Some children are well aware of music's way of hovering just behind the animated and dramatic stories on the TV programs and films they watch, and respond as much to the music as to the scenes it may accompany and enhance. Other children choose to listen to music throughout their waking hours, and fall to sleep with their favorite tapes and CDs playing. Music is also an integral part of the games which children play; the handclapping and jumprope games of children are rarely without the rhythmic chants or sung melodies of the rhyming verses there to amuse them.

Communication

Important sentiments are conveyed through music, and can be understood as well by children as by adults within the same society. From early on, parents and infants share a "prelinguistic alphabet" or code in the form of musical features that both infant–directed speech and infant vocal sounds have in common (Papousek, 1996). Later, music continues to have communicative properties. In my conversations with children as well as in my observations of them at play, children frequently allow their speech to turn rhythmic and even melodic in their inflections. They also receive messages intended to be communicated by the music—from the romantic images conveyed by popular songs to the solidarity and strength expressed by a family's singing of a religious or patriotic hymn. In its function as communication, music enables children to play the roles of both producers and receivers.

Physical Response

To many children, music and movement are inseparable. Infants nod and shake their heads, kick, rock, and click their tongue to musical sounds, while toddlers add bouncing, arm–waving, and swaying to their repertoire. By four, children are hopping, jumping, and marching to music, and by six they can gallop and are on their way to skipping. Some children will acknowledge their attraction to music for dancing; and many who may seem negatively disposed to dancing are nonetheless drawn to the groove of the music as their bodies bob, bounce, and sub–divide to the rhythms they hear. Eight–year–old James, one of my own "informants" on children's musical engagement, explained that adult music of the "sit–there–and–not–move" genre challenged (if not deterred) his patience in listening to it, while twelve–year–old Jonathan described the kinesthetic reality of music for him: "It (music) moves, and it makes you move." Children dance as they play and work; they jump, clap their hands, pat their legs, conduct, swing their towels, tap their pencils in time to the music they hear. Whether choreographed and stylized, or free and spontaneous, movement is a principle means of children's musical engagement.

Enforcement of Conformity to Social Norms

As Merriam explained it, music is sometimes used to provide instructions or warnings. While such functions often may be adult–initiated, children surely receive and respond to them. For example, parents and teachers commonly turn familiar melodies into vessels of learning by altering the words to teach etiquette (songs that reinforce the use of "please" and "thank you") and to remind children of appropriate social behaviors (songs that teach children to share, to wait their turn, to help those that need help). As for music's function in providing a "warning," children respond without provocation to the theme music that signals their favorite television show; they may literally leap to the family sets on hearing the opening pitches of the show's theme, a certain call to attention for them.

Validation of Religious Rituals

Many children have within their song repertoire a selection of songs with religious themes, including such favorites as "Jesus Loves Me," "Kum Ba Ya," and a host of religious "holiday" songs. These they learn at church and temples, in religious schools, at children's services, and of course through family members' introduction and reinforcement of them. In my recent research, I encountered an eight–year–old girl who knew well a repertoire of gospel songs from her regular attendance at church, and an eleven–year–old girl who could sing with little provocation the Gregorian chant from her church choir repertoire. Another six–year–old boy gathered a part of his musical repertoire from his participation in the prayer services of his Indian–born Hindu parents. Families direct children toward worship, it seems, that is musically well–seasoned.

Continuity and Stability of Culture

Music functions in children's lives as a means of linking them to their cultural heritage, and of reflecting the values of their ethnic culture. Even young children perform in ethnic cultural ensembles of young musicians and dancers: for example, certain Los Angeles–based Chicano children who participate in mariachi groups; some of the children of Pittsburgh's Croatian community who perform in junior tamburitza ensembles; the young step–dancers of various Irish–American communities; and hundreds of Khmer children in Seattle, Boston, and Washington, D.C. who continue to learn and perform the historical dance and music traditions of the royal courts of Cambodia. Families and extended communities use music to preserve in children the cultural expressions that are deemed important enough to be transmitted to them.

Integration of Society

Music brings children together, and unites and integrates them within a society. Their "society" is their family, their school group, their neighborhood. Whether they sing together on road trips or at bedtime, play duets and improvise at the piano, or dance together to traditional or popular music, they coalesce and draw closer to one another as they do so. Their singing games bring them into a unions with their friends, just as their participation in school ensembles brings them a sense of belonging to a society of like–minded young people. Children's membership in these social groups that make music together at home and in school is a means of establishing their greater unity through music.

Thus are children drawn to music for its personal and social uses, verbally explained or demonstrated by them through their musicking behaviors. Music's meaning is its function to them, and it may hold its own—center stage—or may enhance another activity in which they are engaged. For each musical experience a child may have, its meaning will be related to its use to them and will be wrapped around the experiences which the individual child brings to bear upon it. Children know music, and they use it in myriad ways. As teachers recognize the prominence of music in children's lives at home and at play, many are persuaded to integrate musical studies within the comprehensive plan for their holistic education. Music is thus seen as more than an ancillary, even subordinate, experience, and more as part–and–parcel of a child's development in school as well as "on the outside."

MUSICAL ENCULTURATION

Enculturation has its roots in anthropology, where it is explained as the life–long process by which people develop their personal and collective cultural identity (Jorgensen, 1997). Children's memberships in particular subsets of society and in specific sociocultural groups are reason for their acquisition of particular types of knowledge, beliefs, values, and attitudes. This process of acquiring cultural knowledge, including music, occurs in broader and more comprehensive ways than the channels of school may provide; it may occur with and without direct instruction and participation in the act of music making. Musical enculturation may seem elusive, but in fact it encompasses the varied musical experiences which children have as they grow up within families, neighborhoods, schools, and various constituent communities. As cultures change, and as children become members of new sociocultural groups (for example, through family relocation or their own maturational processes), they will continue to be shaped by the forces of their environment.

The enculturative learning of children occurs quite naturally, and may often be unintended (or not directly attended to) by adults. Intuitive learning is part of becoming enculturated, and this learning proceeds informally through children's immersion within and exploration of a culture. Children are enculturated prior to schooling as they experience, evolve theories, and learn symbols based upon what they see, hear, taste, smell, and touch. They learn the values and expressions of their culture, and even as schooling begins, this process continues. As their more sophisticated needs are addressed at ever higher stages of cognitive processing within the school curriculum, children continue to be enculturated by parents, teachers, siblings, members of their extended families, friends, and the media.

Through these varied channels, the tenets of musical culture, including valued timbres, musical forms, melodic and rhythmic patterns, are passed on to children. They come to understand the role of music in their lives, as well as to understand their culture in and through the music they hear and in which they participate. Their musical enculturation is holistic in nature, in that their musical selves are a product of the music they have encountered through their multiple experiences in growing up under the influence of their environment.

The music which children possess, the songs and chants which they themselves create and re–create, is in fact demonstrative of their enculturation. Their less formally structured musical "utterances" are products of what they musically know and have internalized from their surroundings. These spontaneously generated phrases, both melodic and rhythmic, exude from them as they play. Kartomi (1991) refers to them as musical doodlings, and they are indeed musical daydreams that seem to flow effortlessly from them. These utterances are typically fragments derived from children's earlier experiences, some of which may gel into finished musical products: their songs.

This music that children make is fascinating for its widespread presence in a variety of contexts, from the playground to the school classroom, in the swimming pool and on the baseball field, in the shopping mall and around the supper table. Melodies fluctuate from seconds and thirds to full octave leaps, while their rhythms are often syncopated—and always pulsive. The songs of children's jumprope and hand–clapping games, as well as their cheers at baseball games, tend to fall within their speaking range, often from about G or A to just over an octave above (b or c'). Pitch is established by the leader of a game or activity, or by the loudest child. Singing games and other songs of play are frequently arranged in strophic form, with each verse sung to the same melody. Nearly without exception, these songs fall into simple duple 2/4 or 4/4 meter.

Children's spontaneous singing—their utterances—are typically open–ended, with beginnings and endings unpredictably developing from and returning to their playful interactions with toys. Some are intermediary forms, performances that sit somewhere between speaking and singing (Nattiez, 1990). They may even consist of semantically meaningless syllables, often peppered by the various dotted patterns found in the popular music they know. The melodies vary with the songs children inadvertently stitch together, and very few of them are stuck in a groove of the descending minor third. Indeed, children's melodic meanderings frequently consist of at least five tones, and they may vocalize two octaves or more. My observations corroborate those of John Blacking (1973), W. Jay Dowling (1984), and Helmut Moog (1976), none of whom could not find much evidence for the universality of an "ur–song" for children. Beyond the use of this minor third in calling chants, the music of children's musical play is far more varied melodically and rhythmically—a reflection of their rich musical enculturation.

Onward through their lives, as children graduate to adolescent and then adult spheres of influence, the songs in their heads typically become more extensive in stylistic range, pitch and rhythm information. Their first music is then surrounded by a series of concentric circles spinning outward, each circle representing the musical styles and forms that comprise their ever–expanding world. As a life–long process, the musical enculturation that began at birth is dynamic in nature and unique to each individual.

MUSICALLY EDUCATED CHILDREN

When children enter school, they have advanced to the stage when formal musical education can greatly benefit them. With their earlier, somewhat intuitive learning in tow, children are capable of developing musical literacy and the conceptual understanding of music as one among many disciplines featured within a school curriculum. The musical competence to sing in tune and step in time, to listen perceptively, to perform from notation, and to create a personal music that is as logical as it is expressive are all skills taught in a music curriculum. These competencies are outcomes of a musical education, musical training that occurs in state–operated and state–approved schools. They are developed when formal training is in balance with what children already know.

Highly structured learning is the stuff of schooling, and of music as it "fits" within the school curriculum. School music is shaped to fit the nature the community's vision for its children. It is shaped by state mandates, and it is also shaped by school culture. Music as a school subject typically proceeds from a carefully laid–out instructional plan that is then sequentially unfolded from one step to the next to ensure learning. The order in which skills and knowledge are presented is designed according to the age and experience of children, but the logical progression of information toward particular goals is evident. Multiplication tables, the grammatical structures of language, and the reading of music are typically accomplished through a sequential process, with teachers intent on delivering strategies that result in their students' learning.

Musical children become more musical yet when experiences are tailored to their individual needs and developmental levels. The placement of music in school curricular programs, along with the hiring of trained music specialists, is vital to the realization of children's musical capacities. Through an education in music, children's listening can become more focused so that they can develop a vocabulary of melodic and rhythmic phrases. This vocabulary, or repertoire, of musical ideas can be revisited through children's experiences as performers, composers, and improvisors. Children can be led to the fuller development of their vocal potential by the training which music teachers can provide, so that the quality, intensity, clarity of their voices, and their ranges and tessituras, will be improved and extended. Likewise, they can be taught the techniques and tools for the performance of percussion instruments, recorders, keyboards, guitars, orchestral and band instruments, and other instruments (like Trinidadian steel drums or Chinese *luogu* drums and gongs) whose presence in the schools is less conventional but fully possible. Children's natural movement responses to music can be further developed, too, as teachers offer them not only a repertoire of gestures, steps, and sequences, but also the means for more attentive listening to music's many events.

The development of musical skills and knowledge requires the guidance of an expert musician–teacher, yet teachers of preschool and primary–grade children have within them music to share as well as ideas for how music can enhance children's development. Music and classroom teachers can—and often do—work in tandem to accomplish musical, social, and academic objectives for children's greater growth. Teachers who sing to their children, who allow children exploratory play with musical instruments and other objects with sound–production potential, who incorporate song and musical (and sound) effects into stories, or who utilize music for transitions from one activity to the next or as tools for teaching language, mathematical concepts, and social values, exemplify the manner in which music can be fully integrated within the curricular plan. Specialists can serve as consultants to classroom teachers, but the presence of music in the daily activities of teachers with young children need not be set aside for "special times" with the highly trained.

Schools exist to pass on to children the heritage of a society, the cultural knowledge that is deemed important for all, not only for children's own survival but also for the continued enlightenment of members of that society in generations to come. Music is part of that societal heritage; it is cultural knowledge which a music teacher has embraced and which she is trained to transmit. All children are steeped in the music of their homes and subcultural communities, but the music of school programs may frequently be that which is historically "American" as well as that which is representative of Western and even world cultures. The schooling of children in music can help to ensure the survival and even flourishing of certain genres and styles, and can effect the likely development of children's attitudes and values for music all their lifetimes long. Musically educated children receive a broader and more balanced outlook not only on music but also on the various components that make up their world.

THE ENCULTURATION–EDUCATION INTERFACE

Learning happens to children as a result of schooling, yet much of their natural ability requires our assistance as teachers. The instruction which children receive requires structure and a well–tailored sequence fit especially to them by those who are knowledgeable in music and pedagogy. It must be accepted, however, that learning also happens in spite of schooling, because children do not always learn what the schools articulate as their goals. Many become "good citizens," but some do not. Many become more humane and more greatly enlightened about their societal heritage, while others choose instead to ignore the school material in favor of what they can acquire at home, through the media, and on the street. Since children are influenced by their own personal and cultural worlds, they typically will examine information they receive from their teachers, match it to their needs and interests, and then discard the parts they do not find relevant. Children can be persuaded of the relevance of certain knowledge through their teachers' explanation and illustration of its application to their lives, although there is no guarantee that they will embrace it wholeheartedly. Often, the school curriculum and its manner of delivery are appropriate for the prototypical "normal" student, but many children's interests and needs are not well–served by a middle–of–the–road, standard, or sometimes even elitist curriculum. Thus, at least some children are unable to accept, acquire, and retain much of their societal heritage; they may allow into their lives only the relevant, intuitive, and environmentally–influenced knowledge.

The musical education which children receive in school can support some of their "outside" enculturative musical learning, however. In fact, it must. Schools that divorce themselves from the challenges of the real world of music in the everyday lives of children, that scale back and simplify beyond recognition the meaning of music, and that give little opportunity for children to apply what musical knowledge and skills they have mastered to new contexts, cannot accomplish the noble goals of transmitting and preserving musical nor cultural heritage. Bright and well–informed young people are the result of schools that honor children's earlier and concurrent pathways of enculturative knowledge of music. Their teachers do not assume this knowledge to be inferior, but find ways to associate what children know of music with what they need to know. Intuitive and informal learning of music beyond the school is a foundation and motivation to a more thorough and lasting understanding of the musical concepts, techniques, and even literacies which schools profess to teach.

REFERENCES

Bateson, G. (1978). *Steps to an ecology of mind*. New York: Ballantine Books.

Blacking, J. (1973). *How musical is man?* Seattle: University of Washington Press.

Bruner, J. (1966). *Toward a theory of instruction*. Cambridge, MA: Harvard University Press.

Campbell, P. S. (1991). The child–song (sic) genre: A comparison of songs by and for children. *International Journal of Music Education, 17*, 14–23.

Campbell, P. S. (1998). *Songs in their heads: Music and its meaning in children's lives*. New York: Oxford University Press.

Dowling, W. J. (1984). Development of musical schemata in children's spontaneous singing. In A. R. Crozier & A. J. Chapman (Eds.), *Cognitive processes in the perception of art*. North–Holland: Elsevier Science Publishers.

Dundes, A. (Ed.) (1965). *The study of folklore*. Englewood Cliffs, NJ: Prentice–Hall.

Ellis, C. J. (1986). *The musician, the university and the community: Conflict or concord?* Armidale, New South Wales, Australia: University of New England Press.

Gaston, E. T. (1968). *Music in therapy*. Lawrence, KS: University of Kansas Press.

Harwood, E. (1987). *Memorized song repertoire of children in grades four and five in Champaign, Illinois*. Doctoral dissertation, University of Illinois, Urbana– Champaign.

Jorgensen, E. (1997). *In search of music education*. Urbana–Champaign, IL: University of Illinois Press.

Kaemmer, J. (1993). *Music in human life*. Austin, TX: University of Texas Press.

Kartomi, M. (1991). Musical improvisations by children at play. *The World of Music, 33*(3), 53–65.

Keil, C. (1994). Participatory discrepancies and the power of music. In C. Keil, & S. Feld, *Music grooves*. Chicago: University of Chicago Press.

Marsh, K. (1995). Children's singing games: Composition in the playground? *Research Studies in Music Education, 4*, 2–11.

Merriam, A. P. (1964). *The anthropology of music*. Evanston, IL: Northwestern University Press.

Merrill–Mirsky, C. (1988). *Eeny meeny pepsa deeny: Ethnicity and gender in children's musical play*. Doctoral dissertation, University of California, Los Angeles.

Moog, H. (1976). *The musical experience of the preschool child*. (C. Clarke, Trans.). London: Schott.

Nattiez, J. (1990). *Music and discourse*. (C. Abbate, Trans.). Princeton, NJ: Princeton University Press.

Papousek, H. (1996). Musicality in infancy research: Biological and cultural origins of early musicality. In I. Deliege & J. Sloboda, Eds., *Musical beginnings*. Oxford: Oxford University Press.

Piaget, J. (1951). *Play, dreams, and imitation in childhood*. London: Routledge and Kegan Paul.

Slobin, M. (1993). *Subcultural sounds: Micromusics of the West*. Hanover: University of New England for Wesleyan University Press.

Sutton–Smith, B. (1995). *Children's folklore: A source book*. New York: Garland Publications.

Whiting, B. B., & Edwards, C. P. (1988). *Children of different worlds*. Cambridge: Harvard University Press.

The underlying premises discussed in this chapter, and some segments of the text, are taken from *Songs in Their Heads: Music and Its Meaning in Children's Lives* by Patricia Shehan Campbell (1998), New York: Oxford University Press. A few additional ideas and segments are derived from *Music in Childhood* by Patricia Shehan Campbell and Carol Scott–Kassner (1995), New York: Schirmer Books. An early version of this chapter was published in 1998 *Research Studies in Music Education*, 11, Dec., 1998. 42-51.

MINETTE MANS

5. PLAYING THE MUSIC – COMPARING PERFORMANCE OF CHILDREN'S SONG AND DANCE IN TRADITIONAL AND CONTEMPORARY NAMIBIAN EDUCATION

How do young Namibian children engage with music? What and when do they play? How are they educated in the performing arts? These are fascinating questions upon which I hope to provide a perspective. By way of introduction, let me explain a few very general principles on which informal, community–based arts education tends to be based in Namibia. I follow this with a look at the principles on which arts education in schools are based, focusing on music and dance. The term music must be understood in an African framework where dance and music are usually holistically integrated and often inclusive of costume, ritual, stories framed within a particular cosmology. Performance is thus "a web of meaning to be read from its surrounding context" (Erlmann, 1996, p. 66). I will be using the terms music, dance and play interchangeably, depending on which aspect is in most sharply focus.

Namibia is an extensive but lightly populated country in south–western Africa. Apart from one city, and sixteen towns of reasonable size, most of the country consists of semi–arid agricultural land thinly dotted with villages. About two–thirds of the population[1] live in the semi–rural and rural areas where the development infrastructure of roads, electricity and communications systems are gradually being implemented. Hence a large proportion of the population does not have day–to–day access to newspapers or television, and entertainment is self–constructed and performed mostly in communal settings. Ironically, the poverty and lack of development of the past has contributed to robust cultural practices, and performances that have long since been discontinued in urban areas retain their vitality in many rural areas.

An interesting characteristic of Namibian cultures is that a major portion of all musical performance amongst different cultural groups is called play[2] not only for children but also for adults. Of course, play is central to our understanding of young children, but we often forget how much of their play is musical play, in which rhythm, movement, characterization, drama or pantomime, and imagination are combined. Play

---

[1] The population totals about 1.5 million, spread over about 825,000 square kilometres.
[2] For example *dhana* means to play, and *uudhano (oudano)* is the form of song–dance–play. /*Hurub* means play, and ≠*ab /hurub* is play with reed–pipes and dance. Similarly children play *omukwenga, outetera, onyando, ondjongo*, and others. Play is more fully discussed in a paper presented at a conference of the Nordiska Afrikainstitutet in Turku, Finland in October 2000 (in press) entitled "Unlocking Play in Namibian Musical Identity".

L. Bresler and C.M. Thompson (eds.), The Arts in Children's Lives, 71–86.
© 2002 *Kluwer Academic Publishers. Printed in the Netherlands.*

usually involves the group collectively singing and clapping while others (ones, twos, or more) take turns at dancing individual variations to fixed rhythmic patterns in the centre of the circle or space. Play often centres around taking turns or surprising another by "giving" a touch, like "tag". Much children's play is a preparation for adult play. Although the notion of play is often relegated to the status of "mere recreation", it is an important facet of communal education, and in the Namibian context it also embodies value systems. It is not mere frivolity but, as Peter Brook (1968) says, play is hard work! Hence "[p]lay is a reflexive activity, and, as most everyone would agree, what is communicated through play, while defined as amusement, can be quite serious indeed" (Arnoldi, 1995, p. 22). Through play, young children are educated not only in a specific music–dance, but in the moral values, conditions of existence, and social relationships of their societies with all their ambiguities and inconsistencies. Music and play can be described as aspects of education for socialization.

Socialization Through Music

Songs illustrate social structures and values through references to kinship and family structure, world views, the importance given to marriage and lineage systems, religious systems, value systems, and production systems. Song not only provides a channel for the transmission of societal values and histories, but is in and of itself a way of knowing and reflecting on self and society. Blacking (1985) states that, "music is an important way of knowing, and the performing arts are important means of reflection, of sensing order and ordering experience, and relating inner sensations to the life of feeling of one's society" (p. 65). Chernoff (1979) underlines this approach by writing that "music's explicit purpose, in the various ways it might be defined by Africans, is, essentially, socialization." Apart from being used as a *means* of socializing young persons, music and dance have long provided the *context* within which socializing education could take place. Philosophical and moral systems of the society are built into the music and dance–making itself. They link with the philosophical and moral systems that lie at the root of social structures, and are seen as a metaphor of life (Dagan, 1997). So much experience and knowledge is implicit in performance. For example, I recently recorded a chantefable called "Nauwa" that surprised me by its extreme brevity. Upon enquiry as to the meaning of the text [3] I was told that a long story preceded the actual chantefable, involving kidnapping of a girl (Nauwa) for marriage by monsters or cannibals, her escape with the help of her mother–in–law–to–be, the chase, and so on. It is only the culmination of the story, where the monster stubs his toe on the stone and cries out against Nauwa that is actually told and sung. The child must know this background story before understanding and participating in the chantefable.

Unlike city living, life in those rural communities without access to television or radio involves musical performances on numerous occasions – "at the drop of a hat" as I was told. These occasions quite naturally include celebrations, weddings, birth and funeral ceremonies, work, change of life stages, seasons, inaugurations, healings and so on. In the past, more than the present, the celebration and ritualization of the cycles of

---

[3] The text basically states a man stubbed his toe on a stone and cursed the girl Nauwa for causing his pain.

life informed and prepared the younger generation in terms of social expectations regarding adult life, kinship and community ethos. Even when young children are not directly involved in performances they are included on the fringes from where they observe and learn.

How does that learning happen? Partly through enculturation or immersion in cultural practices and partly through direct oral/aural instruction. Historically, Namibian cultures have, by and large, been oral cultures.[4] We know that education forms part of all cultures, whether it occurs via the written word or orally. In fact, both African and Western writers today challenge the colonial concept that an oral culture is inferior to one based on a written form (cf. Arom, 1991; Chernoff, 1979; Coplan, 1991; Kubik, 1974, 1986, 1987, 1989; Mazrui, 1990; Okpewho, 1983; Tay, 1989; Vail & White, 1991; and others). Hence, educational practices in Namibian societies prior to government schools included initiation "schools", apprenticeship, "child–to–child" and peer education through which a wealth of specialized life–related knowledge was imparted to the new generation. In these societies teaching or instruction was mainly oral/aural and music, dance, stories, narratives, games and ritual were therefore major means through which knowledge, life skills and social values were transmitted. Nowadays this is not so common, but similar events still take place. An example: in the northern Kunene Region small Ovazemba boys between the ages of four through ten often still attend the circumcision school, *etanda*, usually during a school vacation period. In this time they are circumcised, and while waiting for healing they are instructed about their responsibilities, roles and expected future behavior. They form a named age group with life–long bonds and undergo tests. Even though their mothers may come to care for them, they learn to hunt, to sing special *onyando* songs, create musical instruments and make special palm frond skirts to wear for the dance. *Onyando* songs are performed during the final procession home and the whole community joins in. These songs are some of the most beautiful I have come across in my research! Their educational purpose is considered very valuable in the community, alongside formal schooling which cannot replace these valuable life lessons.

It is common knowledge that children in African societies are likely to be introduced to music and dance at an early age through routine exposure, being integrated into almost all social events,[5] whether they are carried on their mothers' backs, clinging to their skirts, or moving within their own peer group. Damara children on our ranch often break into exuberant choral song even when struggling to carry water to fire fighters in the extreme heat or fetching wood. Children's integration into performance is not mere happenstance. The importance of being drawn into performance becomes clear with the insight that it forms a vital link in the socialization process – a process of Africanization. In many Namibian communities children are considered symbols of the inner strength and "wealth" of a family. They are welcomed

---

[4] This statement does not negate the fact that schooling and literacy in Namibia and all over Africa are steadily on the increase, and so is the publication of written literature as well as academic texts.

[5] I have observed a healing in Katima Mulilo (1994) where the healer's singers were young girls – the leader appeared to be about twelve years old. They were expected to continue their singing throughout the night until the divining (*liyala*) was completed. Considering the crucial role of the singers to the success of the event, this was no light responsibility.

as future helpers and they bring the possibility of future marital ties and kinship
extensions through which familial wealth may increase. Hence, songs and dance
illustrating and teaching about future economic tasks are common practice.[6] The
responsibilities of cattle and goat herding are usually the task of small boys and youths.
Baby care, cleaning and cooking remains the task of girls. Thus one finds songs which
prepare and inform, one example being the songs sung at an Aawambo boy's
name–giving ceremony (*epiitho*) to remind those gathered of the boy's future herding
task. Ovahimba children may not play their musical games inside the home compound,
only adults may. During the day children have chores to perform, but at night all the
children may go outside to a clearing, play *omukwenga* or *ondjongo* and sing about
cattle and dance until late at night. Kxoe, !Kung and Ju/'hoan people have many songs
and dances that teach about the character and habits of animals and birds – important
knowledge for a future hunter. Among Ju/'hoansi there are special songs following the
hunt, indicating whether it was a "good" killing or not.[7] In this event the community is
informed and instructed in terms of the inherent meaning of the hunt and ethical
standards are reinforced. Even when these songs are not performed by children, they
listen, observe and learn through enculturation.

This brings me to ask how children feature in community performances? Ottenburg
(1997) suggests that there are at least three categories of children's dance in most
African societies. These are:

> [T]hose that are unique to children, passed down from generation to generation but not danced by
> adults. A second occurs when children on their own imitate adult dances and dancers if permitted to
> do so, and the third is found when adults organize children to perform specific dances, as at
> initiations and other events governed by adults. (p. 12)

The *onyando* mentioned above is an example of the latter category, while *omukwenga*
and others might be examples of the second. However, although Ottenburg does not
refer to performances created by children for children, it is my experience that, apart
from the above, several such categories exist in Namibia. For example, most forms of
oudano, omukwenga, ondjongo that I have observed have been created by children and
taught peer–to–peer. When children start attending school they share songs from
different cultures and adapt and transform their own as a result. Further, small children
play an observing role at communal (mostly adult) play or events. They may move to
the rear of the play circle or enter and imitate the dances of their elders. Their initial
attempts at participation are generally treated supportively by peers and elders. For
example I've observed a small girl of about two years follow her mother (a good
dancer) into the circle, trying to catch her skirt as she swirls and stamps. Onlookers
encouraged the toddler with shouting and friendly laughter, and swung her out of
harm's way only when the dancers were likely to knock her over.

---

[6] In fact, children in many areas are expected to work very hard and wait until last before receiving food.
Often from the age of about ten years they do not sleep inside the house or compound, but in a room or hut
just outside.
[7] E. Olivier, personal communications, Windhoek, 1996.

(Above) **A SMALL GIRL IN AN ADULT PERFORMANCE OF *UUDHANO*** (captured
from digital video by M. Mans, 1999)

Because of the communal music–making, the ability to sing, clap rhythmically and move the body rhythmically are skills which many children in these situations learn as a matter of course. Uncouth or lazy actions are often treated with embarrassed silence or laughter, but creative and humorous performances are enjoyed immensely. Thus a small boy takes his turn in children's *uudhano* on a hot afternoon in a village in Ongandjera where adults are playing and drinking, and he appears somewhat uncertain. Luckily a good sense of self–preservation prompts him to leap into a statue–like stance reminiscent of a soldier pointing his rifle to the sky. Since the text of the song recalls the shooting skills of freedom fighters this is appropriate, but it is more. By ignoring the set rhythm–stamping patterns of the play and maintaining his dramatic but humorous pose for the full length of his turn, he displays creative individuality and brings the house down!

Below– **HOLDING HIS POSE IN UUDHANO. On the left a girl is using a plastic water container as drum (*ongoma*)** (captured from Digital Video by M. Mans, 1999)

The character of children's music varies throughout Namibia, but there several ways in which children's play differs from that of adults. Even though children as well as adults play *uudhano (oudano), omutjopa, ondjongo, namastap, konsertliedjies, pela,* and so on, the structure and qualities of the performances are seldom identical. Differences are found in the texts, energy levels and movement components, tempo, change–overs and levels of intercultural borrowing. Briefly, texts of children's songs tend to be dependent on whether they are created by children, by adults for children, or in imitation of adults. Self–created texts tend to relate to the activities with which they engage, for example singing about the goats they are herding, about friends, counting games, and so on. Other texts praising the fighting skills of P.L.A.N. freedom fighters or reviling South Africa's ex–President Botha are sung by children too young to remember the freedom struggle (pre–1990). These songs are probably transmitted by older children to their younger siblings, because the dance and its rhythm pattern is not performed by adults. Although I have not heard adults teaching these songs to children, that is also a possibility. The energy levels of children's performance tends to be high, recalling what Thompson (1974, p. 5) refers to as *ephebism*. Energetic movements are performed at full range, often even out of control. Along with this, the basic tempo of most children's categories is faster than those for adults, the change–overs for players are more rapid, and vocal tones as well as movements are strong, experimental and exaggerated. In contrast to this, good adult dancers tend to savor "cool", controlled and sweet movements. Interestingly enough, I find the rhythm patterns of children's *uudhano* more complex than those of adult women, with quick changes between duple and triple pulse, silent pauses and simultaneous start–ups for drum, clapping, song and dance. Lastly, while adults tend to retain their musical culture with relatively little change, if they practice it at all, children seem to pick up whatever sounds and movements are going around. Therefore even in a very remote area settled mainly by Ovahimba, I woke up one night to hear the children playing music–dance that I clearly recognized as Aawambo play. These children were aged between three and about fourteen, had never been to school or a town, yet they knew the music of a group who lived about a hundred and fifty kilometers away! Similarly in northern Kavango I recorded a Kwangali children's song that I knew as a Damara song from central Namibia, eight hundred kilometers away.

Hence, by the time children reach adolescence or adulthood, they know a variety of the songs of their own and other cultures, and if they do not themselves play an instrument, they can assess correct and appropriate execution of musical performances from their area, not only their own culture but those they are exposed to.

There are certain fundamental differences between a traditional or community education and a school–based education. Let's look at the system of traditional community–based education first.

Communal custom–based education

The fact that community teaching and learning in the past occurred through an oral/aural medium had a fundamental influence on the nature of the education process. Rhythm in music and in language is an important instructional medium, animating and shaping the development of consciousness in an oral society. Namibian orature[8] has tended to emphasize pragmatism and holism, along with a very real sense of society and its connection with the spiritual world. In pre–formal or traditional education the methods used were generally pragmatic and the context of indigenous

---

[8] Coined by Ugandan Pio Zurimi and popularised by Kenyan Ngugi wa Thiong'o. Coplan prefers the term auriture. He devised this term to caution against the Western category of literature when speaking of African texts. Coplan feels that the term 'orature' does not overcome the "conceptual separation of verbal, sonic, and rhythmic elements of expression" (1994: 8). Owing to its common usage I retain the use of the term orature.

community–based education was life itself: Every action and every object in the environment had possible educational value, work, beliefs, the environment. The custom of incorporating children into the economic and political life of a village from an early age (through daily chores) meant they assumed responsibilities gradually, each working at a pace suited to his or her own abilities, yet watched over by older siblings or parents. Learning took place through enculturation (immersion in the total cultural environment), by means of imitation, through adult or peer intervention (instruction, induction, apprenticeship), self–instruction, and participation in community activities. This provided learners with a simple but comprehensive education that would benefit the community. As socio–cultural events, music, dance, and stories were central to most Namibian educational practices prior to formal schooling. Taught orally, music and dance in particular were utilized in the development of life skills through rituals, daily tasks and play. All of these contributed not only to individual learning but more broadly to the socialization of the younger generation. Although formal school–based education is now the main means of educating the younger generation, some of these educational practices are still functional in rural parts of Namibia but are increasingly rare.

Along with the discipline of precise transmission an oral system of education can encourage creativity through the development of forms of innovation and problem solving; for example new songs are created or older ones are adapted. Supporting the educational value of orature, it has been suggested that the "associative thinking characteristic of oral culture as against the more rigid propensities of the scribal outlook" demonstrates a more expansive grasp of the cultural universe than the written culture which "reduces reality to static symbols" (Okpewho, 1983, p. 236). On the other hand, the oral transmission of a culture tends to be passed on from an older generation to a younger generation who are expected to listen, observe and conform. This implies that traditional oral cultures tend to transmit only that which is generally accepted and respected. Taken to extremes, oral transmission could, in certain situations, lead to the rigid retention of conservative and familiar forms of behavior rather than innovation and experimentation (Epskamp, 1992, pp. 12–14). Slowly, the older forms of orature are being replaced with a modern one – television. This functions in a similar fasion to earlier oral transmission in that children listen, observe and imitate much of the music and dance. The difference lies in the absorption of value systems. But more research needs to be done in this area of learning.

In relating custom–based to school–based education the challenge would be to strike a balance between conservation of "tried and trusted" knowledge and methods, and those that encourage innovative, generative, expansive and creative knowledge and methods. But traditional community–based methods such as apprenticeship and self–instruction are seldom seriously considered for schools, for reasons of time and continuity.

However, the wealth of traditional materials in any culture is an obvious treasure–house of songs, dances, stories, myths, masks, and characters that appeal to children. In an oral culture the media used to transmit knowledge are sound (music and language), movement (work and dance), vision and touch. In the past there were various ways in which this occurred, for example, oral history was transmitted when people were gathered around the evening fire, or while performing certain tasks. This could occur at cattle posts, when collecting wood, when initiates were being prepared for initiation rites, and when men prepared for the hunt or a raid, for example.[9] Song and dance were used to shape "a specific historical consciousness and identity across generations and the urban/rural divide" (Henrichsen, 1997, p. 27) and to instruct the younger generation in general matters, in both formal and informal situations. Informal instruction tended to take place without specific plans, time frame, aims or settings, for example a young child could be taught to count by means of stones manipulated inside a closed hand, while chanting a little song.[10]

The context and its relationship with musical materials together create the fundamental cognitive and affective structure of musical learning, a complex structure which can be called the child's musical world. Music is something children do and it is always informed by the social context or culture from which the child emerges. Music and dance involve the reciprocal influence of the child and his/her social context. The construction of a "musical world" of a particular culture takes place over a period of time and is embedded in their cosmology. Therefore this musical world reflects existing cultural values and beliefs, while also allowing for the active (re–)construction and change of peoples' values, beliefs and thereby their cultures. Children quickly learn that there is music for everyday and for special occasions. They discover there is music for children, adults, elderly, males, females, commoners, specialists and royalty. Thus groups of people have constructed their musical world or models (Arom, 1991, p. xxi) according to their ways of life, systems of production, values and beliefs – they have enculturated their social system. A musical world includes a background or field of all the music of their culture (songs and their structures, instrumental pieces, instruments used, dances and their structures), as well as all the rules (play frame) guiding the practice of the music. Grauer (1996) states that:

> we cannot normally hear musical passages outside a kind of tonal "force–field" not unlike that which produces, for language, what linguist Ferdinand Saussure called "value." Music, like language, must thus be regarded as "a system of interdependent terms in which the value of each term results solely from the simultaneous presence of the others... Thus, we hear music *virtually*, in terms of essentially mental semiotic *fields* (gestalts produced by systems of differences), not in terms of the material, purely sensory experience of something we might want to call the "sounds themselves." (p. 0.5).

This musical world or field involves the making of the music itself and the rules that guide this practice, as well as the environment or context in which it is situated. Being part of a musical culture involves identification with both the *process* (praxis) and the *environment* of music–making.

Process
In musical terms the process refers to the sounds, patterns and contexts that together form their internalized mental templates (or positive field). Templates or models are specific to cultures or sub–cultures. They are stored in the memory of a people and include knowledge of all the sounds and movements that belong together, the patterns

---

[9] See Williams (1994) for a more complete description of oral history among the Aawambo people.
[10] This was observed by me around 1980, when an elderly, illiterate Damara man taught a child who didn't attend school in this manner.

involved, and the context for use that cultural insiders have developed. Such a template includes all the elements that identify the particular piece of music or song, and that guide the user in terms of its performance. Hence, the process (with which a group identifies) includes the knowledge of appropriate songs, movement patterns, sounds, embellishments, and the ability to create appropriate variations. Based on this aspect of musical identity, members of a group are able to recognize qualities within a musical performance and transmit this recognition of "correct" and "good" sounds and movements to one another. Over time, given that performance by different communities of the same culture may involve different variations, templates undergo changes.

Environment

A musical environment includes all the expectations, rules and understandings referring to the when, where and why of the musical event and is based on culturally organized rules or expectations. Environment includes knowledge of the time, location, function, history, beliefs and values associated with the performance. It also provides reference to whether a performance is private or public, whether it has restricted or open attendance, whether it is urban or rural, and whether it is a power (ritual) performance or recreational. Through regular participation in a variety of events this knowledge is cognitively and affectively internalized.

Contrary to what some people believe, therefore, traditional community–based education through music and dance contains potentially all the major elements required of a good performing arts education. How does this compare with arts education in Namibian schools?

Formal school–based arts education

Since 1990 political changes in this country called for in–depth, not merely cosmetic changes to school curricula in order to improve relevance, breadth, depth and balance of educational programes, so as to provide the best possible educational opportunities for the (mostly previously disadvantaged) masses. According to Herbert Read, "the purpose of a reform of the system of education is not to produce more works of art, but better persons and better societies" (quoted in Small, 1984, p. 218).

Presently the national lower primary arts curriculum (grades one through four) provides only for a combined time slot for performing and visual arts, but states:

> Arts promote the balanced growth, socialization and development of creative ability of a learner. The subject area is a means through which the processes of unfolding, stimulating and capturing the learner's imagination and self expression take place. Through this subject area learners explore their inner selves, their environment, and make discoveries about communication through arts media... (Ministry of Basic Education & Culture, 1997, p. 1).

The early childhood syllabus aims at introducing the basic concepts through a broad experience–based arts curriculum without losing sight of the interconnectedness of activities. It aims to develop a spirit of inquiry and experimentation, foster skills of observation and creativity and reinforce work in other areas of the curriculum. It is basically an outcomes or competency–based curriculum ("the learner will be able to...") and is organized in terms of learning actions that are called domains. They are:

exploring and discovering; performing; creating; communicating; and knowing and understanding (the latter actually being implicit in all of the others). These learning actions can also be linked to known cultural practices.

Underlying the actual syllabus and guiding the complete educational process are several important principles. One of the first reform principles to be addressed was that of *equal access* to education in all areas, to redress the imbalances of the past. Whereas arts education in the past was reserved for the "talented" and financially stable few, arts education in schools in Namibia today is aimed at all learners, from primary level where it is compulsory, through to elective junior secondary levels (grades 1 through 10). This applies to both performing and visual arts. Every learner will have a chance to experience aspects of music, dance, drama and the visual and plastic arts.

This principle relates well to community–based education, where everybody may usually participate, depending on circumstance. In fact, unlike certain traditional performances where gender or status play a role, there are no exclusions to arts education. While there may be some specialized performance roles in a certain lesson, all children in the classroom become involved in the total experience and are encouraged to perform according to their interests and abilities. Children are drawn into planning, creating, performing, appraising, and discussing through the syllabus learning actions required, i.e. exploring, performing, creating, responding and communicating. This means that the principle of equal access is satisfied not only in terms of access to the arts programe, but also in terms of access to the performance. Under ideal circumstances the contribution of each participant synergistically enhances the performance. Reality depends on specific teachers, learners and the situation alike.

A second basic principle is that of *learner–centerdness*. The Namibian Basic Education programe is theoretically at least, based on the needs of the learner first and foremost. Education centred on the learner implies that teaching will not hold the subject or the person of the teacher central, but will place the emphasis firmly on the needs of the learners. A learner–centerd programe stresses the learning actions that each child undertakes, encouraging teachers to listen and look more carefully at what learners actually do. Learner–centered education is located in the specific social context of school and its community and the development of social skills is considered important. It is believed that a learner–centered curriculum promotes self–growth and contributes to the intellectual, physical, emotional and social empowerment of the learner. Therefore, the new arts syllabi are formulated in terms of the competencies that learners need to develop in the various learning areas. The processes of learning, as well as the manifested products of their learning, are important. Processes of learning are monitored through continuous assessment with the emphasis on the ongoing development of learner competencies, and the diagnosis and correction of possible problems. The teacher's role in this approach is that of a facilitator rather than the expert who knows everything. The teacher is expected to stimulate, question, advise, direct, focus and help, in much the same way as a master guides an apprentice.

Once again, this recalls community–based education, where the child is treated as a person in relation to others, one who is situated within particular learning contexts, made up of school, family and society. Goals relating to individual development bear a direct relation to overall goals of socialization.

Musical play such as *uudhano* is learner–centered firstly, because children are actively engaged with sound and movement through performance. They are the ones who explore sound and movement, discover solutions to problems, appraise performances, respond in personal ways, communicate with others and create new variations. This means that learners are not merely objects of instruction, but active agents exploring the world of experience around them. The learning is active in that it involves the learner in decisions and actions through performance; productive by leading to new information being generated and new music and dance being created; effective through repetition which commits learning material to long term memory; and transformative because it effects lasting changes in terms of abilities, skills and understandings.

Secondly, it is learner–centered because learners experience the enjoyment of challenging experiences with music, dance, instruments, costumes, and atmospheric requirements as well the experimentational and competitive aspects of play. Playing the music remembers and celebrates cultural origins, but also explores new forms of cultural expression. Through the processes of engaging with music and dance (making or doing it), and through the inner response and appraisal of their own and others' work, learners can enhance their awareness and imaginative capacities. Teachers need to consider how best to provide enjoyable yet challenging experiences in the classroom. This requires a pleasant classroom atmosphere with interesting and challenging materials and methods. Through the communal and egalitarian participation in music–dance–play events, situations which create anxiety or frustration because the challenge is too great, or boredom because the challenge is too little, are less likely to occur.

Thirdly, learners are involved in education of the whole person – physical, intellectual, emotional, and social. Whether in community or school, the performance of music and dance such as *onyando* or *ondjongo* involves physical knowing–in–action (Elliott, 1995, p. 54), expression of personal responses, and communication with others within a context of communal participation. In this way the process of educating the whole child is enhanced, illuminated and expanded. If music and dance center on learners in their contexts, it results in knowledge, skills and attitudes which can be applied outside of schools, which can easily be expanded into further exploration and study, and which leaves lasting positive results for life. The focus moves away from "subject discipline" to what learners know, understand and can do.

The teacher should know "when to intervene in the learning process and when to stay out of the way" (Small, 1984, p. 225). Although she plans, guides, supports and assesses the competencies of the children, the character of play should not be lost. Group play has an energy and life of its own and this may be eroded by too much control. Experts from the community are sources of information and inspiration, and can serve as a wonderful way of bringing school and community closer to one another. The teacher creates a positive, nurturing classroom atmosphere where teacher and learners respect one another and where learners are supported in their attempts to experiment and improvise. In local communities adults correct children's performance by means of comments, shouts, ululations, and other means. In a modern classroom the same informal kind of feedback can have positive effects.

Of course school arts education has to take sequence, coherence and consistency along with breadth and depth of learning experiences into consideration. But it is specifically in satisfying the criterion of *relevance* of education that I believe that an arts programe that is informed by the values, methods and materials that have developed over time amongst the people would have the greatest success. A relevant education meets both the present and the future needs of the learner. Even young children have to feel that what they learn is meaningful. Relevant education means that they develop competencies and understandings that are transferable in a variety of real life situations. Content and methods should be practical, interesting, stimulating, and valued by the learners. To be relevant, the wider population must be taken into consideration, so that contents do not only reflect a dominant culture, but the cultural capital of the whole class. A culturally relevant content is likely to make use of the cultural practices from which the learner emerges. The teacher can draw from the learner's experience and can ensure that there is a connection between content and learner. Therefore these children's own songs and games are an excellent starting point.

Education is made relevant through music and dance because it contributes to the social and personal development of learners. In community–based customs I have shown that learning through music and dance was directed primarily towards everyday life and had direct applicability, creating a framework through which individuals could relate to one another. It is through the practice of music and dance, language, kinship and lifestyle that people distinguish themselves from one another and develop cultural identity. In the classroom too learners can discover more about themselves in the context of the peer group because music and dance provides a conduit through which they discover how to express themselves. They develop an understanding of place in the larger social context by having to take turns to play in a specific order (or not), by discovering individual strengths and weaknesses, disparate abilities, interests, backgrounds and needs. This approximates the community in town or village where an event may include old and young, rich and poor, powerful and weak, skilled and unskilled. The classroom performance can therefore provide a mode of exploration and expression by means of which children continue to experience society at large.

Some education realities

In conclusion therefore, it seems as though the school arts program for early childhood does take culture, background, and values into consideration. Unfortunately however, there are several factors that hinder the smooth implementation of arts education in Namibia.

Firstly, teachers in this country can rarely perform music other than that which they have woven into their own cultural identity, whether it is Western classical music, commercial pop, reggae, gospel, *soukous, rhumba, kizomba,* church or a specific cultural music. This is a result of the convoluted history of the region, involving different colonial occupations, "apartheid" and war. Music graduates, mainly of European descent, either feel uncomfortable with music of black cultures, or they see indigenous folkloric musical practice as inferior to the "high musical art" of European origin. On the other hand, very few black music or arts teachers have completed

They often feel inadequate to the task, cannot play musical instruments or verbalize musical concepts, and some even support the notion that the "cultural music" that they know is inferior and not worth teaching to children. A senior Minister in government recently made the comment to me that he considered research and education in terms of cultural musics such as *uudhano* and *Namastap* as worthless because "they can be learnt on the street".[11]

Secondly, facilities are generally poor to non–existent. Not all schools have classrooms, only about half have electricity, only singular schools have special music rooms. Music books, instruments and electronic media are generally not provided by education authorities. This means that there are no simple solutions and teachers are compelled to resort to creative and innovative means of presenting music and dance classes. As a combined result of the above, music education in schools is presently both limited and limiting, while dance education is almost non–existent.

The result of this educational climate and situation is that the curriculum principles described above remain theoretical because they are either not properly understood, or teachers do not have the confidence to explore musics and dance other than those they know well. Generally Namibian extended family environments provide the necessary emotional support for children to feel free to perform and experiment. The sad thing is that as more and more children leave homes to attend school in towns and follow modern trends, the social structures within which children were educated communally in and through the arts are disintegrating. During my field trips it is becoming more and more difficult to find a group of children who know the same songs and play. Small children are able to sing many songs in English but few in their mother tongue. To counteract this state of affairs, I have discovered children of four to eight years old at gatherings who now sing songs and rap by Toni Braxton, TLC, LL Cool J and others. Children seem to pick this up (orally) from radio, television and observing their older siblings, all of whom they imitate and emulate (beautifully I might add). At community celebrations like our annual Christmas party Damara children are eager to perform and they demonstrate whatever new and cool move or song they have learnt and practiced. This is very entertaining, but the communal involvement one finds in play has disappeared and is replaced by individual performance.

Therefore, I suspect that unless at least some of the play traditions described above, and the methods of learning them, are incorporated into formal schooling, they will soon be forgotten. In modern Namibia few people have the time to engage in community–based arts education. While the children are away the grandmothers tend the fields, the mothers go out to work and few have the time or energy to teach children songs after school (or even before). To play *uudhano, omukwenga, //gais* or *omutjopa* properly you need at least ten or more kids who get together regularly. Nowadays this is not always feasible. Perhaps the global emphasis on individual stardom and achievement cannot, after all, live side by side with communal, egalitarian participation in performance. But what a pity when the community–based methods and materials are so varied, available and fun!

---

[11] Informal conversation with the Minister of Mines and Energy. The Honourable Toivo ya Toivo, Windhoek, September 2000.

REFERENCES

Arnoldi, M. J. (1995). *Playing with time. Art and performance in central Mali.* Bloomington: Indiana University Press.

Arom, S. (1991).*African polyphony and polyrhythm. Musical structure and methodology.* (M. Thorn, B. Tuckett & R Boyd, trans.). Cambridge: Cambridge University Press.

Bjørkvold, J–R. (1992). *The muse within: Creativity and communication, song and play from childhood through maturity.*(H. Halverson, trans.). Aaron Asher Books. New York: Harper Collins.

Blacking, J. (1985). The context of Venda possession music: Reflections on the effectiveness of symbols. *1985 Yearbook for Traditional Music, 17*, pp. 64 – 87.

Brook, P. (1968). *The empty space.* New York: Atheneum.

Chernoff, J. M. (1979). *African rhythm and African sensibility. Aesthetics and social action in African musical idioms.* Chicago: Chicago University Press.

Coplan, D.B. (1991). Ethnomusicology and the meaning of tradition. In P. Bohlman & S. Blum (eds.) *Ethnomusicology and modern music history.* Urbana: University of Illinois Press.

Dargie, D. (1996). African methods of education: Some reflections. *African Music. Journal of the International Library of African Music. 7*(3), pp. 30 – 43.

Dagan, E. (Ed.) (1997). *The spirit's dance in Africa. Evolution, transformation and continuity in Sub–Sahara.* Montreal: Galerie Amrad African Art Publications.

Erlmann, V. (1996). *Nightsong. Performance, power, and practice in South Africa.* Chicago: University of Chicago Press.

Elliott, D. J. (1995). *Music matters: A new philosophy of music education.* New York: Oxford University Press.

Epskamp, K. (1992). *Learning by performing arts. From indigenous to endogenous cultural development.* CESO Paperback no. 16. The Hague: Centre for the Study of Education in Developing Countries.

Grauer, V. A. (1996). Toward a unified theory of the arts, *Music Theory Online.* The Online Journal of the Society for Music Theory, *2.6.* http://www.societymusictheory.org

Henrichsen, D. (1997). *A glance at our Africa. Facsimile reprint of SOUTH WEST NEWS SUIDWES NUUS 1960. The only non–racial newspaper in the territory. Mehindji ojo otijaitonga ndji hina mbangu komihoko djerike.* Basel: Basler Afrika Bibliographien.

International Development Consultancy (Compiler) (2nd Ed.). (1996/1997). *Namibia regional resources manual.* Friedrich Ebert Stiftung. Windhoek: Gamsberg Macmillan.

Kubik, G. (1974). Music and dance education in mukanda schools of Mbwela and Nkongela communities. *Review of Ethnology, 4*(7–9), pp. 49–65.

Kubik, G. (1986). Stability and change in African musical traditions. *The World of Music, XXVIII*(1), pp. 44 – 68.

Kubik, G. 1987. Musical activities of children within the eastern Angolan culture area. *The World of Music, XXIX*(3), pp. 5 – 25.

Kubik, G. (1989). Àló – Yoruba chantefables: An integrated approach towards West African music and oral literature. *African Musicology: Current Trends, Vol. 1. A Festschrift to J.H. Kwabena Nketia.* Los Angeles: University of California, African Studies Center.

Mans, M. E. (1997). *Namibian music and dance as Ngoma in arts education.* Unpublished dissertation presented in partial fulfilment of the requirements for the degree Doctor of Philosophy, Music Department, University of Natal.

Mans, M. E. (2000). Unlocking play in Namibian musical identity. Paper presented at the conference "Playing with Identity in Contemporary African Music," Nordiska Afrikainstitutet in Turku, Finland.

Mans. M. E. *Uudhano* as a symbol of renewal and growth. Paper presented at the ESEM Conference, John Blacking's Legacy, Queen's University, Belfast.

Mazrui, A. A. (1990). *Cultural forces in world politics.* London: James Currey.

Ministry of Basic Education and Culture (1995). *Lower Primary Phase. Arts. Grade 1 and 2. Syllabus.* Okahandja: National Institute of Educational Development.

Ministry of Basic Education and Culture (1997). *Lower Primary Phase. Arts. Grade 3 and 4. Syllabus.* Okahandja: National Institute of Educational Development.

Okpewho, I. (1983). *Myth in Africa. A study of its aesthetic and cultural relevance.* London: Cambridge University Press.

Olivier, E. (1994). Musical repertoires of the Ju/'Hoansi: Identification and classification. *Proceedings of the Meeting Khoisan Studies: Multidisciplinary Perspectives.* Köln: Rüdiger Köppe Verlag.

Ottenburg, S. (1997). Some issues and questions on African dance. Introduction to E. Dagan (Ed.) *The spirit's dance in Africa. Evolution, transformation and continuity in Sub–Sahara.* Montreal: Galerie Amrad African Art Publications.

Serafine, M. L. (1988). *Music as cognition.* Columbia University Press.

Small, C. (1984). *Music . Society . Education.* London: John Calder.

Tay, A. K. B. (1989). *'Child –to– child' in Africa: Towards an open learning strategy.* Paris: UNESCO–UNICEF Co–operative Programme.

Thompson, R. F. (1974). *African art in motion. Icon and act.* Berkeley and Los Angeles: University of California Press.

Vail, L. & White, L. (1991). *Power and the Praise Poem. Southern African Voices in History.* London: James Currey.

Development Interlude

I was upset when my art teacher told me that I had to draw the sky all the way down to the bottom of the page. She explained to me that the sky did not just meet the top of the trees. I admit part of the reason I was so upset was because now I had more to color, but I was also confused. I would look outside and see the blue sky and then I would see the trees and then the ground. To me, they were all independent of one another. I did not see the blue sky touching the grass. It was just air. The air was white or clear and I did not understand how I could represent the air when I could not even see it.

The undergraduate student who recalled this incident from childhood in such vivid detail reminds us of a premise fundamental to developmental psychology: Although adults and young children may inhabit the same universe, they often see things from very different perspectives. A lifetime of looking at photographs and paintings and landscapes, as well as an acceptance of the prevailing consensus about the way things are, had convinced Sarah's teacher that the sky meets the ground at the horizon line. She undoubtedly considered the band of uncolored paper bisecting the middle of Sarah's drawing a mistake which could easily be corrected by reminding her of the facts. For Sarah—and, undoubtedly, for many of her classmates—however, the adult convention of coloring in sky until you met ground was incompatible with the reality they experienced, of sky overhead and air—colorless, transparent, blank—all around.

Everyday, in every corner of the globe, in matters large and small, young children are misunderstood. As Saint–Exuperey's Little Prince (1943) observed of this situation, "Adults never understand anything by themselves, and it is tiresome to be always and forever explaining things to them." Developmental theory implicitly recognizes the existence of a gulf between the worlds of children and adults and attempts, in various ways, to bridge that gap. Often this is done by describing the behavior of children, the way they think and act, in terms that may help to explain the logic that undergirds thoughts and actions which may seem eccentric, from an adult point of view. Frequently such explanations, no matter how objectively they are presented, seem to contain and suggest appropriate responses. A teacher who believes that no inaccuracy should be allowed to pass unnoticed in children's conceptions or in their drawings, for example, will find many of the things young children tend to do when they draw aggravating. On the other hand, a teacher who understands that it is normal, typical, and defensible on logical grounds for children of a certain age to construct their drawings with skies above and ground below, who knows that this is a formula that almost every child adopts and eventually discards as experience and intentions for drawing conspire to suggest other solutions, is likely to tolerate, if not appreciate, this deviation from conventions of representation.

For many, many years, art educators accepted as a fact of life the proposition that young children construct visual images according to a logic that is not readily apparent, in a language that must be learned. Those who were involved in the education of other teachers considered descriptions of typical passages and patterns of development in children's drawings foundational knowledge, the basis of informed sensitivity to

L. Bresler and C.M. Thompson (eds.), The Arts in Children's Lives, 87–92.
© *2002 Kluwer Academic Publishers. Printed in the Netherlands.*

children's projects and purposes. And so generations of young teachers have viewed examples of baselines and skylines, houses with chimneys perched precariously on pitched roofs, humans with arms spouting from what seems to be a head balanced atop pairs of freestanding legs, animals strangely human in form and expression. The similarities among children, across cultures, over time are remarkable. The details may differ, particularly as children reach school age and begin to incorporate in their drawings the small but telling details unique to their time and place, but the organization, the basic "groundplan" (Cox, 1992; Golomb, 1992) of children's images maintains an almost eerie consistency. What's more, the changes in structure and organization that occur in children's drawings as they grow older and begin to explore broader territories in their drawings seem to occur predictably and, for a period in children's lives at least, without the necessity of strenuous intervention from adults.

What do we make of this phenomenon? Does the apparent universality and predictability of artistic development in childhood absolve us from exerting any effort to cultivate the activity? Is art–making an activity of childhood which is self–sustaining and self–limiting, an occupation that runs its course and then disappears from most lives, resurfacing in nostalgia for the smell of crayons and the special toothy surface of manila paper? Or is the expression of thought and feeling through art a uniquely human propensity which develops only so far as it is encouraged and supported, an endeavor so basic to human well–being that its absence from our existence diminishes life and reduces our capacity to make sense of our experience, as Buber (1965; see also Thompson, 2001), Sarason (1990), and many others suggest?

If we concede that art is a significant aspect of human experience, a capacity that all children possess, one that deserves and requires attention, respect, and support from parents and teachers, we are left to ponder what we should make of the apparent regularity of the process through which this capacity emerges and develops. How should generalizations about development influence and inform our teaching? Should we simply appreciate the logic of the things children do in their drawings, such as their determination to avoid overlapping forms in order to insure that there is no confusion about the identity of each object they depict? Should we stand back and enjoy what comes naturally, and hope that our supportive response is all that is needed to maintain children's involvement in the process when they inevitably encounter graphic problems for which they can find no satisfactory solutions? Or should we assume that many of the characteristics that appear in children's drawings are evidence of "innate graphic biases" (Wilson & Wilson, 1982) which can, and perhaps should, be superseded by instruction? Is it most appropriate to think of developmental change as primarily stage–like or gradual, idiosyncratic or predictable, progressive or simply mutable? Should we avoid confusing the child by teaching beyond the child's present capacity or should we regard the things that the child can accomplish independently as a platform upon which a scaffold can be built, allowing the child to exceed his or her grasp?

What is the value of developmental theory? Can we understand individual children well enough without some sense of what is typical of most children and what may be truly distinctive in the children we teach? Can we appreciate what is unique without recognizing that much of the experience of being a child is shared, even across time and space? Do we do children (and their teachers) a disservice by insisting that no generalizations are possible? Are some behaviors so ubiquitous, so immediately apparent to experienced teachers of young children, that they must be regarded as testimony to the deepest structures of the human spirit?

These questions, and many more, surround discussions of development in visual arts education, a field with a strong tradition of developmentally–based theory and practice, particularly in the approaches it has sanctioned for parenting and teaching young children. Other art forms, with very different and distinctive pedagogical traditions, may emphasize, accumulate and value very different kinds of developmental information, with different levels of specificity and different measures of confidence. Yet there are certain fundamental issues implicit in the concept of development that are essential to defining relationships between teachers and students, and between the beginning performances of children and the thoughts and works produced by adult practitioners of an art, a craft, a skill, or a discipline.

No adult can approach children devoid of expectations for their behavior, with no predispositions to interpret the things they say and do according to particular ideas about childhood. These ideas are absorbed in the process of living within a particular family, community, culture, and moment. Anyone who has taken a very small child to dinner in a moderately upscale restaurant can attest that the public response of adults who encounter a toddler in their midst varies widely, from amusement to fascination to barely disguised—sometimes overt—hostility: The same child can be regarded as rambunctious, bold, or spirited, depending upon the concept of the ideal child held by individual observers stationed around the room. For those adults who meet children rarely and then at a safe distance, a "vague average understanding" (Heidegger, 1962, p. 25) of what such creatures are like may suffice. However, children have a right to expect that the adults who figure most prominently in their lives, their parents and teachers, will develop a more sensitive, informed, and particularized "image of the child" (Malaguzzi, 1993, p 10). Indeed, teacher education in its broadest sense is the project of helping others to develop interpretive frames that allow them to make sense of children, attitudes and orientations that must be more comprehensive and coherent than those which may suffice for adults who have not elected to stand in a pedagogic relationship (van Manen, 1991) toward children.

As Jo Alice Leeds (1989) pointed out in an historical overview of attitudes toward child art, adult's understanding of child art is influenced both by prevailing conceptions about the nature of art, as well as attitudes toward childhood. During the early Modernist period and into the days of Abstract Expressionism, for example, the spontaneous paintings and drawings of very young children were greatly admired by artists who coveted their fresh and uninhibited qualities, the boldness of execution, lack of premeditation, and absence of recognizable subject matter that is the stock–in–trade of preschool painters. More recently, as narrative painting became increasingly dominant in the official art world, the type of surreptitious, sometimes scatological drawings that embellish the margins of notebooks in middle schools and junior high schools were recognized as worthy of artistic and scholarly attention (Korzenik, 1981; Wilson & Wilson, 1982). Although appreciation of the various kinds of art that children produce may originate in a distant cultural avant–garde, neither teachers nor parents are immune to the force of these judgments. The value others place on children's artistic products and performances may at least inspire them to look twice.

In a similar manner, prevailing notions about the ways in which young children develop and learn have undergone gradual but fundamental changes in recent years (Walsh, 1993; Wilson & Wilson, 1982). For much of this century, largely under the influence of Jean Piaget, the process of development was described in "maturationist, romantic, and idealist" (Walsh, 1993, p. 19) terms. Development was seen as a unitary process, most clearly represented in the evolution of logical and scientific reasoning. Children passed through stages, each qualitatively different and more sophisticated than the one before and each representing a fundamentally different approach to thinking about and acting upon the world. Opportunities to interact with materials and act upon the environment were deemed crucial to this process, while human intervention was decidedly less important. In the worst of cases, untoward adult interference was seen as actively detrimental to the child's learning. In the Piagetian view, nothing should be taught, and nothing could be learned, that the child was not developmentally prepared to grasp. Children's developmental levels set boundaries for teaching.

An alternative view, proposed most powerfully by the Russian psychologist, L.S. Vygotsky, has gained credence in recent years. In Vygotsky's view, development is inextricably intertwined with the process of learning, even dependent upon it. Vygotsky (1978) maintained that the development of an individual child cannot be understood without reference to the social milieu—both interpersonal and institutional—in which the child exists (Tudge & Rogoff, 1989). In this perspective, children learn both through their interactions with materials and through dialogue and activity shared with parents, teachers, and other children. Vygotsky's central claim was that development and learning are sociocultural phenomena. The mastery of the tools and symbols valued by the child's home culture and the acquisition of "higher mental processes" are made possible by the child's immersion in society (Wertsch, 1985, 1998).

This sociocultural view of development permeates the chapters that follow. Both the child and the culture are seen as active agents who influence the course of development and learning. The powerful influence of parents, teachers, and peers is recognized as primary, determining the extent to which artistry in its various forms will develop, and even children's basic opportunities to encounter the arts and to engage them as realms of meaning.

Daniel Walsh suggests that it is time to abandon the developmentalists' traditional quest for rules that apply to all of the children, all of the time. Instead, he recommends that we teach ourselves to honor exceptions as well as rules, to measure the exceptionality of every child by recognizing that children are shaped in profound and decisive ways by the experiences available to them. Even in early childhood education, Walsh reminds us, access to meaningful education in the arts is not universally available. As long as this is the case, we prevent children from constructing artistic selves, and deprive them of rich resources for constructing meaning.

Graham Welch reminds us that development is far more domain specific than was supposed in the past, when many forms of activity were forced uncomfortably into an epistemological mode that honored logical thought about all other human capacities.

Even within a single art form, many forms of engagement are possible, far more than were dreamt of, even in the four categories of disciplinary involvement proposed by the Getty Center for the Arts in Education (1985). Not only is it possible that different strands of development can proceed rather independently of one another—that a child can sing a complex melody more expertly than she can produce a steady beat with rhythm instruments, for example; it is also true that the process of mastering one skill can be impeded by development and learning occurring simultaneously in other symbol systems. The complexity of the processes of development and learning are apparent in the detailed descriptions Welch provides of component skills and processes. Equally intriguing is the type of information that is available about early musical development. The specificity and the nature of the information that Welch provides suggests a distinctive research orientation in music education that reflects the centrality of the body as instrument and the importance of physiological growth and development in determining what children are able to do.

By contrast, Christine Thompson's chapter acknowledges the role that children play in shaping their own development. The lives of young children in North America have been affected profoundly by the dramatic social changes that have occurred in the lives of adults in the past three decades, negatively and positively, in ways which we are only beginning to understand. Some form of education or care in a setting outside the home, once an exception, has become the rule for a great majority of children in their preschool years. Young children are now far more likely to spend their days in the company of peers, and to reach many of the milestones of early learning in their company and with their help. Much of what we know about early artistic development was learned through intimate, informal observations of children drawing in the presence of fascinated adults. It is possible that our shared conceptions of the progress of artistic development in early childhood is outmoded and in need of fundamental revision. Thompson describes instances of peer tutoring and collaboration observed in preschool and kindergarten art classes, and speculates on the impact these experiences may have on the process of learning to draw.

Shifra Schonmann examines the engagement of young audiences in Israel with the art form of theater, focusing on the essential issue of young children's ability to maintain an appropriate "aesthetic distance" as the view events transpiring on stage. Schonmann explores the relationships between imagination and reality, between play and art as aspects of children's experience that bear directly upon their understanding of the creations of imaginary worlds, detached from the everyday and commonsensical world of their own experience.

Finally, in this section, Kieran Egan and Michael Ling challenge the basic assumptions about development that prompt us to regard young children as intellectually deficient, or, at least, significantly less capable than adults. They suggest that there are certain aspects of intellectual activity at which young children excel, far surpassing their elders in the imaginative and metaphoric ways of thinking that are central to the arts. Egan and Ling suggest that prevailing developmental theories focus on what young children do least well, and, in doing so, present a distorted view of children's minds which, in turn, mislead the adults who make curricular decisions in their behalf.

REFERENCES

Buber, M. (1965). *Between man and man*. New York: Macmillan.

Cox, M. (1992). *Children's drawings*. New York: Penguin.

Getty Center for Education in the Arts. (1985). *Beyond creating: The place for art in   American schools*. Los Angeles: The J. Paul Getty Trust.

Golomb, C. (1992). *The child's creation of a pictorial world*. Berkeley: University of California Press.

Heidegger, M. (1962). *Being and time* (J. Macquarrie & E. Robinson, Trans.). New York: Harper & Row. (Original work published in 1926).

Korzenik, D. (1981, Sept.). Is children's work art? Some historical views, *Art Education*, 20 –24.

Leeds, J. A. (1989). The history of attitudes toward child art. *Studies in Art Education*, 30(2), 93–103.

Malaguzzi, L. (1993, Nov.) . For an education based on relationships (Lella Gandini, Trans). *Young Children*, 9–12.

Saint–Exuperey, A. (1943). *The little prince*. New York: Harcourt Brace Jovanovich.

Sarason, S. B. (1990). The challenge of art to psychology. New Haven: Yale University Press.

Thompson, C. (2001). Martin Buber. In J. Palmer, D. Cooper, & L. Bresler (Eds.), *One hundred key thinkers on education* (volume 2: contemporary thinkers). London: Routledge (forthcoming).

Tudge, J. & Rogoff, B. (1989). Peer influences on cognitive development: Piagetian and Vygotskian perspectives. In M. H. Bornstein and J. S. Bruner (Eds.), *Interaction in human development* (pp. 17–40). Hillsdale, NJ: Lawrence Erlbaum Associates.

van Manen, M. (1991). *The tact of teaching*. Albany: State University of New York Press.

Vygotsky, L. S. (1978). *Mind in society* (M. Cole, V. John–Steiner, S. Scribner, & E. Souberman, Eds.) Cambridge, MA: Harvard University Press.

Walsh, D. (1993, July/Aug.). Art as socially constructed narrative: Implications for early childhood education. *Arts Education Policy Review*, 94(6), 18–23.

Wertsch, J. V. (1985). *Vygotsky and the social formation of mind*. Cambridge, MA: Harvard University Press.

Wertsch, J. (1998). *Mind as action*. New York: Oxford University Press.

Wilson, M. & Wilson, B. (1982). *Teaching children to draw: A guide for parents and teachers*. Englewood Cliffs, NJ: Prentice Hall.

KIERAN EGAN & MICHAEL LING

6. WE BEGIN AS POETS:

Conceptual Tools and the Arts in Early Childhood

INTRODUCTION

In this chapter we want to focus on what seems to be one of the main obstacles to the wider recognition of the value of the arts to education. We will locate the obstacle in a set of ideas about children's learning that have become very widely believed. The chapter will sketch the ideas, try to show why we should be skeptical of them, and offer an alternative way of conceiving young children's learning. In proposing the alternative, we will draw on Lev Vygotsky's work that shows how we make sense of the world in terms of the cognitive tools that we pick up while growing up within a particular culture.

Let us begin with a local example, which, we are sure, finds endless echoes across the continent. In its newsletter to parents a local school has been boasting that it offers its students "job–ready skills." It has been tailoring its curriculum to "produce" precisely what various local employers seem to want. This responsiveness to the "marketplace," to "the consumer of the schools' products" is considered entirely admirable by many local politicians, who are the schools' paymasters. This pressure on schools is felt not only at the senior secondary level, but is evident throughout the system. It is also evident in young children. When Cedric Cullingford (1985, 1986) asked a wide sample of primary school children what they were at school for, he was surprised to hear from all the children that they understood the first purpose of school was to prepare them for "jobs."

At present it is easy to justify curriculum time being spent on activities that seem to lead directly to skills that will be of practical use in adulthood. So the "basics" of education are usually thought to be the early development of literacy and numeracy. It is now proving easy for those who promote "computer literacy" to argue for curriculum time on the grounds that computer skills will be of practical value for jobs in the future. It is becoming another "basic." How can the arts defend themselves from being increasingly marginalized by the insistence that schools give more and more curriculum time to those "basic" skills that will be of practical value in future society?

We want to suggest that the problem we find ourselves in—sidelining the arts increasingly even though we recognize their centrality to education—is in part tied up in our having accepted a set of basic educational ideas that are mistaken. That is, we

93

L. Bresler and C.M. Thompson (eds.), The Arts in Children's Lives, 93–100.
© 2002 *Kluwer Academic Publishers. Printed in the Netherlands.*

want to make the uncomfortable case that the root of the problem is a set of ideas that most readers of this chapter probably take for granted.

These ideas have a long history and were put into their modern familiar form by the English philosopher Herbert Spencer (1820–1903). They were then adapted by American psychologists, philosophers, and educators such as William James, John Dewey, G. Stanley Hall, and Edward Thorndike. The ideas also influenced, as we shall see, Jean Piaget. These influential thinkers and researchers have reinforced Spencer's ideas and helped to make them taken–for–granted truisms about children's thinking and learning.

These ideas are, in Spencer's words, that in educating children "we should proceed from the simple to the complex . . . . from the indefinite to the definite . . . . from the particular to the general . . . . from the concrete to the abstract . . . . from the empirical to the rational" (1969, p.75). "Every study, therefore," he argued, "should have a purely empirical introduction . . . children should be led to make their own investigations, and draw their own inferences. They should be told as little as possible, and induced to discover as much as possible" (1969, p. 75).

The problem with these ideas is that they assume that children's intellectual development follows a path like our biological development. Spencer adapted these ideas from evolutionary biology and applied them directly to education. Jean Piaget's influential theory is similarly built on a biological conception of development. It is an "hierarchical integrative" theory, in which the child is represented as accumulating skills in stages, each set of which is incorporated and enlarged by the further skills acquired in the subsequent stage. The process leads ideally to the complete unfolding and fullest "development" of all the skills that existed in embryonic forms in earlier years. The adult is thus seen as an elaboration of all the capacities that are simply embryonic in childhood.

The result of Spencer's ideas, and of the support Piaget has lent to them, is a view of the basics of education as setting in place the skills that gradually grow to maturity and practical use in adult society. What is wrong with this?

We begin as poets

What is wrong is that the human mind does not develop like the rest of the biological world in one educationally very important way. Human children are equipped with some specific intellectual capacities that reach their peak in our early years and remain in some residual form through the rest of our lives. For example, our ability to recognize and generate appropriate metaphors reaches its peak by age five, and declines, following an irregular profile, thereafter (Gardner & Winner, 1979; Winner, 1988). Metaphoric fluency is crucial in language development, but also, of course, for a range of other intellectual activities, and particularly to that range of activities we call "the arts." Dance, painting, acting, and play in general all rely crucially on the child's ability to see something in terms of something else—this line represents a tree, this movement represents a feeling, these words represent an action.

Those intellectual capacities we rather vaguely refer to as "the imagination" similarly experience energetic deployment early in life and, typically, gradual decline as we grow older. We tend to develop arteriosclerosis of the imagination in adulthood.

Consider for a moment the kind of food you most hated when you were five years old. And try to recapture if you can the degree of loathing you felt for it. In my case it was cheese. I couldn't bear to let cheese near my mouth. Now I eat cheese quite appreciatively, and for some time thought this was a triumph of character—when, alas, it's largely the result of a decay of taste buds. Unfortunately, it isn't only the taste buds that go into decline after about age five or six; a whole range of intellectual capacities that are necessary to quickly orient us to a language, a society, and a cosmos are evolutionarily developed to become less useful after about age five and to go into decline. Unfortunately, again, these tools of the imagination are precisely those needed to keep us intellectually flexible, creative, and energetic in modern societies. That is, our evolution is at odds with our educational needs—which helps to explain why the educational job is so hard.

The profile of the development of imagination in our lives seems quite unlike that ever–rising progress from childhood to adulthood that is represented in hierarchical–integrative, biology–derived developmental theories. While we lack any precise image of the development of imagination, even the most casual observation of human beings at various ages suggests that it would be absurd to claim that imagination is only embryonically present in young children and becomes increasingly more evident, elaborate, and rich as we grow older. Give a box to a typical adult and to a typical child and ask them to work out different uses for it; when the adult gives up after a few minutes with six uses, the child is into the fiftieth and just warming up.

If we look at children's imaginative lives, rather than their slowly–accumulating logico–mathematical skills, we do not see intellectual activity dominated by the concrete, the simple, the indefinite, the empirical, and so on. We see prodigal metaphoric invention, talking middle–class rabbits, titanic conflicts of good and evil, courage and cowardice, fear and security, and so on. We see, that is, the kinds of intellectual activity that are central to the arts.

It seems not unfair to say that current developmental theories that have been influential in education have emphasized what young children do least well—those logico–mathematical capacities that slowly develop through our early lives—and have largely ignored those things that young children do best intellectually, and better typically than adults—those imaginative skills attached to metaphor and image generation, and to narrative and affective understanding. Those developmental theories, while proponents of the arts in education have accepted them and tried to use them, have consistently depreciated the child's central set of intellectual tools and skills. They have served rather to support the view that the central skills we must attend to are those logico–mathematical skills whose practical social utility seems most obvious.

If we conclude that Spencer's principles are inadequate in giving us a picture of the child as a learner, and hence are wrongly identifying what are the most secure basics for education, to what alternative can we turn for a more adequate conception of children's development and so the basics of education?

The arts

If language is the crucial fact of early human development—the true basic of all our education—and early childhood is the period during which children are developing oral language at a prodigal rate, let us consider what intellectual capacities—what tools of understanding—are involved in generating and using an oral language. To put it generally, what, intellectually, comes to children along with language?

"Language, in a preliterate society lacking the apparatus of a modern information–state, is basically for telling stories" (Donald, 1991, p. 257). Our inventory of what comes along with language, then, might begin with stories.

What are stories? Stories are unique kinds of narratives in that they have, in their basic forms, ends that satisfy some tension generated by their beginnings. They can thus fix the hearer's affective orientation to the events, characters, ideas, or whatever, that make them up. They allow us the satisfaction that life and history—which are, without the stories we try to lay on them, just one damn thing after another—deny us. The story was perhaps the most important of all social inventions, in that it provided the bond for languaged people to tie themselves into societies, emotionally committed to shared social and cosmic stories. Stories, basically, are little tools for orienting our emotions.

Languaged people without writing need to preserve their store of knowledge, feelings, hopes, and fears in living memories. To do this most effectively—oral cultures discovered long ago—people learned to deploy a set of techniques that were a part of language itself. So rhyme and rhythm could help the process of remembering: "Thirty days hath November . . . " If one does not have writing, the preservation of lore in the living memory leads to a mind that re–sounds with a store of rhymes and rhythms. These tools we see most simply in language also, of course, find expression in other arts—patterns of line and color and music, routines of movement and performance, etc.

The need to preserve lore in the memory also led to the discovery that language could be used to stimulate vivid images in the mind, and lore coded into such images was more easily remembered and so reliably preserved across generations. Generating images from words seems invariably to involve some emotional component (Warnock, 1976)—which helps to account for the greater richness we typically experience from generating our own images from text or listening to an oral story than from seeing images presented to us on film or television. Those vivid images become also central to achievements in other arts; they are what we can seek to express in movement or in paint or in sound.

If we consider the kinds of fantasy stories young children are most powerfully engaged by—and it is a rare adult who does not recall in detail, say, Cinderella, while the same adult may remember nothing of the more "relevant," "issues–oriented" stories read to them as children—we may see that their underlying structure is usually a simple binary conflict based on security/fear, courage/cowardice, good/evil, and so on. Now so much has been written lately about binary opposites, critical of their pernicious influence, that we need to be careful in pointing out that the generation of opposites and mediating between them seems to be basic to human thinking. (For a discussion of this issue, see Egan, 1997, Chs. 2 and 6.) Three simple observations might be made about these binary structures; first, they are abstract, second, they are affective, and, third, they can "expand" understanding to anything in the universe that can be organized in terms of their basic affective concepts.

Their abstractness perhaps merits emphasis in the face of the near–ubiquitous assertion in education that young children are "concrete thinkers." That young children do not commonly use abstract terms explicitly does not mean that they do not constantly use abstractions in their thinking. Indeed, one might reasonably make a case for "the primacy of the abstract" (Hayak,1970) and for children's ability to make sense of the concrete only to the degree that the concrete elements are tied to some affective abstraction (Egan, 1989).

The point about the binary oppositions and mediation is that once you grasp from experience such oppositions as solitude/company, for example, you can make sense of a solitary like Obi–Wan Kenobi in *Star Wars*. That is, you don't need to "expand" the child's horizons gradually from something familiar till you can make star warriors, monks, or witches meaningful; they can be grasped directly in terms of such abstract binary terms.

These, then, are just a few of the intellectual tools that come along with language. With metaphor, story, binary–opposition and mediation, affective abstraction, image–generation from words, rhyme and rhythm, we are beginning to construct our inventory of "basics" in education. They look very like the basic set of tools we have traditionally associated with the imagination and with the arts in general. And so, while we have been emphasizing the application of these "tools of understanding" to language specifically here, from a certain point of view, these same tools in some way also form the bases for other expressive forms, like drama, dance, music, and visual art.

Furthermore, we could say that all forms of artistic expression are ultimately forms of storytelling; they are articulations of moments in which one describes "what is important," a statement of some desire to express a view of the world, some statement about how one finds the world and oneself. They describe a moment in which we are invited to attend to the arc of a narrative, that is, some description of a trajectory from one point to another, with significant events and tensions presented in between, and in so doing, they "fix a hearer's affective orientation." If we can recognize the arts as elaborations of the skills and capacities of "language" and "storytelling," then we can see how important are explorations in these various domains to the developing consciousness of young people. The significance of all this with regard to children's learning is that the arts, and thus the basic cognitive tools employed in their expression, are the fundamental means with which we find and experience ourselves and the world.

By focusing on cultural development rather than biological development, the principles of children's learning we infer seem quite different. Just to sketch quite casually some of the alternative principles, we might suggest that:

1. children are abstract as well as concrete thinkers;
2. children's thinking is powerfully affective;
3. children readily understand content organized into story forms;
4. children are readily engaged by forming images from words;
5. children are prodigal producers and consumers of metaphors;
6. children's learning is stimulated by rhyme and rhythm;

7.   children's learning can proceed by forming binary oppositions and   mediating them.

(It would be possible to go on with this fairly casual list. We'll stop at 7 because that's how many principles Spencer enunciated.)

There seem to be significant implications for teaching that follow from these alternative principles.

Implications for teaching

The first implication, to quote the title of a book we seem to remember seeing somewhere, is that one might begin to think of "teaching as story telling" (Egan, 1986). This is not to suggest that we should spend our time telling children lots of fictional stories, though more emphasis on such stories may be one result of this alternative approach, but rather that we think of the content of the curriculum more as great stories to tell than as objectives to attain. We might, then, think of "story" much in the sense a newspaper editor asks a reporter, "What's the story on this?" That is, we will not look for a fiction related to the content but rather seek out the affective meaning—the emotional resonance—within the content. This primary focus on the affective rather than some content or plan can lead us to recognize that the arts can be our route into other disciplines. Again, while we use "the story" as our paradigmatic form here, we want to emphasize that the constituents of storying can be elaborated to many important aspects of other arts, as indicated above.

So, instead of using a planning model derived from Ralph Tyler's (1950) useful, but industry–influenced (Callaghan, 1962), objectives–content–methods–evaluation scheme, we might construct an alternative model derived from some of the principles sketched above. We have called it "mythic" because so many of the features of children's thinking on which it is based are shared by the central features of mythic thinking:

Mythic planning framework

1.   Identifying importance
     What is emotionally important about this topic? What is affectively engaging about it?
2.   Finding binary opposites
     What binary concepts best capture the affective importance of the topic?
3.   Organizing the content into a story form
     3.1 First teaching event
          What content most dramatically embodies the binary concepts, in order to provide access to the topic? What image best captures that content and its dramatic contrast?
     3.2 Structuring the body of the lesson or unit
          What content best articulates the topic into a clear story form? What vivid metaphors does it suggest?

4. Conclusion

What is the best way of resolving the conflict inherent in the binary concepts? What degree of mediation is it appropriate to seek? How far is it appropriate to make the binary concepts explicit?

5. Evaluation

How can one know whether the topic has been understood, its importance grasped, and the content learned?

We will give a quick example of how this model might be used, taking an example from a book written by three Australian teachers who have been using the model for a few years (Armstrong, Connolly, & Saville, 1994). Among the units of study they outline in the book is one on the environment.

They identified the importance—the emotional importance to them and to the children—in the sense that what the individual does can and does make a difference to the environment, and that the environment they influence is the one they will grow old in and the one they will pass on to their children.

The binary opposites they identified, based on their exploration of their feelings about the environment, were despair and hope.

They began organizing the content into a story structure by choosing something that provided a dramatic exemplification of those binary opposites. They used the book and video *The Man Who Planted Trees* by Jean Giono. It tells the story of Elzéar Bouffier, who, over a lifetime, filled a whole region with hope by his solitary efforts to reforest a desolate area of the French Alps. From this beginning they built activities and knowledge that conveyed an understanding of the environment by constantly contrasting hope with despair. They included in the process a range of arts activities—for example, painting, play–acting, aesthetic involvement in designing improvements to a local area of despoiled scrub land.

As they regenerated the waste land, the students concluded by seeing the positive aesthetic results of their work, feeling the hope that working along with nature gave them, and recognizing that over the years what they had done would have significant beneficial consequences. Their purpose was less mediation than the confirming of hope. The unit of study also involved personal development activities, religious study, science and mathematics, language, and other arts, all integrated into the single extended story about human hopes and despairs concerning the environment.

Evaluation was based on the students' grasp of the story of regeneration they played a part in, the clarity and accuracy of their predictions for the results of their work, discussion of their emotions and thoughts about their work, their enthusiasm, commitment, and involvement, their ability to extract relevant information that would have practical beneficial effects and to present this in confident and competent oral and written forms, and their ability to cooperate in a group to achieve agreed on goals.

The trouble with this model, without more examples than we can give here (but see Egan, 1988, 1989), is that it is difficult to begin by locating within oneself something affectively engaging, something emotionally moving, about the content. Yet, we have suggested, it is only by connecting with that emotional association that the content can be made meaningful and engaging to children. The affective engagement with content does not go away as we grow older. The model draws attention to those characteristics that we share with young children—even if our emotional and imaginative grasp on content will often be less vivid. The model tries to make these elements central for us to focus on when planning. It also, far from incidentally, suggests that the beginning of our thinking about planning teaching should be tied up with the arts.

CONCLUSION

Spencer's (1969) principles derive from thinking of children's minds largely in terms of literacy–induced capacities, and forgetting that before they are literate, and also after they are literate, they also have the capacities of orality. The central fact of our minds from an educational point of view is not their biological nature, and all that follows for conceptions of development, but their cultural nature. We begin as poets, using the techniques that language allows us to make sense of our world. The basics of our cultural lives are the arts. It is through deployment of those tools and skills that are central to early language development—story, metaphor, rhyme and rhythm, binary structuring and mediation, image formation from words, affective abstraction, and so on—that we lay down the true basics of education.

REFERENCES:

Armstrong, M., Connolly, A., & Saville, K. (1994). *Journeys of discovery.* Melbourne: Oxford University Press.
Callaghan, R. (1962). *Education and the cult of efficiency.* Chicago: University of Chicago Press.
Cullingford, C. (1985). *Parents, teachers and schools.* London: Robert Royce.
Cullingford, C. (1986). "'I suppose learning your tables could help you get a job'—Children's views about the purpose of schools." *Education 3–13,* 14 (2), 41–46.
Donald, M. (1991). *Origins of the modern mind.* Cambridge, MA: Harvard University Press.
Egan, K. (198–). *Primary understanding.* New York: Routledge.
Egan, K. (1986). *Teaching as story telling.* Chicago: University of Chicago Press, 1989.
Egan, K. (1997). *The educated mind: How cognitive tools shape our understanding.* Chicago: University of Chicago Press.
Gardner, H. & Winner, E. (1979). The development of metaphoric competence: Implications for humanistic disciplines. In S. Sacks (Ed.), *On metaphor.* Chicago: University of Chicago Press.
Hayek, F.A. (1970). The primacy of the abstract. In A. Koestler & J.R. Smythies (Eds.), *Beyond reductionism.* New York: Macmillan.
Pinker, S. (1994). *The language instinct: How the mind creates language.* New York: Morrow.
Silin, Jonathan G. (1995). *Sex, death, and the education of children: Our passion for ignorance in the age of AIDS.* New York: Teachers College Press.
Spencer, H. (1969). *Herbert Spencer.* Ann Low–Beer (Ed.) London: Collier–Macmillan.
Tyler, R. W. (1950). *Basic principles of curriculum and instruction.* Chicago: University of Chicago Press.
Warnock, M. (1976). *Imagination.* London: Faber.
Winner, E. (1988). *The point of words: Children's understanding of metaphor and irony.* Cambridge, MA: Harvard University Press.

This chapter is based on and uses some material from "The Arts in Basic Education: In *Childhood Education.* Vol. 73 No. 6. 1997, pp. 241–345.

DANIEL J. WALSH

7. CONSTRUCTING AN ARTISTIC SELF: A CULTURAL PERSPECTIVE

In this chapter I argue that cultural psychology (e.g., Bruner, 1996; Cole, 1996; Goodnow, Miller, & Kessel, 1995; Shweder et al., 1999) provides useful insights into the artistic development of young children. Cultural psychology, wrote Bruner (1990), is "an interpretive psychology [that] seeks out the rules that human beings bring to bear in creating meanings in cultural contexts" (p. 12). Historically psychology has limited itself to biology and evolution to explain development while ignoring the critical roles of *culture* and *situation* (Bruner, 1996). This chapter will focus on culture and situation.

I make three points and contrast them to dominant themes in the discourse on early schooling. I then explore implications of these points and end by making specific recommendations for pedagogical practice. My first point is that children are historical or contextual, not universal. Second, the self is contextual rather than bounded. Third, learning and development are more domain–specific rather than domain–general. I discuss each idea in detail below and show how it differs from the dominant discourse.

THE HISTORICAL CHILD

Sixty years ago Vygotsky urged developmentalists to end the vain quest for "the eternal child." He urged them to instead pursue "the historical child" (1934/1987, p. 91). The historical child does not transcend culture and history. As Minick put it, she learns and develops "under particular social and historical conditions" (1989, p. 162).

The notion of a child who lives beyond time and place is so counter–intuitive I find it difficult to understand how the eternal child was ever taken seriously. It should be transparently clear to anyone who has compared his own childhood to that of his children's, contrasted her own children born a few years apart, or observed children learning and developing in different cultures, that children and times change rapidly.

Still, developmentalists have largely ignored Vygotsky's advice. The quest for the eternal child continued. As a result, our understanding of young children's development, despite massive empirical and theoretical efforts, remains limited. Developmentalists have vainly sought laws that apply to children's development in all places at all times. Ironically, they have looked less at children themselves and how they are situated in their daily worlds than at children as "windows onto universal psychological laws or as indicators of treatment effects" (Graue & Walsh, 1995).

Guided by a dominant theoretical framework that has been predominantly structural, individualistic, at times maturationist, and limited in scope to matters biological and evolutionary (Bruner, 1996), the pursuit of the eternal child has continued.

L. Bresler and C.M. Thompson (eds.), The Arts in Children's Lives, 101–111.

The dominant developmental theories of this century have been structural in that they view children as proceeding through successive stages—as children move from one stage to the next, underlying structures change. The structures underlying, for example, the theories of Gesell, Piaget, and Freud vary, as do the stages they describe. But in structural theories, children move through predictable, invariant, and domain–general stages.

Theoretical explanations of development have also been, as has Western academic thought generally, individualistic. Bruner described the emphasis thus:

> there is some inherently individualistic Self that develops, determined by the universal nature of man, and that is beyond culture. In some deep sense, this Self is assumed to be ineffable, private. It is socialized, finally, by such processes as identification and internalization: the outer, public world becoming represented in the inner, private one. (1987, p. 85)

The influence of a romantic maturationism on the discourse of early schooling has been strong. Walsh (1991) argued that it has been dominated in the last decades by a "vulgar–Piagetian" theory—Piagetian terminology overlaid on maturationist concepts

As noted above, developmental theories, like psychological theories in general, have attended to those aspects of development that can be explained in terms of biology and/or evolution. Culture and situation have been ignored. Cole (1996) demonstrated that psychology, in its emphasis on measurement and experimentation, failed to attend to Wundt's "second psychology"—psychological development in culture.

Given the influence of developmental theory on early education, it is no surprise that educators have expended a great deal of effort toward educating the eternal child. Witness the present emphasis on "developmentally appropriate practice," which is based on a narrowly conceived developmentalism (Walsh, 1991). The discourse speaks, for example, of preoperational and operational, ready and unready children, and of what is "appropriate" for 3–year–old children as opposed to fours. Allowance is made for individual differences, for special–needs children, for children from subcultures, but the assumption remains that there is a universal norm. The "particular social [and cultural] and historical conditions" in which children develop and learn receive lip service at best.

The object, or subject of schooling, is the cultural–historical child, the child who lives in particular social, cultural, and historical situations, and ends up in particular classrooms. She does not live beyond time and place. She lives here and now.

From the perspective of a cultural psychology, development is envisioned as the process of growing into culture. Growing into culture involves growing into shared meanings, into the shared narratives that, as Geertz (1973) noted, people tell themselves about themselves. Children learn associations—what goes with what and when to do what they do where they do it with whom they do it and why. They learn what is sensible, what is probable, and what is possible. They learn to find their ways through the intricate and constantly changing systemic webs of meanings that comprise contemporary American culture.

Development does not, in this perspective, exist *in* the child. It is found in the complex cultural system of which the child is part (Pianta & Walsh, 1996). Development occurs in the interactions between the child and others, in the context of beliefs about and attitudes toward children, and in the many contexts in which children both construct their selves and their selves are constructed.

I emphasize that as we think of artistic development, we are not looking within the child but at the world into which the child is growing. Selves are formed not *within* but *between*, in interactions, in the system.

THE INTERDEPENDENT SELF

As a developmentalist, my goal is to understand how the historical child develops, how she constructs that sense of who she is that we have come to call the *self*. Shweder et al. (1999) suggest that, "the self can be conceptualized as a primary locus of culture–psyche interaction and of culture–specific being....It is where the individual, a biological entity, becomes a meaningful entity—a person, a participant in social worlds" (p. 895).

Markus and Kitayama (1991) show that across cultures two contrasting conceptions of self have developed: the independent self, typical of Western cultures in general and of Western psychology in particular; and the interdependent self, typical of many Asian cultures.

The independent self, as Geertz (1975) described it, is, "a bounded, unique, more or less integrated motivational and cognitive universe, a dynamic center of awareness, emotion, judgment, and action organized into a distinctive whole and set contrastively both against other such wholes and against a social and natural background" (p. 48).

Markus and Kitayama go on to say that this conception of self "gives rise to processes like 'self–actualization,' 'realizing oneself,' 'expressing one's unique configuration of needs, rights, and capacities,' or 'developing one's distinct potential'"(p. 226).

> In marked contrast, the interdependent self takes a view of the self as part of an encompassing social relationship and recognizing that one's behavior is determined, contingent on, and, to a large extent organized by what the actor perceives to be the thoughts, feelings, and actions of *others* in the relationship....An interdependent self cannot be properly characterized as a bounded whole, for it changes structure with the nature of the particular social context. Within each particular social situation, the self can be differently instantiated. (Markus & Kitayama, p. 227)

The view of the self as independent is deeply embedded in Western psychology. The extent to which it is deeply embedded in Western cultures is not as clear. The idea of the inherent social nature of the self has long been emphasized in Western thought. Bruner, drawing on the work of Mead (1962) and others, notes that "self–awareness requires as its necessary condition the recognition of the Other as a self" (1996, p. 35).

As Western psychology changes and becomes more cultural, the underlying conceptions of self are also changing and are shifting to a more interdependent view. Markus and Kitayama propose, "Perhaps Western models of the self are quite at odds with actual individual social behavior and should be reformulated to reflect the substantial interdependence that characterizes even Western individualists" (p. 247).

Selves

Within this view of the highly contextualized self, I find it useful to think of the self as a, more or less, integrated collection of *situated* or *contextualized* selves. Let me give an personal example by briefly describing how I wrote this chapter. Four selves vied for control of the keyboard. I am a professor and researcher, who regularly writes about topics relating to young children and early schooling, like this chapter. But I am also a former teacher, a parent, and musician, all of whom have something to say about young children, development, and art. Incidentally, these last three selves abhor the stilted way my professor self, left to his own devices, writes.

Let me describe these selves briefly. I muddled through a dozen years teaching urban prekindergarten and kindergarten children, trying to make sense of how they learned. I despised pompous professors then, and I still do. When the professor starts professing, the teacher demands, "What do you know?"

I am the father of two young children, and much of what I know about children I learned because on occasion I had the sense to attend carefully to them. Of course, my professorial self dismisses such knowledge as "anecdotal" and hopelessly biased.

Finally, I am a minor musician who plays and sings whenever I can squeeze in a few moments. Years ago I played in bar bands, but singing "Me and Bobby McGee" for the thirty–three–hundredth time at two in the morning lost its appeal. Now I play and sing for and with my kids. Why introduce this self? Because this is my artistic self. When I get stuck on the keyboard, I move my fingers to the fret–board. It helps.

It gets more complicated. Since I wrote the first draft of this chapter, I lived in Japan for 8 months, doing fieldwork in kindergartens and day cares. I have an understanding of the interdependent self from daily living that I did not have before, one that affected me as professor, father, former preschool teacher and so on. Some combination of these and other selves comprise the self whom I identify as me, but that self varies in important ways depending on the context. To the extent that I am a "balanced" person it is because my various selves offset each other.

My point is that when we think about art education for young children we are not about developing artists, but about developing children with a well integrated collection of varied selves, one of which is artistic. To develop an artistic self, children have to have artistic contexts within which to spend significant time. They require contexts within which the development of an artistic self is supported.

These contexts cannot exist independently of the larger culture and the meaning and value of the artistic within it. I was struck by the high level of drawing skills of kindergarten children in my work in Japan, and I was also struck by how the aesthetic permeates the larger culture in all almost all aspects. Art is really not central to our culture. One may decry that reality, but that is the culture that kids are developing into, and it should understood: Not necessarily accepted but understood.

DOMAIN–SPECIFIC DEVELOPMENT

To see development as a domain–general process, as it is seen in structuralist accounts, is to see the human being developing in a very unitary way, that is, at any time a child is at a given stage of development across the various domains of development. Thus, to know something about a child's cognitive development is to know something about her emotional and social development, as they are constrained by the same underlying structures, whether those structures be Gesell's biological ones or Piaget's logic–mathematical ones. Information, then, about a child's developmental level will be equally predictive of his progress in literacy and art.

To see development as domain–specific is to see the human being as developing at different rates and in different ways depending on the given domain and the various cultural and situational factors constraining development in that domain. It is to see the *situated* nature of development. Knowing something about a child's (or adult's) developmental level in one domain may or may not be instructive of the child's level in another domain.

One reason for talking above about situated *selves* is to emphasize the domain–specificity of development. I do not deny that one develops what can usefully be called a *self* or the importance of doing so. My point is simply that underlying this self is a collection of many situated selves, some more developed than others, and that this collection may be more or less coherent given contextual factors. Development is, most definitely, more than simply a collection of varying competencies across many domains. To borrow a central concept from systems theory, the whole is always greater than the sum of the parts. Developmentalists ultimately want to understand the process by which the child comes to be the child she is. But often one can build a better understanding of the whole by attending to the parts, remembering not to isolate them.

Learning and development are very domain–specific. One's developmental level in one domain, for example, mandolin playing, may bear little relationship to one's level in another, for example, piano playing. Some domains may be more related than others, and what one learns in one may transfer to another, for example, mandolins and fiddles are tuned the same. But the point is that children's development as artists is very domain–specific. Development is situated.

Beginning from the Specific

Development proceeds from the specific. One cannot just become a generic artist. One must start somewhere concrete. Evidence is building (Inagaki, 1992) that children's understanding is better enhanced by learning a lot about one domain than a little about a lot of domains. Unfortunately, much of what is done in schooling looks more like the latter. Children develop artistic selves by learning to do one thing and learning to do it well. It is not important that they learn to do many things. It is important that they learn to do one or a very few things well.

What children learn to do well depends on accessibility or familiarity. General constraints, physical or cognitive, have less to do with how children develop than cultural constraints—what is accessible and valued. To take an example from my own children's development, children's development as hockey players is much more dependent on the accessibility of ice and how much time they spend on it and whether they are getting good instruction, than on individual physical constraints. I have seen many three– and four–year–old kids whizzing around the ice, doing things that I suspect some early childhood colleagues would say children that age are not "ready" to do. Ready or not, the ice rink is a very familiar domain to these kids.

The importance of familiarity and accessibility should be obvious. The more familiar one is with something, the more one can learn about it. The more accessible something is, the more likely one is to be highly skilled in activities related to it. The more familiar children are with a domain, the more competent they become operating there.

Development is, of course, more than the acquisition of skills. Development involves change. Let me return to skating for an example. One of the most fascinating things about watching children learn to skate is that not only do they learn skills, they learn to become skaters. The child who on dry land is very ordinary, even klutzy, becomes transformed on the ice. The opposite is also true—the very competent dry land athlete can be reduced to a board–hugging novice.

Young skaters, artists on ice, construct selves with special skills. They become *aware* of those selves. They change the way they hold their bodies. Their eyes take a very different cast. They enter a world to which they have a very different relationship from the one they have to the dry–land world. They construct a skating self—a very situated self. When they leave the ice, they leave some of their skating self, some or much of that grace there, until they return.

Human Sense

Donaldson (1978) argued that young children develop by making sense of the world, beginning with that tiny corner in which they are situated. Through this sense–making process they bring the world and their own thinking under control. She referred to the sense that children make of the world as their *human sense*. Human sense is another way of saying that experience of the world is very situated. One knows the part of the world with which one is familiar.

Adults have a fairly well developed human sense in that they have learned to operate formally, that is, they can engage in what Donaldson calls "disembodied" thinking, that is, thinking removed from concrete experience. Thus when encountering a problem on a test that describes Bill and Mary and how fast the trains on which they are riding are traveling, they do not give up and move on to the next problem because they do not know Bill and Mary, or the Bill and Mary they know have never ridden the trains from Des Moines and Denver. They understand what text book problems are about.

Children's human sense is very much tied to their experiences, to the world they inhabit. All human beings have difficulty in unfamiliar circumstances disembedding their thinking from their experience. But much more of the world is unfamiliar to children than to adults. Adults do not always find disembedding easy, but children are in many ways more situated than adults. Consider how little control children have over their daily lives—they seldom are able to pick their schools, teachers, babysitters, or even their daily routines. If a child is having difficulty in kindergarten, he cannot "change majors" like his brother at the university who, finding that engineering interferes with his social life, switches to sociology. He is stuck in kindergarten. He cannot even change to the kindergarten across the hall.

All human learning begins with a person's human sense. In order for children to learn, they must be able to relate what they are to learn to their understanding of the world, to their human sense. To the extent that what is presented to them is distant from or irrelevant to their human sense, it will be minimally available to them.

I emphasize that the argument being made is not one of *should*, that it is better to do it this way. It is an argument of *is*—that which we cannot connect to our human sense we cannot learn. Nor is the argument one of building only on children's interests, a most narrowly romantic and limiting perspective that Dewey ably critiqued 90 years ago in "The Child and the Curriculum" (1902/1964). Children's interests need to be guided and expanded and changed.

The unfamiliar must first be tied to children's sense of what the world is, how it works, and their part in the whole process. A student asked me once if I was saying that we should not teach young children here in middle Illinois about the ocean. There was much very animated discussion. I pointed out that within a few hundred yards of where she and her four–year–old daughter lived was a creek. Eventually the water in that creek makes its way, via the Sangamon and Illinois Rivers, into the Mississippi and thence to the Gulf of Mexico. If you want to take a child in middle Illinois to the ocean, start with the creek down the road. This advice holds true for more than creeks and oceans.

SUMMARY

I have described a culturally and historically situated child, whose self is contextual, and whose development is more often domain–specific than domain–general. What does this mean for art education? I will make a few general suggestions.

First should be a rejection of biological explanations for artisitic capabilites. In our culture in general and in the discourse of early schooling in particular, biological explanations for children's abilities are prevalent, even if couched in other terms. But the general notion is that biology not only causes children to have different rates of development, it also causes them, because of their genetic makeup, to develop different capabilities and/or different levels of those capabilities. As a result, some children are born with certain talents, while others are not, particularly it seems, in matters artistic.

In matters of creativity, the discourse in schooling becomes very hereditarian—some kids have it, some don't, and there's not much we can do about it. As a culture, we may value—and even this is arguable—the importance of hard work and persistence in other areas, for example, science, but we firmly believe that artists are born not made. This belief is troubling. Genetically oriented explanations ignore the situated nature of all life. Genes, whatever their impact, do not exist outside a given place and time. The smartest things that geniuses like Wayne Gretzky and Wolfgang Amadeus Mozart did was to be born at the right place at the right time to the right families. The history of music and hockey would be very different had Gretzky been born in 18th century Austria and Mozart in 20th century rural Canada.

A second suggestion is that the quest to find universals on which to base pedagogical theory should end. If there are universals in development that cross cultures and history, they are going to be due to biology and/or evolution. Surely commonalities across the human race and in the way children develop exist. But they are of trivial importance when compared to the developmental trajectories constrained by culture and situation. American children become Americans; Japanese children become Japanese. The differences are significant.

Historically, apparent commonalities have often been the result of reductionism—for example, reducing language development to "p" and "o" words, or Piaget giving children "novel, nonsignificant problems, and adopt[ing] a rigorous criterion for assessing their understanding, i.e., stating formal–logically coherent justification" (Hatano & Inagaki, 1986, p. 265). Language development is about learning to communicate within a culture. It cannot be reduced to vocabulary. When children perform tasks that are familiar and significant, that make sense to the children, and when we attempt to look carefully at their understanding and adopt sensible criteria for judging their understanding, children's performance is very different than Piaget concluded.

Pedagogy is a cultural endeavor and must be sensitive to the realities of culture. One example: Masami Toku (1999) undertook a massive cross–cultural comparison of American and Japanese children's drawings. She found that 95% of the American drawings could be placed into one or more of Eisner's (1967) spatial categories. She also found that only 65% of the Japanese drawings fit. Learning to draw in the U.S. and in Japan are two very different processes.

Third, I suggest careful attention to the concept of the artistic self. The traditional Western view of the self is limited and increasingly suspect both theoretically and empirically. Selves are formed in context. Who a child is very much depends on the kinds of context she has access to. The cultural–historical child should be enabled to construct an artistic self that is sensitive to his situatedness in history and culture. The goal is not a society of artists, any more than a society of athletes or physicists, but a society of people with many well developed selves, one or more of which is artistic.

When we then investigate the cultural–historical child's development of an artistic self, we have to look very carefully at that development in specific domains. Also required is a respectful sense of young children's capabilities. It is a trivial task to set up situations in which children, or anyone, will perform incompetently. Various critics have argued that schools do exactly that for many children. The challenge is to set up situations that support and extend children's remarkable capabilities. The challenge is also to provide artistic endeavors that are worthy of their capabilities.

SPECIFIC RECOMMENDATIONS

I will end with some specific recommendations that are drawn from Hatano, Inagaki, and Oura (1993). Hatano and his colleagues specifically addressed the issue of art education from what they then called a "post–Piagetian" perspective, which has much in common with a cultural perspective. They end their article with a series of "admittedly very tentative" (p. 150) suggestions for practice—suggestions that can serve as the basis for fertile discussion. I have selected those implications I find most applicable to young children and have expanded upon their discussion.

A first suggestion builds on the notion of the domain–specificity of development, as well as on the importance of familiarity. They suggest that teachers should choose for children one very narrow artistic domain, for example, a specific style of painting or sketching or making montages. Children then should be given the support and the opportunity to develop a level of expertise in this domain. Objections are often made that this approach limits children by not exposing them to many artistic domains. But such arguments are based on a false alternative. The alternative to a expertise in one domain is not expertise in many domains, but expertise in none.

Price described the importance of giving children a "prolonged, pressure–free period of familiarization" (1982, p. 282) in which to learn and develop. Supporting children's development in one very well specified domain can do just that.

A second suggestion builds on the first. Having selected the specific artistic domain, teachers should specify for themselves as well as for the children, in as much detail as possible what skills they want the children to acquire and to find *socially meaningful contexts* within which children can acquire the target skills. As cognitive developmentalists, their emphasis on skills in "socially meaningful contexts" goes beyond a narrow notion of behavioral objectives. Skill is more than simply doing, and, as they argue, it should be contextualized.

Making sense of the world is supported for the child when the immediate world makes sense to the child and when what the child is doing in that world has meaning. This suggestion relates very closely to what Bruner calls "the instrumental tenet," one of nine tenets he sets out to "guide a psycho–cultural approach to education" (1996, p. 13). What one learns in school has consequences both for now and later. For the development of an artistic skill to have meaning, for it to contribute to the construction of an artistic self, it must have social meaning. It must serve some social function, that is, it must go beyond simply self–expression. For a skill to become meaningful it must become part of one's cultural toolkit, thereby allowing one to engage more fully within the culture itself.

A third suggestion is to begin with children's prior skills and ideas and build upon their knowledge and their competence. This advice should be obvious to any skilled teacher but is often given more lip than actual service. All knowledge begins as *local* knowledge in particular situations (Donaldson, 1978), and this situated, very particular local knowledge forms the basis for all further development. Discovering this knowledge and skills requires teachers to attend very carefully to children and to the stories that they are telling about themselves. It also requires that teachers have a strong sense of children's competence and of the importance of beginning with the familiar and with children's human sense.

A fourth suggestion is to support their efforts by using various tools and aids, to use the popular term, *scaffold* the children's efforts. For example, Hatano et al. report a study that found that college students were much more capable singers when accompanied by a *karaoke* tape than by piano. The importance of supporting children's efforts cannot be overemphasized. A most important lesson from Vygotsky is, of course, that competence should be defined not in terms of what children can do on their own but what they can do with support. I suspect that in most areas of the curriculum educators still have much to learn about what tools and aids are most useful in this regard. Are there analogs, for example, to karaoke tapes in other forms of art? And if the idea of using karaoke tapes is off–putting, why? Not all good educational ideas begin in the university.

A final suggestion involves self evaluation. Give children ample opportunities to reflect upon their efforts. "It is very important for students to develop...evaluative criteria of their own. They should come to be independent and creative experts" (p. 151) in their artistic domain. From this awareness comes a most critical sense of control. Donaldson wrote, "What is now at stake, however, is the child's more general awareness of his own thought processes—his self–awareness. For Vygotsky rightly says: '...control of a function is the counterpart of one's consciousness of it'" (1978, p. 96).

Self evaluation is critical also for building identity. Bruner argues that a sense of self has two components, agency and evaluation, and that together they are "central to the construction of a concept of Self" (1996, p. 38), certainly to the construction of an artistic self.

CONCLUSION

The cultural–historical child has the right to an artistic self. I reemphasize that point as I end. A democratic society very much depends upon the multidimensionality of its citizens, citizens whose sense of Self is built on a range of well integrated selves.

In the fall of 1997, I attended a conference of early childhood teachers (APEI) in Lisbon, Portugal. I was struck from the beginning by how important the aesthetic was to these teachers' identity as an organization. The opening session was held in a magnificent theater in an old part of the city. The session began with port wine and ended with four wonderful story tellers. Between sessions and workshops throughout the four–day conference were music performances. The conference ended with a teacher summing up the events of the previous days in a long exuberant and playful poem—a performance that was answered by the most spontaneous and heartfelt standing ovation I have ever witnessed.

This sense of the importance of the aesthetic is missing from early schooling in this culture. It is also missing from our sense of who we are and who we should be as a culture. But we are historical, not eternal. We construct who we are. And we can change those constructions. We can, as Rorty (1989) has urged, replace the imposed descriptions with our own descriptions, in our own language.

We will be a stronger culture if we raise our children to have artistic selves. This is the challenge. I see it as the central challenge to art educators at this particular historical moment.

REFERENCES

Bruner, J.S. (1987). The transactional self. In J.S. Bruner & H. Haste (Eds.), *Making sense: The child's construction of the world* (pp. 81–96). London: Methuen.

Bruner, J. (1990). *Acts of meaning.* Cambridge: Harvard.

Bruner, J. (1996). *The culture of education.* Cambridge: Harvard.

Chung, S., & Walsh, D. J. (1999, April). Unpacking "child–centeredness": A history of meanings. Paper presented at the Annual Meeting of the American Educational Research Association, Montreal.

Cole, M. (1996). *Cultural psychology: A once and future discipline.* Cambridge: Harvard.

Dewey, J. (1902/1964). The child and the curriculum. In R. D. Archambault (Ed.), *John Dewey on education* (pp. 339–358). Chicago: University of Chicago.

Donaldson, M. (1978). *Children's minds.* New York: W.W. Norton.

Eisner, E. W. (1967). *A comparison of developmental drawing characteristics of culturally advantaged and culturally disadvantaged children.* Project No. 3086 (U.S. Dept. of Health, Education, and Welfare).

Geertz, C. (1973). *The interpretation of cultures.* New York: Basic Books.

Geertz, C. (1975). On the nature of anthropological understanding. *American Scientist, 63,* 47–53.

Goodnow, J. J., Miller, J. P., & Kessel, F. (1995). *Cultural practices as contexts for development.* San Francisco: Jossey–Bass.

Graue, M. E., & Walsh, D. J. (1995). Children in context: Interpreting the here and now of children's lives. In A. Hatch (Ed.), *Qualitative research in early childhood settings.* Westport, CT: Praeger.

Hatano, G., & Inagaki, K. (1986). Two courses of expertise. In H. Stevenson, H. Azuma, & K. Hakuta (Eds.), *Child development and education in Japan* (pp. 262–272). New York: Freeman.

Hatano, G., Inagaki, I., & Oura, Y. (1993). Changing conceptions of development and their implications for art education. *The Bulletin of the Faculty of Education, Chiba University, 41*(1), 137–153.

Inagaki, K. (1992). Piagetian and post–Piagetian conceptions of development and their implications for science education in early childhood. *Early Childhood Research Quarterly, 7,* 115–133.

Marcus, H. R., & Kitayama, S. (1991). Culture and self: Implications for cognition, emotion, and motivation. *Psychological Review, 92,* 224–253.

Mead, G. H. (1962). *Mind, self, and society from the standpoint of a social behaviorist.* Chicago: University of Chicago.

Minick, N. (1989). Mind and activity in Vygotsky's work: An expanded frame of reference. *Cultural Dynamic, 11*(2), 162–187.

Pianta, R. P., & Walsh, D. J. (1996). *High risk children in schools: Constructing sustaining relationships.* New York: Routledge.

Price, G. G. (1982). Cognitive learning in early childhood education: Mathematics, science, and social studies. In B. Spodek (Ed.), *Handbook of research in early childhood education* (pp. 264–294). New York: Free Press.

Rorty, R. (1989). *Contingency, irony, and solidarity.* Cambridge: Cambridge University Press.

Shweder, R. A., Goodnow, J., Hatano, G., LeVine, R., Markus, H., & Miller, P. (1999). The cultural psychology of development: One mind, many mentalities. In William Damon (Ed.), *Handbook of child psychology (5th ed.): Volume 1, theoretical models of human development* (pp. 865–937). New York: Wiley & Sons.

Toku, M. (1998, March). *Spatial representations in children's drawings: Why do Japanese children draw in particular ways?* Paper presented at the Annual Meeting of the National Art Education Association.

Vygotsky, L. S. (1934/1987). Thinking and speech. In R.W. Rieber & A.S. Carton (Eds.), *The collected works of L.S. Vygotsky (Vol. 1): Problems of general psychology.* New York: Plenum.

Walsh, D. J. (1991). Reconstructing the discourse on developmental appropriateness: A developmental perspective. *Early Education and Development, 2,* 109–119.

An early version of this chapter was published in 1999 *Visual Arts Research, 25* (2), 1999, pp. 4-13.

GRAHAM F. WELCH

8. EARLY CHILDHOOD MUSICAL DEVELOPMENT

INTRODUCTION

In her ethnographic study of community music in the modern English town of Milton Keynes, Finnegan (1989, p.194, p.305, *et seq*) charts the significance of the family in the promotion of "pathways" that induct successive generations into the dominant musical cultures. Whatever the musical genre – classical, rock, or jazz – children's successful engagement with that music depends more on parental interest than social or economic background. Finnegan (1989, p.311) draws parallels with the hereditary arts of non–industrial cultures in which specific families provide expertise for society as a whole in activities such as drumming or in particular forms of dancing and singing. But, unlike such non–industrial cultures, music making in this modern English setting is not confined to a few "expert" families, but is far more widespread. Commitment to particular musical genres is often lifelong, with a communal depth and breadth that contradicts the often received wisdom that music is an "inborn gift," confined to the few.

Finnegan's anthropological and sociological study can be seen as one significant contribution to a larger mosaic of evidence, drawn from many different disciplines, that demonstrates the universality and diversity of music in human cultures (*cf.* Blacking, 1976). Music's persistence across generations appears to be a product of biological/neurological predisposition (Gardner, 1983; Trehub & Trainor, 1993), socialization (Davidson et al., 1995/6; Finnegan, 1989; Lecanuet, 1996) and the existence of a gamut of artworks constituting the world's musics which have symbolic and affective meaning (Reimer, 1997). Consider these three examples of young children's musical behavior:

> In the first music play session, Caroline chooses the Chinese gong and begins to strike it with the mallet provided. Her movements are repetitive and quick as she listens to the sounds. Pausing, she looks around the room. Soon, she begins to repeat patterns of 8 to 10 beats, from faster to slower, softer to louder. She repeats this pattern 15 times in succession. She pauses again and repeats the same pattern 7 more times. The play episode lasts 20 minutes. Caroline's improvisation with the gong contained organized musical elements of tempo, dynamics and rhythm in a pattern of audible structure. A week later when Caroline returned to the music setting, she went directly to the gong and repeated the pattern again. Caroline's creation had remained long after play was over, in her own memory (Littleton, 1992, p.55).
>
> When seated at the piano, TG explored the sounds, carefully searching out and finding consonance. Favoured combinations of sounds were intervals of the third, sixth and, most particularly, the octave. These were occasionally supplemented by the perfect fourth and fifth, but never the second and seventh. She also played major scales of one octave. All these activities used the top three octaves of the piano.... Once found, the consonant interval would

L. Bresler and C.M. Thompson (eds.), The Arts in Children's Lives, 113–128.
© 2002 *Kluwer Academic Publishers. Printed in the Netherlands.*

be repeated up to a dozen times. These sound explorations were not limited to the white keys; on the contrary, she seemed to enjoy varying the tonality by employing many black notes (Welch & Backhouse, 1987, p.35).

Eddie's first recital for me was very brief. Asked to play the Christmas carol "Silent Night", he gave a fairly good rendition. The melody was well articulated, the tempo appropriate, and there was a nice rolling broken chord figure in the bass. Eddie's hands, which had difficulty holding a pencil, were clearly at home on the keyboard.... When he had finished playing, his teacher and I clapped enthusiastically, and Eddie smiled in appreciation. There certainly seemed to be something special here, and I promised to come back soon (Miller, 1989, p.2).

Caroline and Eddie are five years old; TG is six. All three children exhibit musical behaviors. Yet, while Caroline attends a mainstream pre–school nursery, TG attends a special residential first school for children with severe visual disability and additional problems; TG exhibits limited motor activity, restricted vision and only the beginnings of spoken language. Nevertheless, notwithstanding differences in their general intellectual and physical development, Caroline and TG appear to be very similar in their observed musical behavior. By comparison, five–year–old Eddie's behavior is much more musically advanced since he is already demonstrating competence in keyboard skills and in the reproduction of cultural repertoire. However, like TG, Eddie is legally blind with motor delay and only rudimentary language; he also attends a special day center for children with multiple disabilities.

To different degrees, the musical behaviors of all three children have much in common with those of adult musicians. Despite their young age, individually and collectively they demonstrate a sensitivity to elements that are inherent in many musical compositions, such as scales, recurrent patterns, contrasting timbres and harmonic consonances. In doing so, the children exemplify three essential ways that we as humans make sense of music, namely through the perception of *psycho–acoustic features* (such as pitch, loudness, duration, timbre), *structures* (detecting/constructing patterns, regularities) and *syntactic and communicative elements* (the potential for musical sounds to be characterized by a grammatical function within the musical context as a form of language) (Spender, 1987). In addition, music also has strong *emotional* associations (Gardner, 1983, p.105), and there is evidence that differing personality types are attracted to music of varying genres (Kemp, 1996, p.138). Musical perception, cognition, emotion and behavior are species–specific capabilities (*cf.* Blacking, 1976) that, like language, originate in basic neurological structures (*cf.* Gardner, 1983; Geschwind, 1979; Mehler & Christophe, 1995; Papousek, 1996; Thurman & Welch, 2000).

The manifestation of musical behavior at any given age, including childhood, is dependent on a wide range of factors, embracing basic biological potential, maturation, experience, opportunity, interest, education, family, peers, and socio–cultural context. Through their initial socialization into the dominant culture, children are exposed to many different musical genres. Concomitantly, such socialization determines which particular groupings of perceived sounds are to be classified as "music" within the culture, for this is something learned and not absolute (Finnegan, 1989, p.194). Different cultures (and subcultures) emphasize different sound combinations as musical features: for example, a descending melodic line is an important archetype in the music of the northern Ewe people of Ghana (Agawu, 1995, p.182), whereas microtonal intervals (*'srutis*) juxtaposed against drones are characteristic of an Indian *rag* (Farrell, 1997, p.49). In today's (post)modern polycultural societies, many musics co–exist, synthesize and transform, both at the macro–level (such as in the African, Western and Oriental musical traditions of Kenya (Floyd, 1996, p.202)) and also at the micro–level (through the diversity of musics within families, schools and the local community, *cf.* Finnegan, 1989).

THE FOUNDATIONS OF MUSICAL DEVELOPMENT IN INFANCY

As the brief descriptions of Caroline, TG, and Eddie suggest above, musical behavior is not necessarily related to other aspects of intellectual development such as language, nor to current physical abilities. Musical behavior is a unique yet common human trait, one particular and distinctive form of intellectual functioning (Gardner, 1983, p.99 *et seq*; O'Neill, 1996) that may be observed from the very youngest age (Howe et al, 1995; Papousek, 1996; Ries, 1987). For example, there is now a wealth of research data on the musical significance of the fetal sound environment and of how the fetus responds to musical stimuli (Abrams & Gerhardt, 1997; Lecanuet, 1996). From the twentieth to the thirtieth weeks of fetal life, the human auditory system becomes sufficiently developed for response to external sound stimuli. Significant among such external sounds are those present in the mother's daily environment, including music and the mother's voice in both speech and song. The auditory response of the fetus can give rise to learning that subsequently controls postnatal behavior (Lecanuet, 1996). Neonates two to five days old, for example, have been shown to modify their sucking behavior (an indication of increased attentiveness) when exposed to the music of the maternal culture (defined as the music that the mother listened to during pregnancy) compared to music of other cultures (Woodward et al, 1996).

After birth, the infant's musical intelligence continues to be shaped and fostered by interaction with its immediate sound environment. In particular, early vocalization influences both linguistic and musical development, with parents tending to utilize musical elements to support the acquisition of speech in infants (Papousek, 1996, p.50). The research evidence indicates a universality of parental behavior in offering vocal sounds to infants, regularly encouraging and rewarding their infant's vocal imitation and adjusting parental interventions on a moment by moment basis.

As the child grows and develops, the actual musical behaviors and capabilities that emerge are the product of a complex interaction between general intellectual predisposition and potential, the species–wide capacity for musical behaviors, and particular environmental experiences that, to a greater or lesser extent, "match" and allow such potential to be realized (see figure 1). Subsequent success in the dominant cultural forms of musical performance can be seen in retrospect to embrace a developmental "route," unique to each individual, that involves a certain continuity and non–arbitrary progression of experiences (Howe et al, 1995, p.51).

The concept of developmental "routes" actually taken by individuals in their journey towards formal musical competence compliments the notion of societal "pathways" that provide a structure for the individual to experience and be inducted into the dominant musical traditions. Furthermore, at any given moment of development, the child's observable musical behavior can be

Figure 1: the ontogenesis of musical behavior

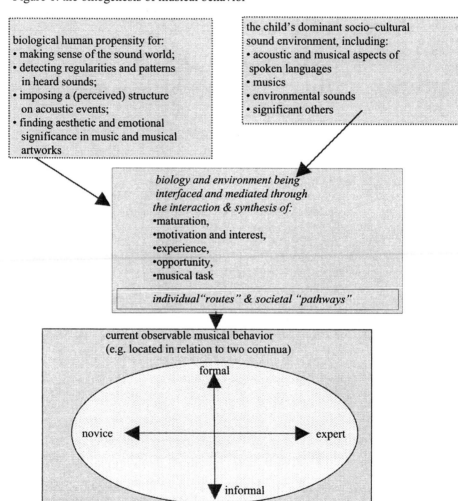

located on two continua that interface. Depending on experience and expertise, the behavior can be characterized (a) by the degree to which it contains certain defining features of the dominant musical culture(s) (such as the skilled ability to play a musical instrument and the exhibition of formalized features of the dominant musical grammars, e.g. musical phrasing, evenness of timbre and stability of tonality) and (b) in relation to a particular skill level, ranging from novice to expert in relation to the particular musical genre and task. A child's theorized "location" between these continua is relative, in that it is defined both socially and musically, and subject to developmental change.

It was once thought, for example, that "absolute pitch" ability, the ability to identify a sound in terms of its frequency, was an exceptional natural "gift," confined to less than 1% of the general population. Recent research, however, has revealed that early learning in a musical environment requiring specific control of pitch is important, such as in learning a stringed instrument (Sergeant, 1969). Also, kindergarten children can improve this ability significantly with a short period of training (Crozier, 1997). Furthermore, there is evidence that absolute pitch ability is present in large numbers of congenitally blind children, up to 50% of those sampled in a study by Welch, (1988). This large representation is thought to be a byproduct of such children's need for increased auditory acuity in an essentially unsighted world.

ASPECTS OF MUSICAL DEVELOPMENT IN EARLY CHILDHOOD

Young children's musical development is primarily evidenced by their overt musical behaviors within the dominant musical genre(s) . Although these behaviors are subject to interpretation by adult/expert musicians in relation to expected norms, such observations provide insight into the children's current musical intelligence, understanding and phase of development. Musical behaviors can be spontaneous, standing alone or concurrent with another play activity (singing while you work), or in response to a particular musical task (as in the more formal world of the elementary school classroom). Three key behaviors are elaborated below as exemplars of the nature of young children's musical development. These are *playing and composing* (in the sense of both playing with sound and of creating sound structures and forms that have musical features), the *notating of musical experiences* and, virtually ubiquitously from the earliest age across cultures, *singing*. A common permeating feature of all of these is the young child's growing comprehension of the nature of sound organization and music as sonic objects within the culture.

Playing and Composing

According to Kratus (1994, p.131), the main compositional processes are exploration, development and repetition. Exploration is defined as the unfolding of new ideas, with development being their revision and repetition their review. A study of elementary school children (Kratus, 1989) revealed that younger children (aged 7) composed primarily by exploring sounds, whereas older children (age 11) used much more development and repetition. The younger subjects were able to generate musical ideas, but [appeared] less able to manipulate or repeat them (Kratus, 1994, p.136).

A more detailed analysis of children's compositions (Swanwick & Tillman, 1986; Swanwick, 1991), based on samples in two different countries, England and Cyprus, provides further evidence of an underlying pattern to compositional development and musical understanding. Using a broad–based definition of composing, embracing the briefest utterances as well as more sustained and rehearsed invention (Swanwick, 1991, p.23), the data from these two studies suggest that young children:

- have an initial interest in the sensory aspects of sounds, such as timbre and dynamic levels, with sound organization being spontaneous and unstructured up to age 3;
- then enter a more manipulative phase where the interest is in handling instruments, in controlling the sounds intentionally; music making is affected by the instruments, physical structure, and layout at ages 4 and 5;
- develop further through an imitation phase that embraces a gradual establishment of dominant musical conventions, such as phrasing, glissandi, metrical organization, ostinati and the general patterning of sounds; compositions draw on other musical experiences, such as singing and listening between ages 5 to 8.

The prime difference between the two countries is that the English children appear to be more developmentally advanced in their compositions with increasing age. That is, although there was no difference between samples at ages four and five, by the ages of seven and eight a greater percentage of the English children were at the imitation phase, making more use of general musical conventions, perhaps as a result of different educational experiences. Nevertheless, the observed developmental sequence was the same in both countries and accords with other research into phases of musical development (e.g. Hargreaves, 1996, p.156).

The interaction of this developmental phase sequence with the music making opportunities within the child's socio–cultural environment is evidenced in the effects of early schooling. For example, Fash (1990, p.59) describes how the provision of a free play music corner for her four– and five–year–olds, just starting school, facilitates development:

> By the end of the second term the children's work takes on a distinct and audible structure and phrasing that seems to have its own internal logic. After the random striking and spasmodic changes of volume that characterize the early stages[,] we begin to hear sound patterns that are repeated over the same intervals of time[,] even though the instruments or parts of the sequence are changed. Sometimes a sequence is repeated, but interspersed with other ideas of widely differing length, and sometimes there are distinct changes of mood or tone that are repeated. The music is still experimental and exploratory but it is more than an exploration of the instruments themselves. The children begin to move towards controlled, often quiet pieces with elements of repeated patterns and rhythmic structure or dramatic phrasing. From sociable sound–making, more and more the children begin to enjoy playing alone or with a specific musical partner.

Furthermore, even though the 'free play' situation was controlled by the children and away from the direct intervention of the teacher, it has been argued

(Young, 1995, p.56) that the listening adult nearby is 'intimately bound' to the learning and developmental process because the children's musical products are heard, interpreted and often subject to teacher comment.

Other evidence of the potential significance of adult interaction to musical development is provided by research which focused on an analysis of children's response to changes in musical mode (Costa–Giomi, 1996). Although a brief training period had little effect on pre–schoolers' perception of musical mode, by contrast, an identical training permitted kindergarten children to perceive mode changes. Furthermore, following such training, five–year–olds were also able both to identify major and minor and to use correctly the appropriate verbal label.

Notating Musical Experiences

Notation is an important feature of the high art tradition of Western musical culture, not least because of its customary association with the repetition of musical composition in performance. Notation is an analogy for sound, a visual symbolization for auditory events. The nature of young children's abilities with regard to notation is of developmental interest because of its hypothesized association with musical understanding, particularly with respect to rhythm and pitch (*cf.* Bamberger, 1991; Domer & Gromko, 1996; Gromko, 1994; Poorman, 1996; Smith, Cuddy & Upitis, 1994) and with musical performance (Smith, Cuddy & Upitis, 1994).

Children vary developmentally in the degree to which they associate visual symbols with sounds. Such symbolization can be through drawing (Bamberger, 1991; Welch, 1991) or in the manipulation of shaped, textured or colored materials (Poorman, 1996; Walker, 1985). Notational development is characterized by several phases, with four commonly described in the research literature (Hargreaves, 1996). In the earliest *scribbling* phase, graphic representation is distinguished by "action equivalents," with the young child making marks on paper which correspond to physical actions and which may match the timing of sounds heard (Goodnow, 1971); otherwise no obvious graphic–sonic relationship is evident. The next two developmental phases have been labeled under the umbrella term *figural* (Bamberger, 1991) because the child's invented notation somehow corresponds to particular features of the perceived sounds, firstly in relation to a single dimension (such as approximate duration) and secondly to several dimensions at once (such as approximate duration and intensity) (*cf.* Durrant & Welch, 1995, p.69 & p.89; Hargreaves, 1996, p.156). In the fourth formal phase, notation is metrically accurate and corresponds to the established form of traditional (Western) music, including an accurate representation of duration. Formal notation is closely associated with formal musical training (Bamberger, 1991). These phases in notational development correspond with those mentioned earlier for composition, with notational scribble being associated with sensory impressions and figural notations embracing development across the manipulative and the imitative (vernacular) phases (*cf.* Hair, 1993; Barrett, 1997).

The child's actual notational response, however, is likely to be task specific (at least in part) and related to the nature of the musical stimulus. A sung stimulus, for example, has both metric and durational information because the sounds can be sustained by the voice, but a clapped stimulus loses information about duration. As a result, the notation of a clapped stimulus can be less developed, particularly for those children who do not yet read music (Mills, 1991). So, like other musical abilities, notational behavior is both task specific and susceptible to adult intervention and training. Pre–schoolers' invented notations, for example, showed qualitative changes after twelve weeks of music instruction, particularly for those children who already were more experienced musically (Domer & Gromko, 1996). At the end of the training period, fewer of the children's melodic representations of stimulus songs were at the "scribble" stage, and more were interpreted as either "enactive," accurate representations of the continuous pulse of the whole song, or "melodic," systematic and relatively accurate visual representations of the song's actual melodic contour. Such susceptibility to appropriate external stimuli is yet another example of how musical behaviors change and develop rather than being immutably fixed.

Recently, Barrett (1997, 1998) has demonstrated both the task–specific nature of pre–schoolers' invented notations and also how such notations are flexibly applied, depending on the features that the child perceives as being dominant within a particular musical task. Notational strategies for singing tasks, for example, were often different from those employed for instrumental tasks. With singing tasks, the words of the songs often appeared to be the dominant perceptual feature underlying invented notation, with some children even stating that they were unable to notate a song because "I don't know my letters yet." However, these same children were able to focus on specific musical features when notating their instrumental work (Barrett, 1998, p116).

Singing

Of all musical behaviors, singing is one of the most universal, commonly observed and long established (Nettl, 1983). The oldest known song is Sumerian and dates from around 1400 B.C.; yet its first modern performance in 1974 (shortly after its discovery) revealed familiar (Western) musical structures such as in a lullaby, hymn or folk song (Trehub, Schellenburg & Hill, 1997, p.113). Arguably, the persistence of common musical structures across thousands of years is another example of how existing socio–cultural musical genres interact with inherent biological design and patterns of child–rearing to be re–invented across generations. Recent neurological research into the complex functioning of the brain provides evidence of common neural contributions to the active processing of intonation in speech (Van Lancker, 1997, p.3) and also of melodic contour (Patel & Peretz, 1997, p.197). Perceptual studies of two–month–old infants provide evidence that they are already able to discriminate prosodic features of the dominant (maternal) language such as intonation and rhythm (Mehler & Christophe, 1995, p.947). Moreover, an analysis of lullabies and infant songs from different cultures reveals that their musical structures are characterized by perceived simplicity, descending intervals and contours, with relatively few contour changes, paralleling some prosodic features of infant–directed speech (Unyk *et* al, 1992, p.25).

The foundations for singing development are established during infancy because of the physical and structural interrelatedness between early infant vocalization, infant–directed speech, infant–directed singing, and the existence (and persistence) of songs designed for an infant audience within the maternal culture. During these first few months of life, parents consistently guide the infant towards at least three levels of vocal expertise (Papousek, 1996, pp.44–45). These levels gradually emerge during preverbal vocal development.

- **level 1:** initial fundamental voicing develops into prolonged, euphonic cooing (around the age of 8 weeks); subsequently leading to phrasing and melodic modulation;
- **level 2:** the vocal stream becomes segmented into syllables due to the use of consonants; mothers facilitate this development through the use of rhythmic games and rhythmic melodies;
- **level 3:** canonical syllables appear and are treated by parents as protowords to which they attribute meanings, assigned in a declarative manner to the naming of persons, objects and events.

Adult–child dialogue is characterized by rich melodic modifications during these first months of life (Papousek, 1996, p.48), with repetitions, frequent glides, a prevalence of basic harmonic intervals (3rds, 4ths, 5ths, 8ves) and sometimes dramatic changes in intensity.

Given the bipotentiality of early interactive vocalization, it is not surprising to discover that the borders between singing and speech are often blurred, particularly for the young child (Davidson, 1994; Davies, 1994; Sergeant, 1994; Welch, 1994a; Welch, Sergeant and White, 1996). Such blurring is characteristic of one of the first phases of singing development for many young children (see figure 2)[1]. For a small minority, this phase can persist into later childhood and result in singing that is labeled as out–of–tune because, in the absence of useful information on how to

---

[1] The existence of individual pathways in development permits some children to become relatively skilled in the dominant musical song genre(s) at a very early age. At present, there is insufficient evidence as to whether such children proceed through the developmental phases of the model much more quickly, whether some phases are missed out or collapsed together, or whether they experience an alternative developmental process. Davidson (1994, p.114), for example, suggests that more developed singers have a wider variety of melodic contour schemes available at an earlier age. Nevertheless, the basic model draws on a wide range of existing research data and is thought to be applicable to the majority of young children. In addition to the London–based research (detailed in the chapter) other studies by Davidson (1994) and Rutkowski (1996) offer useful perspectives of the nature of the developmental sequence, each taking complimentary aspects.

consciously change vocal pitch, the early vocal behavior continues to be inappropriately repeated (and rehearsed) in response to singing tasks (Kalmar, 1991; Welch, 1985a; 1985b; 1994b). Nevertheless, caution is required in the use of this or similar labels, because "in–tune" singing is culturally defined, perceptually experienced (through categoric perception) and task specific. For example, studies of children's singing development in non–Western cultures whose languages are tonally–based (where tonal patterns are involved in conveying meaning) reveal the close association between speech and singing contours (Addo, 1995; Chen–Haftek, 1996). Overall, early childhood singing development is sequential in character, with certain singing behaviors having primacy over others (Davidson, 1994; Rutkowski, 1996; Welch, 1994a; Welch, Sergeant and White, 1996, 1997).

Longitudinal research evidence from a sample of one hundred and eighty–four five–, six– and seven–year–olds in their first three years in London elementary schools (Welch, 2000; Welch et al, 1996, 1997) supports the key features of the model while indicating that singing development is multi–faceted and complex, with differences emerging in relation to the children's age, sex and singing task.

Figure 2: a model of vocal pitch–matching development[2]

- **Phase 1** The words of the song appear to be the initial center of interest rather than the melody, singing is often described as chant–like, employing a restricted pitch range and melodic phrases. In infant vocal pitch exploration, descending patterns predominate (e.g. Davidson, 1994; Davies, 1992; Dowling, 1984; Fox, 1982; Goetze, 1985; Levinowitz, 1989; Moog, 1976; Reis, 1987; Rutkowski, 1987; Thurman & Klitzke, 1994; Welch, 1986; Young, 1971);
- **Phase 2** There is a growing awareness that vocal pitch can be a conscious process and that changes in vocal pitch are controllable. Sung melodic outline begins to follow the general (macro) contours of the target melody or key constituent phrases. Tonality is essentially phrase based. Self–invented and "schematic" songs borrow elements from the child's musical culture. Vocal pitch range used in "song" singing expands (e.g. Davidson, 1994; Davidson et al., 1981; Davies, 1986, 1992, 1994; Fujita, 1990; Fyk, 1985; Hargreaves, 1986, 1996; Minami & Umezawa, 1990; Moog, 1976; Papousek, 1996; Rutkowski, 1987; Welch, 1986; Welch et al., 1991; White, Sergeant & Welch, 1996)

---

[2] This model is a revision of the original as published in Welch (1986) and was first presented to the 1993 British Voice Association annual conference. The model has been updated in the light of ongoing research findings from across the world. It should be noted that the suggested model of singing development is based on a research literature that is firmly rooted in Western musical genres. Singing development in relation to non–Western musics may be different because differing musical traditions and structures shape auditory perception and, potentially, vocal production (e.g. Addo, 1995; Chen–Haftek, 1996; Imada, 1994; Walker, 1994). Although singing is a commonplace human activity, it is also culturally diverse.

- **Phase 3**   Melodic shape and intervals are mostly accurate, but some changes in tonality may occur, perhaps linked to inappropriate singing register usage. Overall, however, the number of different reference pitches is much reduced (e.g. Davidson et al., 1981; Dowling, 1984; Fyk, 1985; Welch, 1986; Wurgler, 1990).
- **Phase 4**   No significant melodic or pitch errors in relation to relatively simple songs from the singer's musical culture (e.g. Davidson et al., 1981; Fyk, 1985; Rutkowski, 1987; Welch, 1986, 1994a).

The longitudinal data reveal an explicit hierarchy in children's developing singing competences. At each age, children were much more accurate in their vocal pitch matching when asked to copy simple glides (uni– or bi–directional, being equivalent to simple melodic contours), single pitches and (from age 6) melodic fragments, compared to complex glides (multi–directional contours) and songs (see figure 3). There was also clear evidence of a general, systematic and statistically significant improvement in pitch matching skills from school year to school year, with the exception of pitch matching in song singing, which was consistently judged as being much poorer in comparison (Welch et al., 1996).

The reasons for this developmental disparity between songs and other forms of pitch matching appear to be closely related the generic nature of songs. An examination of the project data reveals a significant difference in the children's singing abilities in relation to two key constituent parts of the test songs, namely the words (song text) and the music (pitches) (Welch, 1997). In each of the three years of testing, the children's ability to reproduce the words of the chosen songs were rated extremely highly by the judges (see figure 4). Moreover, in each year, the ratings for word accuracy were significantly better than the ratings for pitches. In contrast, the ratings for melodic interval pitch accuracy showed no significant improvement until the third year of testing (age seven) and even in this third year, pitch accuracy was still rated as significantly worse than text accuracy.

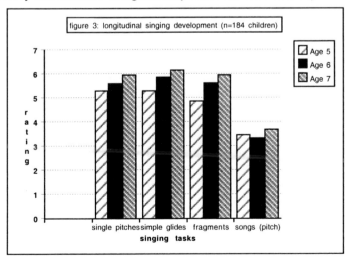

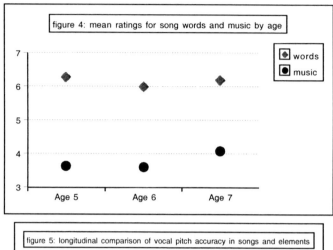

figure 4: mean ratings for song words and music by age

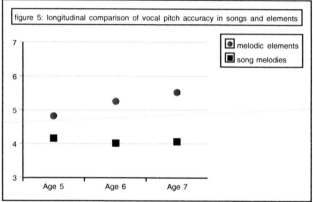

figure 5: longitudinal comparison of vocal pitch accuracy in songs and elements

In general, the data indicate that children enter compulsory schooling with an ability to learn the words of songs. For many children, this linguistic competence would appear to be significantly in advance of their ability to learn the melodic contour and musical intervals of the same songs. The evidence from this study is that children arrive at school "programmed" to be responsive to words and perhaps "biased" towards words when these are attached to specific melodic contours as in songs. Related evidence of such bias may be found in the perceptual dominance of textual features when pre–schoolers' invent notations of songs (see Barrett 1997, 1998).

Further evidence of the effects of text on vocal pitch matching development is evidenced from an analysis of judges' ratings for subjects' pitch accuracy in matching melodic elements (single pitches, simple glides and melodic fragments) compared to their pitch accuracy on test song melodies (see figure 5). The results indicate that, in each year of the longitudinal study, the children scored more highly for their vocal pitch matching of melodic elements compared to melodies in songs, even though these were identical samples of pitches. If these children's overall musical development were to be judged solely on the accuracy with which they could reproduce song melodies, a false picture would be created which belied their developing (and more competent) singing skills when presented with non–song tasks.

CONCLUSION

In summary, systematic observation of young children's musical behavior reveals a rich and diverse pattern of development and musical competencies. Although development may be faster or slower for particular individuals, there is sufficient evidence to suggest that, with appropriate support, all young children can achieve a degree of mastery in the contemporary musical idioms of the maternal culture. Moreover, a child's present mastery level is always subject to qualitative change, especially in a supportive environment. The complex interaction between the basic structure of the human intellect and the opportunities provided by the socio–cultural environment determine the nature and extent of musical development in early childhood and on through the lifespan. Observed differences reflect individual developmental "routes" along the socially constructed musical "pathways."

REFERENCE

Abrams, R.M. & Gerhardt, K.K. (1997). Some aspects of the foetal sound environment. In Deliege, I. & Sloboda, J. (Eds), *Perception and cognition of music* (pp. 83–101). Hove: Psychology Press.

Addo, A. (1995). *Ghanaian children's music cultures: A video ethnography of selected singing games.* Unpublished PhD Thesis, University of British Columbia, Canada.

Agawu, K. (1995). *African rhythm.* Cambridge: Cambridge University Press.

Bamberger, J. (1991). *The mind behind the musical ear: How children develop musical intelligence.* Cambridge, MA: Harvard University Press.

Barrett, M. (1997). Invented notations: A view of young children's musical thinking. *Research Studies in Music Education, 8,* 2–14.

Barrett, M. (1998). Modal dissonance: An analysis of children's invented notations of known songs, original songs and instrumental compositions. *Proceedings* (pp. 110–120). Seventeenth International Society for Music Education Research Seminar 11–17 July, Magaliesberg, South Africa.

Blacking, J. (1976). *How musical is man?* London: Faber.

Chan–Haftek, L. (1996). *Effects of the pitch relationship between text and melody in Cantonese songs on young children's singing.* Unpublished PhD Thesis, University of Reading, UK.

Costa–Giomi, E. (1996). Mode discrimination abilities of pre–school children. *Psychology of Music, 24*(2), 184–198.

Crozier, J.B. (1997). Absolute pitch: Practice makes perfect, the earlier the better. *Psychology of Music, 25*(2), 110–119.

Davidson, J.W., Sloboda, J.A. & Howe, M.J.A. (1995/1996). The role of parents and teachers in the success and failure of instrumental learners. *Bulletin of the Council for Research in Music Education. 127,* 40–44.

Davidson, L., McKernon, P. & Gardner, H. (1981). The acquisition of song: A developmental approach. *Documentary Report of the Ann Arbor Symposium.* Reston, VA: MENC.

Davidson, L. (1994). Songsinging by young and old: A developmental approach to music. in R. Aiello & J.A. Sloboda (Eds), *Musical perceptions* (pp. 99–130). Oxford: Oxford University Press.

Davies, C. (1986). Say it till a song comes: Reflections on songs invented by children 3–13. *British Journal of Music Education, 3*(3), 279–293.

Davies, C. (1992). Listen to my song: A study of songs invented by children aged 5 to 7 years. *British Journal of Music Education, 9*(1), 19–48.

Davies, C. (1994). The listening teacher: An approach to the collection and study of invented songs of children aged 5 to 7. *Musical connections: Tradition and change.* (pp. 120–127). Auckland, NZ: International Society for Music Education.

Dowling, W.J. (1984). Development of musical schemata in children's spontaneous singing. In W.R. Crozier & A.J. Chapman (Eds), *Cognitive processes in the perception of art.* (pp. 145–163). Amsterdam: Elsevier.

Domer, J. & Gromko, J.E. (1996). Qualitative changes in preschoolers' invented notations following music instruction. *Contributions to Music Education, 23*, 62–78.

Durrant, C. & Welch, G.F. (1995). *Making sense of music.* London: Cassell.

Farrell, G. (1997). *Indian music and the West.* Oxford: Oxford University Press.

Fash, L. (1990). Changing perceptions of music with reception children. *British Journal of Music Education, 7*(1), 43–65.

Finnegan, R. (1989). *The hidden musicians.* Cambridge: Cambridge University Press.

Floyd, M. (1996). Promoting traditional music: The Kenyan decision. In M. Floyd. (Ed). *World musics in education* (pp. 186–206). Aldershot: Scolar Press.

Fox, D.B. (1982). *The pitch range and contour of infant vocalizations.* Unpublished Doctoral thesis, Ohio State University.

Fujita, F. (1990). The intermediate performance between talking and singing – from an observational study of Japanese children's music activities in nursery schools. In J. Dobbs (Ed), *Music education: Facing the future* (pp. 140–146). Christchurch, NZ: ISME.

Fyk, J. (1985). Vocal pitch–matching ability in children as a function of sound duration. *Bulletin of the Council for Research in Music Education, 85*, 76–89.

Gardner, H. (1983). *Frames of mind.* London: Heinemann.

Geschwind, N. (1979). Specializations of the human brain. *Scientific American, 241*(3), 158–168.

Goetze, M. (1985). *Factors affecting accuracy in children's singing.* Unpublished Doctoral thesis, University of Colorado.

Goodnow, J. (1971). Auditory–visual matching: Modality problem or translation problem? *Child Development, 42*, 1187–1210.

Gromko, J.E. (1994). Children's invented notations as measures of musical understanding. *Psychology of Music, 22*(2), 136–147.

Hair, H.I. (1993). Children's descriptions and representations of music. *Bulletin of the Council for Research in Music Education, 119*, 41–48.

Hargreaves, D.J. (1986). *The developmental psychology of music.* Cambridge: Cambridge University Press.

Hargreaves, D.J. (1996). The development of artistic and musical competence. In I. Deliege & J. Sloboda (Eds). *Musical beginnings* (pp. 145–170). Oxford: Oxford University Press.

Howe, M.J.A., Davidson, J.W., Moore, D.G. & Sloboda, J.A. (1995). Are there early childhood signs of musical ability? *Psychology of Music, 23*, 162–176.

Imada, T. (1994). *Escaping the historical influences of the West on Japanese music education.* Unpublished Masters thesis, Simon Fraser University, British Columbia.

Kalmar, M. (1991). Young children's self–invented songs: Effects of age and musical experience on the singing improvisation of 4–7 year-olds. *Canadian Music Educator: Research Edition, 33*,75–86.

Kemp, A.E. (1996). *The musical temperament.* Oxford: Oxford University Press.

Kratus, J. (1989). A time analysis of the compositional processes used by children ages 7 to 11. *Journal of Research in Music Education, 37*, 5–20.

Kratus, J. (1994). The ways children compose. In H. Lees (Ed), *Musical connections: Tradition and change* (pp. 128–140). Auckland, N.Z.: ISME.

Lecanuet, J–P. (1996). Prenatal auditory experience. In I. Deliege & J. Sloboda (Eds). *Musical beginnings* (pp. 3–34). Oxford: Oxford University Press.

Levinowitz, L.M. (1989). An investigation of preschool children's comparative capability to sing songs with and without words. *Bulletin of the Council for Research in Music Education, 100*, 14–19.

Littleton, D. (1992). Ecological influences in children's musical play. In H. Lees (Ed), *Music education: Sharing musics of the world* (pp. 53–58). Christchurch, N.Z.: ISME.

Mawhinney, T.A. & Cuddy, L.L. (1984). *A factor analytic investigation of tone deafness.* Unpublished paper, Music Educators National Conference, Chicago.

Mehler, J. & Christophe, A. (1995). Maturation and learning of language in the first year of life. In M.S. Gazzaniga (Ed), *The cognitive neurosciences* (pp. 943–954). Cambridge, MA:MIT Press.

Miller, L.K. (1989). *Musical savants.* Hillsdale, N.J.: Lawrence Erlbaum Associates.

Mills, J. (1991). Clapping as an approximation to rhythm. *Canadian Music Educator: Research Edition, 33,* 131–137.

Minami, Y. & Umezawa, Y. (1990). 'The situation in which a child sings an original song. In J. Dobbs (Ed). *Music education: Facing the future* (pp. 131–134). Christchurch, NZ: ISME.

Moog, H. (1976). *The musical experience of the preschool child.* (trans. C. Clarke). London: Schott.

Nettl, B. (1983). *The study of ethnomusicology.* Urbana: University of Illinois Press.

O'Neill, S. (1996). The influence of ability, effort, motivation and teaching context on achievement during the first year of learning to play a musical instrument. *Proceedings,* 7th International Seminar of the ISME Early Childhood Commission, Winchester, UK.

Papousek, H. (1996). Musicality in infancy research: Biological and cultural origins of early musicality. In I. Deliege & J. Sloboda (Eds), *Musical beginnings* (pp. 37–55). Oxford: Oxford University Press.

Patel, A.D. & Peretz. I. (1997). Is music autonomous from language? A neuropsychological appraisal. In I. Deliege & J. Sloboda (Eds). *Perception and cognition of music* (pp. 191–215). Hove, UK: Psychology Press.

Poorman, A. Smith (1996). The Emergence of symbol use: prekindergarten children's representations of musical sound. *Contributions to Music Education, 23,* 31–45.

Reimer, B. (1997). Should there be a universal philosophy of music education? *International Journal of Music Education, 29,* 4–21.

Reis, N.L. (1987). An analysis of the characteristics of infant–child singing expressions: Replication report. *The Canadian Journal of Research in Music Education, 29*(1), 5–20.

Rutkowski, J. (1987). The effect of restricted song range on kindergarten children's use of singing voice and developmental music aptitude. *Dissertation Abstracts International, 47,* 2072A.

Rutkowski, J. (1996). The nature of children's singing voices: Characteristics and assessment. *Proceedings,* 7th International Seminar of the ISME Early Childhood Commission, Winchester, UK.

Sergeant, D.C. (1969). Experimental investigation of absolute pitch. *Journal of Research in Music Education, 17,* 135–143.

Sergeant, D.C. (1994). Towards a specification for poor–pitch singing. In G.F. Welch & T. Murao (Eds), *Onchi and singing development* (pp. 63–73). London: David Fulton.

Smith, K.C., Cuddy, L.L. & Upitis, R. (1994). Figural and metric understanding of rhythm. *Psychology of Music, 22*(2), 117–135.

Spender, N. (1987). Psychology of music. In R.L. Gregory (Ed), *The Oxford companion to the mind* (pp. 499–505). Oxford: Oxford University Press.

Swanwick, K. (1991). Further research on the musical development sequence. *Psychology of Music, 19*(1), 22–32.

Swanwick, K. & Tillman, J. (1986). The sequence of musical development. *British Journal of Music Education. 3*(3), 305–339.

Thurman, L. & Klitzke, C. (1994). Voice education and health care for young voices. In M.S. Benninger, B.H. Jacobson & A.F. Johnson (Eds), *Vocal arts medicine: The care and prevention of professional voice disorders* (pp. 226–268). New York: Thieme Medical Publishers.

Thurman. L. & Welch, G.F. (2000). *Bodymind and voice: Foundations of voice education.* Revised Edition. Iowa City: National Center for Voice and Speech.

Trehub, S.E. & Trainor, L.J. (1993). Listening strategies in infancy: The roots of music and language development. In S. McAdams & E. Bigand (Eds). *Thinking in sound. The cognitive psychology of human audition* (pp. 278–327). Oxford: Oxford University Press.

Trehub, S.E., Schellenberg, G. & Hill, D. (1997). The origins of music perception and cognition: A developmental perspective. In I. Deliege & J. Sloboda (Eds). *Perception and cognition of music* (pp. 103–128). Hove, UK: Psychology Press.

Unyk, A.M., Trehub, S.E., Trainor, L.J. & Schellenberg, E.G. (1992). Lullabies and simplicity: A cross–cultural perspective. *Psychology of Music, 20*(1), 15–28.

Van Lancker, D. (1997). Rags to riches: Our increasing appreciation of cognitive and communicative abilities of the human right cerebral hemisphere. *Brain and Language, 57*(1), 1–11.

Walker, A.R. (1985). Mental imagery and musical concepts; some evidence from the congenitally blind. *Bulletin of the Council for Research in Music Education. 85*, 229–237.

Walker, A.R. (1994). Will karaoke teach the world to sing in tune? In Welch, G.F. & Murao, T. (Eds) (1994). *Onchi and Singing Development* (pp. 8–17). London: David Fulton/ASME.

Welch, G.F. (1985a). Variability of practice and knowledge of results as factors in learning to sing in tune. *Bulletin of the Council for Research in Music Education, 85*, 238–247.

Welch, G.F. (1985b). A schema theory of how children learn to sing in–tune. *Psychology of Music, 13*(1), 3–18.

Welch, G.F. (1986). A developmental view of children's singing. *British Journal of Music Education, 3*(3), 295–303.

Welch, G.F. (1988). Observations on the incidence of absolute pitch (AP) ability in the early blind. *Psychology of Music. 16*(1), 77–80.

Welch, G.F. (1991). Visual metaphors for sound: A study of mental imagery, language and pitch perception in the congenitally blind. *Canadian Journal of Research in Music Education. 33*, 215–222.

Welch, G.F. (1994a). The assessment of singing. *Psychology of Music, 22*, 3–19.

Welch, G.F. (1994b). *Onchi* and Singing Development: Pedagogical Implications. In Welch, G.F. & Murao, T. (Eds). *Onchi and singing development* (pp. 82–95). London: David Fulton/ASME.

Welch, G.F. (2000). The developing voice. In L. Thurman & G.F. Welch (Eds). *Bodymind and voice: Foundations of voice education* (pp. 704–717). Iowa City: National Center for Voice and Speech.

Welch, G.F. & Backhouse, J. (1989). Musical potential and behaviour in visually–handicapped children. *Journal of Blind Welfare, LXXI* (838), 33–36.

Welch, G.F., Rush, C. & Howard, D.M. (1991). A developmental continuum of singing ability: Evidence from a study of five–year–old developing singers. *Early Child Development and Care, 69*, 107–119.

Welch, G.F., Sergeant, D.C. & White, P. (1996). The singing competences of five–year–old developing singers. *Proceedings*, Fifteenth International Society for Music Education Research Seminar, 9–15 July, 1994, Miami, USA. *Bulletin of the Council for Research in Music Education, 127*, 155–162.

Welch, G.F., Sergeant, D.C. & White, P. (1997). Age, sex and vocal task as factors in singing "in–tune" during the first years of schooling. *Proceedings,* Sixteenth International Society for Music Education Research Seminar, 15–22 July, 1996, Frascati, Italy. *Bulletin of the Council for Research in Music Education, 133*, 153–160.

White, P., Sergeant, D.C. & Welch, G.F. (1996). Some observations on the singing development of five–year–olds. *Early Child Development and Care, 118*, 27–34.

Wurgler, P. (1990). *A perceptual study of vocal registers in the singing voices of children.* Unpublished Doctoral Thesis, University of Ohio.

Woodward, S.C., Fresen, J., Harrison, V.C. & Coley, N. (1996). The birth of musical language. *Proceedings*, 7th International Seminar of the ISME Early Childhood Commission, Winchester, UK.

Young, S. (1995). Listening to the music of early childhood. *British Journal of Music Education, 12*(1), 51–58.

Young, W.T. (1971). An investigation into the singing abilities of kindergarten and first grade children in east Texas. *ERIC* EDO 69431.

An early version of this paper was published in *Research Studies in Music Education*, 11, Dec., 1998, 27–41.

CHRISTINE THOMPSON

9. DRAWING TOGETHER: PEER INFLUENCE IN PRESCHOOL–KINDERGARTEN ART CLASSES

A year ago, when they were four, Peter and Kevin might not have chosen one another as friends. As a preschooler, Kevin was mildly interested in the children who attended Saturday art classes with him: He silently watched others draw and monitored their conversations, but he seldom entered in. Peter, new to the business of schooling, was unaccustomed to the clamor that attends gathering of young children. He seemed neither comfortable with, nor impressed by, those around him. Peter simply wanted to draw, and his drawings required absolute concentration. During the weeks between Saturday classes, Peter created large complex scenes which were even more elaborate and sophisticated than those he inscribed each week in the pages of his sketchbook. Kevin's drawings represented more typical four–year–old fare, in content and in execution.

This January, Kevin and Peter found themselves in the same Saturday art class. Kindergarten has convinced Peter that popularity has its rewards and has taught him the fine art of playing to the crowd. Kevin, a year later, remains quiet, calm, and intent. Peter's drawings are as fluid and intricate as ever, but the zoo animals and forest creatures which filled last year's sketchbook have been vanquished by Teenage Mutant Ninja Turtles. Kevin now draws X–Men, star–shaped superheroes surrounded by a complex mythology of their own which Kevin is eager to share with all who will listen. His drawings are more schematic than Peter's, hewing closely to a formula which, Kevin proudly admits, was taught to him by a friend. Nonetheless, it doesn't take long to recognize a kindred spirit, particularly when his allegiances are displayed in such a public and accessible way in his drawings. By the second week of Saturday classes, Peter and Kevin, attended by their younger brothers, Sam and Vincent, had formed a stable and impenetrable alliance.

By tacit agreement, whichever pair of brothers arrives first reserves a space on the floor for their tardy friends. The boys watch and wait for one another, and show real concern when illness or Illinois weather cancels their weekly meetings. Other children seem to recognize this relationship as sacrosanct; few venture to join the group. The boys remain close to one another throughout the morning. But it is sketchbook time—the twenty minutes at the beginning of class reserved for children to draw whatever they wish in their own bound volumes of blank paper—that they consider most clearly *their own,* a time in which they are free to indulge their shared passions for drawing and for recounting the exploits of the animated figures who occupy their imaginations.

L. Bresler and C.M. Thompson (eds.), The Arts in Children's Lives, 129–138.
© 2002 *Kluwer Academic Publishers. Printed in the Netherlands.*

In a few short weeks, Peter and Kevin have established a personal relationship in which both similarities of interest and differences of expertise are acknowledged and accepted. They sometimes collaborate in activities initiated by their teachers, and occasionally conspire to dispense with the day's work as quickly as possible to expedite a return to their sketchbooks. But when the boys are drawing the characters they value most highly, Kevin consistently defers to Peter's expertise, and Peter readily accepts the role of tutor. At times, Kevin simply watches Peter draw, as a spectator might watch any skilled performance, admiring the technique and command displayed. Peter is clearly flattered by Kevin's attention to his drawings, and more than happy to rehearse his knowledge of Ninja Turtle lore and lineage for the edification of his captivated audience.

Recently, Kevin has ventured increasingly into Peter's territory. After trying his hand at the depiction of Ninja Turtles, Kevin sought direct instruction from the master. Peter gladly obliged, demonstrating, step–by–step and with notable patience, how to draw Donatello. Peter drew a section of the character, and waited as Kevin replicated that form in his sketchbook, continuing this process until a Turtle materialized in reasonable facsimile on Kevin's page.

The time designated for drawing in sketchbooks is always punctuated by conversations among children, as ideas and images are shared, admired, critiqued, and appropriated with abandon. Seldom, however, do preschool and kindergarten children form tutorial relationships as intentional or as formal as the one which evolved between Peter and Kevin. Peter assumed the role of teacher in a way which seemed to make sense to both boys: He provided step–by–step demonstration, waiting patiently for Kevin to complete each phase of the drawing, talking his student through the process, and finally proclaiming the apprentice's work satisfactory. Peter seemed to accept the principle that teaching another person how to draw involves modelling the process of constructing an image from beginning to end. This emphasis on following–the–leader reflects a classic approach to drawing instruction that remains prevalent in how–to–draw books and, perhaps more decisively, in the ways that parents or older children might teach a young child to draw a rabbit or a face or a cartoon character. Damon and Phelps (1989), who studied peer tutoring among young children, note that these exchanges frequently follow a transmission–of–knowledge model which does not necessarily conform to the definition of "developmentally appropriate practice" (Bredekamp & Copple,1997) to which many teachers of young children subscribe. But peer tutoring sessions do allow for more give–and–take than might occur if similar teaching procedures were adopted by an adult. Kevin felt free to question Peter, to ask for clarification, to adjust the pace of the demonstration, to indicate frustration or confusion.

The drawing Kevin produced with Peter's help was less organized and integrated, certainly less assured, than the example Peter provided. Peter has methodically practiced and perfected his own way of drawing Ninja Turtles. Because Peter's images were borrowed from popular culture—and to draw them well meant to do justice to the originals—Peter had invested considerable time and energy in this task. Kevin, on the other hand, seemed to move in circles in which Ninja Turtles are not as well known, nor as immediately compelling, as they are to Peter. Peter's history with these images and with the characters the images represent was far more extensive. In this very specific area of knowledge and of skill, Peter was truly the more experienced—and dedicated—peer.

Kevin seemed satisfied with the results of this drawing lesson, pleased that he had produced a drawing which resembled the model Peter provided, and that he had taken this opportunity to work closely with his new friend. In the weeks that followed, Kevin interspersed drawings of Ninja Turtles among other drawings, of volcanic eruptions and X–men, in his sketchbook. But these Ninja Turtles were clearly drawn by Kevin, modified to fit the star–shaped bodies that had become his schema for humans and humanoids alike. Apparently, Kevin appropriated what he was able to use at the moment from Peter's drawing lesson. The ultimate consequences of any teaching or learning event are unpredictable, but it is likely that Kevin absorbed more from this encounter than he was immediately prepared to understand or apply: food for thought about the process of composing a drawing, a specific strategy or two, an attitude about what is important when one's purpose in drawing is to provide fit tribute to a subject who is greatly admired. And Kevin was not the sole beneficiary of this event: Peter appeared to be pleased that his expertise was recognized by an audience whose opinion he valued, and happy to share his methods with his friend. Just as surely, Peter was served, as all teachers are, by the effort to clarify and articulate processes of thought and action in order to communicate them to others.

Interactions such as this are very much a part of the ongoing artistic and intellectual life of early childhood classrooms. Yet, Anne Haas Dyson (1990), a language arts educator interested in young children's symbolic learning, observed that, "Researchers who study children's graphic symbolism stress the interaction between children and their own products. . . .In centers and classrooms, though, the dialogue between children and their papers can include other people, as children's skills as collaborative storytellers and players infuse their drawings" (p. 54). Early artistic development was traditionally characterized as a solitary process of exploration and emergence, a matter of natural growth unfolding, and perhaps thriving most successfully under circumstances of benign neglect. But solitary moments are rare in the lives of young children who spend their days in nursery schools and playgroups, preschool and kindergarten classrooms.

In the past two decades, many widely–held beliefs about young children have come into question as a more complex and challenging and realistic vision of early childhood has gained favor. This reconsideration represents a convergence of theory, research, and praxis far too complex and far–reaching to adequately summarize here. In no small way, however, it was reality that demanded attention: As young children began to gather in preschool classrooms in unprecedented numbers, and to act and interact in ways that contradicted our best predictions, teachers and researchers were forced to confront assumptions that seemed increasingly faulty, partial, and unreliable.

Primary among those assumptions was the Piagetian concept of the young child as egocentric, preoccupied with the world of objects and substances, unable to interact with others or to learn from interaction with them. Bruner (1983) described this egocentric child as a "solitary explorer. . .virtually alone. . .[in] a world of objects that he must array in space, time, and causal relationships" (p. 138). The child that Piaget envisioned and introduced to us *was* powerful, active, intelligent, resourceful. At the same time, there were limits to what that child could do, or think, or consider, limits that seemed inflexible, developmental, innate, unyielding. Teachers of the very young were taught to expect children who talked incessantly but with little or no desire to communicate, children who appeared to be playing together but were in fact pursuing private dramas in a public place, children whose patience for conversations or collaborative ventures was virtually nonexistent.

But the children that we know and care for are neither chronically self–centered nor completely self–contained: They are inherently social and skillful in their approach to the world (Genishi & Dyson, 1984; Paley, 1999). From earliest infancy, they learn from us and from other children, entangle themselves in situations in which learning from others is possible. Barbara Rogoff and her associates (Rogoff, Malkin, & Gilbride, 1984) remind us that the forms of assistance which young children draw from those around them often require deft interpretation and have enduring influence on the child's ways of making sense of the world. As they look to see how a parent responds to a loud noise or an animal bounding into view or a sudden tumble, children not only seek safety and reassurance: They also acquire interpretive frames, ways of responding to this experience and to similar experiences in the future. There is often a moment of hesitation when an injured toddler stops to consider, "Is this worth crying about?" The answer to that question is instinctively sought in the expression of the nearest and most trusted adult.

The writings of the Russian psychologist, L. S. Vygotsky (1962, 1978, 1983), are frequently invoked by those who believe that children develop and learn through the interplay of personal initiative and intersubjective experience. Vygotsky believed that the relationship between development and learning is intimate and intersustaining, He also believed that neither development nor learning could occur without the mediation of others. Young children are just beginning the process of learning to use the tools and interpret the symbols through which the culture preserves and passes on its beliefs and aspirations, its questions and its certainties. Lacking immediate access to many cultural forms of mediation, young children are quite dependent upon the direct assistance of other people, in Vygotsky's view. He suggested that learning occurs in a "zone of proximal development," an area that lies just beyond what a child can accomplish independently, but within boundaries where that child can succeed if appropriate forms of assistance are available. Vygotsky stressed that the assistance a child needs to perform a particular project can be provided by an adult or by a more capable, or experienced, peer, someone who is able to perform at a level slightly in advance of the learner's present capability. A child who has successfully participated in an activity or explored an idea in conversation can repeat and practice that activity or experiment with that idea with increasing independence. Eventually, the knowledge, skills, and behaviors children encounter through others are appropriated and internalized, subsumed into their own repertoires of thought and action: "What the child can do in cooperation today he can do alone tomorrow" (Vygotsky, 1983, p. 268).

Vygotsky suggested that teaching as a deliberate and intentional activity relies upon the same instructional strategies that people within a particular culture use as they attempt to share ideas, information, and skills in the course of their daily lives.

Vygotsky recognized, as Martin Buber did, that the relationship between teacher and student is unique, "lifted out of the purposelessly streaming education by all things, and. . .marked off as purpose" (Buber, 1965, p. 89). But he believed that the informal and unintentional teaching that occurs as children observe and participate in activities valued by those around them is a potent source of learning, particularly for young children. As Barbara Rogoff (1990) points out, the social world exerts subtle and pervasive influences in the early childhood years: The structure of young children's days, the activities and routines that surround them, the company they keep, "the scenarios and cast of characters in children's lives" (p. 87), provide natural boundaries and guides—constraints and supports—for children's explorations.

As Vygotsky consistently emphasized, much of children's learning originates in their interactions with peers. Other children may bring more extensive experience or simply their own distinctive perspectives to a conversation or joint project. The designation "more capable peer" is a situational one: Every child has some unique form of expertise to share. Kevin understands clay far better than does Peter, for example. Peter has focused so exclusively on drawing, and the ways of thinking and acting that drawing entails, that his ambitions are frequently thwarted by other, less tractable media. Kevin assisted Peter in various ways during a recent series of lessons which featured experiences with clay: Kevin suggested a more attainable but thematically–related alternative to Peter's initial plan to model a Ninja Turtle in full regalia, and he provided some help with construction problems. Less directly, Kevin demonstrated ways of working with clay and thinking with the medium that he developed through countless sessions working with a material that, according to Kevin's preschool teacher, has long been his favorite. His enthusiasm seemed to sustain Peter's attention despite his frustrations.

As William Corsaro (1985) and many others (see, for example, Katz & McClellan,1997) have noted, the life–worlds and social development of preschool and kindergarten children "are dramatically affected by their entrance into peer culture" (p. 51). Children must marshal considerable social skills and personal resources in order to initiate and maintain friendships and to enter into the fleeting alliances that characterize the social world of preschool and kindergarten. Donaldson, Grieve, and Pratt (1983) suggest that young children reach decisive conclusions about themselves on the basis of their ability to "enter the social world beyond the family and establish themselves, more or less easily and successfully, as members of a community of their peers" (p. 1). Our own experiences remind us that "finding oneself among one's friends" (Dyson, 1989) is undoubtedly among the most crucial of childhood's experiences, but only recently have we begun to realize how early that search for acceptance and identity begins. Damon and Phelps (1989) suggest that children contribute to one another's learning in complex and unexpected ways:

> Repeated studies have shown that peer interaction is conducive, perhaps even essential, to a host of important early achievements: children's understanding of fairness, their self–esteem, their proclivities toward sharing and kindness, their mastery of symbolic expression, their acquisition of role–taking and communication skills, and their development of creative and critical thinking. (p. 135)

Numerous studies of children's interactions in preschools and kindergarten classrooms support David Hawkins' (1974) proposition that enduring and productive relationships between any two people must be based on an interest or activity those two people share together. "Young children's interactions with one another are almost always supported by some play object, game, or play activity" (Scarlett, 1983, p. 36). Children do things together; they do not simply coexist. Research suggests that the nature of the activity and materials at hand influences the interactions which occur within a setting (Genishi & Dyson, 1984): Young children tend to interact more freely when a manageable variety of materials and range of choices is provided in their classrooms, but their social impulses may be overwhelmed by a surfeit of riches.

Certain activities that are a part of life in many early childhood classrooms seem to be particularly likely to attract other children's attention, to inspire dialogue and collaboration and communal action (Corsaro, 1985; Dyson, 1989, 1990, 1997; Gallas, 1994, 1998). The arts—in the form of dramatic, constructive, or symbolic play—serve their primordial function in early childhood classrooms: They bring people together, display and celebrate their community, declare their pleasure in being together and their pride in being special. As Jones and Reynolds (1992) suggest, in the preliterate culture of preschool classrooms, children "rely on, and continue to create, an oral tradition shared in face–to–face encounters. . . .Simultaneously, given the availability of tools for the purpose, they are creators of images. . . .Drawing and building together, children create the shared imagery that makes their community of experience visible" (p. 4).

Children's drawings may be particularly important and instrumental to the formation of the community of artists and writers, according to Dyson (1989). In the kindergarten classroom Dyson studied, early writing experiences involved drawing, dictating, or writing entries in personal journals. The children, experienced in drawing but new to the conventions of the written word, found drawing a far more comfortable, fluent, and flexible medium of representation. And drawing had additional advantages: "Its meaning was more accessible to a curious peer. Moreover, that drawing was often surrounded by audible talk, as children labelled and elaborated upon the meaning of those drawings; this talk too engaged the interest of peers" (p. 3).

Often, children's thinking about the images they are drawing is available, not only in the drawings themselves (Forman, 1993), but also, and perhaps more explicitly, in the talk that accompanies drawing events. Because this private, planning speech conforms so closely to the style and structure of normal conversation, other children frequently overhear and respond to comments which may not have been intended as public statements (Thompson & Bales, 1991). Even when children's interactions begin with a misunderstanding of this type, the opportunity to enter into a shared undertaking is often so attractive that such transgressions are readily forgiven.

When preschool and kindergarten children draw in close proximity to others, they initiate interactions overtly as well as inadvertently. In Saturday art classes, the most sustained and intentional collaborative partnerships tend to emerge between children who know each other well outside the studio setting. A year ago Natalie and Andrea spent every available moment over a period of six weeks engaged in a highly structured and serious project, in a manner very similar to the apprenticeship model that Peter provided for Kevin to follow. Natalie would draw a form in her sketchbook, and

Andrea would replicate that form, somewhat less precisely, in her own. Unlike Peter and Kevin, Natalie and Andrea seemed to have no preordained goal in mind. Andrea was simply content to follow Natalie's lead. When the girls finally completed these two drawings, they turned in unison to fresh pages, and Natalie plucked two orange markers from the basket, uncapping both and handing one to Andrea before a new round of drawing began. A year later, Natalie and Andrea continue to draw together and share ideas when they can: The most recent drawing in each girl's sketchbook is a full–length portrait of her friend. But Andrea has come to pride herself on her independence, and the practice of directly replicating another child's images is no longer compatible with her intentions.

James, David, and Andrew are kindergarten classmates and neighborhood friends who share interests in robots and machinery, mazes and highways, and dinosaurs, particularly those with long necks. Although the boys are clearly absorbed in the activity of drawing, it seems clear that they would find that activity less rewarding if it did not present so many and varied opportunities for dialogues with friends. Teachers, who tend to know little about the workings of electronic devices or the nomenclature of prehistoric beasts, make excellent audience members, providing ample pretext for expounding one's knowledge of the topic at hand. Drawing together, James, Andrew, and David frequently devise challenges for one another. A series of mazes, containing, by Andrew's estimate, "two hundred circles," occupied the boys' energies for several weeks and inspired a similar effort by four–year–old Corey.

The process though which images are selected and emulated is often very subtle, though there is seldom any attempt at subterfuge or concealment. Copying another child's drawing seems to be considered the highest form of flattery, accepted as a legitimate way of entering an activity in progress and declaring common cause with another child. At times, no verbal interaction is involved as children simply draw companionably side by side. And, at times, inspiration for drawing emerges as children compare their experiences in the world beyond the transitory society they share in their art class.

Vivian Gussin Paley (1981), Anne Dyson (1989, 1990), and William Corsaro (1985) each point out that the things that young children most want to know are frequently things that only other children can teach them. Occasionally children teach one another things we would rather they did not, but the appeal of learning to draw a conventional symbol—a hand turkey, or a rainbow, or a five–pointed star—from another child is not to be denied, even in preschool. There are, certainly, limits to what children can teach one another, and limits to the alternatives they have at their disposal when they attempt to teach. When Meg admired the dog that her friend Jessica had just completed, Jessica responded immediately, assuring a nearby student teacher, "I'll show her how." The student teacher asked, "Why don't you *tell* her?" and so Jessica tried to guide Meg through the process, using her own completed drawing as a model. "You make an oval," Jessica began, pointing to the body of her dog. Meg hesitated: "I don't know how to make an oval." But she looked at Meg's drawing and made an attempt which turned out well enough to prompt a very surprised declaration: "I *can* make an oval!" Despite Meg's success, Jessica had grown tired of the process, eager to finish the task and return to her own drawing. She decided it would be more efficient simply to draw a dog in Meg's sketchbook, and completed her mission with dispatch. In the interest of replicating the drawing Meg had admired as fully as possible, Jessica remembered to include the label "Old dog" at the top of the drawing she had completed for Meg. Both girls seemed satisfied with the arrangement.

In similar fashion, five–year–old Mick greatly admired his classmate, Kody's, facile drawings of dinosaurs, but seemed to have no strategy ready at hand that would enable him to make use of Kody's repeated demonstrations of his technique. In response to Mick's requests that Kody teach him to draw a dinosaur, Kody executed a series of three dinosaurs in Mick's sketchbook, in his characteristically spare, expressive, and precise linear style. Because Mick failed to watch, much less listen to Kody's quiet instruction, he reached the end of this session no better informed about ways of depicting dinosaurs than he had been when Kody reluctantly interrupted his own work to help Mick out. Mick sighed deeply and shook his head. "Look how good he draws those things. Now the problem is. . . " Jennifer, an interested onlooker, rushed to finish Mick's sentence, ". . .you don't know how to draw." She shrugged her shoulders, palms raised in a gesture of deep resignation to larger truths, as she informed Mick, "You just have to practice, practice, practice." Jennifer's advice struck a chord with Kody, affirming his own experience in acquiring and perfecting his signature imagery. He concluded the conversation, "Yeah. I practiced. First I just drew teeth, then eyes, then claws. . ."

Perhaps there was something for Mick to carry away from this lesson after all, something more enduring and essential to his continued growth as an artist than the goal he initially sought, when his desire was simply to acquire a more sophisticated formula for drawing an appealing creature than he might have developed on his own. Few things are more important to know, and less obvious, than this: that drawing is a skill developed through patient practice and continual refinement, through a process of reflection that is both personal and social, and dependent upon both the intentions of the artist and the extent to which those intentions are mirrored or deflected in the response that one's work evokes in others.

What do children make of these drawing lessons? Like the ideas and techniques that children encounter in lessons presented by teachers or parents, some are attempted and forgotten, while others persist to be practiced and perfected and gradually internalized, as part of a child's own repertoire. What is certain is that the "exposure to others" (Cocking & Copple, 1979, p. 124) that occurs as young children draw together expands their conceptions of the drawing process and shapes their understanding of its possibilities in decisive ways.

Writing in the middle of the twentieth century, Viktor Lowenfeld (1957) remarked that art is different for children. Vivian Gussin Paley (1999) suggests that this difference may reside largely in the extent to which the artistic process for young children relies upon the presence of other children, the forms of "interference" which she equates with "the kindness of children" (p. 95). She shares a quote from Proust in which he claims that "Ideas are goddesses who deign at times to make themselves visible to a solitary mortal at a turning point in the road. . .but as soon as a companion joins him they vanish. In the society of his fellows no man has ever beheld them" (in Paley, 1999, pp. 94–95). "Unlike Proust's solitary thinker," Paley observes, "the children's ideas take wing in the company of their peers. When one is young, the need to be discovered is greater than the need for privacy" (p. 100). Reynolds and Jones (1997) agree that children may differ from adults in this regard, that "Adult writers, artists, and actors are inclined to practice their craft in private. Young children are more generous in allowing us a window on the emergence of their ideas" (p. 4).

It may well be that the process of learning to form and to use symbols cannot be accomplished successfully in private that the ability to originate communicative symbols, certainly symbols that carry meaning, must be practiced within a community where children's expressions are measured against the responses of their peers. Mikhail Bakhtin (1981,1986) sees language in this way, as intrinsically dialogical:

> In this view, learning to use language involves learning to interact with others in particular social situations and, at the same time, learning to be, so to speak, within the dominant ideologies or "truths" about human relationships; that is, it involves learning about the worlds   available in a particular situation to a boy or a girl, to a person of a particular age, ethnicity, race, class, religion, and so on. (Dyson, 1997, p. 4)

Children's visual images, even when they draw upon a child's own experiences, are not self–expressive in a narrow sense: They do not simply externalize some interior reality. Robert Coles (1978) described the process of symbolization as "a manner of looking at the world, then reaching out for company." For very young children, the company they reach for is close at hand. With the response of these companions comes affirmation of the child's competence, her sensitivity to the objects, images, and ideas that are valued within the group of which she is a part. As Dyson (1997) noted, "we reach out to social companions with our stories, and we wait to see what they make of both the stories and us" (p. 11). Other children may be favored audiences for children's work because they may be the people who are most willing, and most able, to provide the immediate and reliable responses that children need, to extend themselves as critics and teachers to others in their community of artists.

REFERENCES

Bakhtin, M.   (1981).   *The dialogic imagination: Four essays by M. Bakhtin* (C. Emerson & M. Holquist, eds.). Austin, TX: University of Texas Press.

Bakhtin, M. (1986). *Speech genres and other late essays.* Austin, TX: University of Texas Press.

Bredekamp, S., & Copple, C. (Eds.) (1997). *Developmentally appropriate practice in early childhood programs* (revised edition). Washington, DC: National Association for the Education of Young Children.

Bruner, J. (1983). *In search of mind: Essays in autobiography.* New York: Harper Colophon.

Buber, M. (1965). *Between man and man.* New York: Macmillan.

Cocking, R. R., & Copple, C. E. (1979). Change through exposure to others: A study of children's verbalizations as they draw. In M. K. Poulsen & G. I. Lubin (Eds.). *Piagetian theory and its implications for the helping professions* (Proceedings, Eighth Interdisciplinary Conference, Vol. II), (pp. 124–132). University Park, CA: University of Southern California Press.

Coles, R. (1978, October 2). The search, 1. *New Yorker*, 43–110.

Corsaro, W. (1985). *Friendship and peer culture in the early years.* Norwood, NJ: Ablex.

Damon, W., & Phelps, E. (1989). Strategic uses of peer learning in children's education. In T. J. Berndt & G. W. Ladd (Eds.), *Peer relationships in child development* (pp. 135–157). New York: John Wiley & Sons.

Donaldson, M., Grieve, R., & Pratt, C. (Eds.) (1983). *Early childhood development and education (Readings in psychology).* Oxford: Basil Blackwell.

Dyson, A. H. (1989). *Multiple worlds of child writers (Friends learning to write)*. New York: Teachers College Press.

Dyson, A. H. (1990, Jan.). Symbol makers, symbol weavers: How children link play, pictures, and print. *Young children, 45*(2), 50–57.

Dyson, A. H. (1997). *Writing superheroes: Contemporary childhood, popular culture, and classroom literacy*. New York: Teachers College Press.

Forman, G. (1993). Multiple symbolization in the long jump project. In C. Edwards, L. Gandini, & G. Forman (Eds.), *The hundred languages of children (The Reggio Emilia approach to early childhood education)* (pp. 171–188). Norwood, NJ: Ablex.

Gallas, K. (1994). *The languages of learning: How children talk, write, dance, draw, and sing their understandings of the world*. New York: Teachers College Press.

Gallas, K. (1998). *"Sometimes I can be anything:" Power, gender, and identity in a primary classroom*. New York: Teachers College Press.

Genishi, C. & Dyson, A. H. (1984). *Language assessment in the early years*. Norwood, NJ: Ablex.

Hawkins, D. (1974). *The informed vision (Essays on learning and human nature)*. New York: Agathon Press.

Jones, E., & Reynolds, G. (1992). *The play's the thing (Teacher's roles in children's play)*. New York: Teachers College Press.

Katz, L. G. & McClellan, D. E. (1997). *Fostering children's social competence: The teacher's role*. Washington, DC: National Association for the Education of Young Children.

Lowenfeld, V. (1957). *Creative and mental growth* (3rd ed.). New York: Macmillan.

Paley, V. G. (1981). *Wally's stories*. Cambridge, MA: Harvard University Press.

Paley, V. G. (1999). *The kindness of children*. Cambridge, MA: Harvard University Press.

Rogoff, B. (1990). *Apprenticeship in thinking (Cognitive development in social context)*. New York: Oxford University Press.

Rogoff, B., Malkin, C., & Gilbride, K. (1984). Interaction with babies as guidance in development. In B. Rogoff & J. Wertsch (Eds.), *Children's learning in the zone of proximal development* (pp. 31–44). San Francisco: Jossey-Bass.

Scarlett, W. G. (1983). Social isolation from agemates among nursery school children. In M. Donaldson, R. Grieve, & C. Pratt (Eds.), *Early childhood development and education (Readings in psychology)* (pp. 34–45). Oxford: Basil Blackwell.

Thompson, C. M., & Bales, S. (1991). "Michael doesn't like my dinosaurs:" Conversations in a preschool art class. *Studies in art education, 33*(1), 43–55.

Vygotsky, L. S. (1962). *Thought and language* (E. Hanfmann & G. Vakar, Trans. & eds.). Cambridge, MA: Harvard University Press.

Vygotsky, L. S. (1978). *Mind in society*. Cambridge, MA: Harvard University Press.

Vygotsky, L. S. (1983). School instruction and mental development. In M. Donaldson, R. Grieve, & C. Pratt (Eds.), *Early childhood development and education (Readings in psychology)* (pp. 263–269). Oxford: Basil Blackwell.

An early version of this chapter was published in *Visual Arts Research, 25* (2), 1999, 61–68.

SHIFRA SCHONMANN

10. FICTIONAL WORLDS AND THE REAL WORLD IN EARLY CHILDHOOD DRAMA EDUCATION

This chapter seeks to broaden the scope of research in theatre/drama education by placing the neglected issue of *the child as spectator* in the mainstream of thought on the uses of drama in education. The fine boundary between imagination and reality is studied from the viewpoint of the child watching a theatre performance. This is based on observational research in which I examined if and how children aged 5–8 live the aesthetic experience of a performance, and how their involvement in the performance affects the reduction of *aesthetic distance*. Research on the young child as spectator and his or her perception of aesthetic distance in a theatre performance is new and ground–breaking. It aims at developing an instrument for assessing aesthetic distance in early childhood.

FRAMEWORK

Declarations such as "Drama develops the imagination," "Drama means self–expression," and "Drama has a therapeutic effect" are frequently made. But such claims could also be made for music, painting, and dance. It is therefore important to present the special nature of theatre as distinct from the other arts. Its uniqueness lies in its materials and its tools. The essential elements of drama and theatre are human materials; the themes are always associated with people, their spirit and body in the context of life and death. The tool of the theatre is the actor's body. The actor has no violin or piano or paintbrush or anything else with which to realize his or her creation. Body language, movements, gestures, and mimicry serve to unfold the actor's art. The unique advantages of this form of expression also give rise to its dangers. Theatre art is direct; it has force, power, and influence. Plato understandably excluded drama from the arts in his ideal republic, although he allowed it as something "which only the slaves may perform."

Drama education theorists as well as practitioners have long debated issues of *the playing child*, arguing about the purposes of play: promotion of personal growth, a means of social development, or a learning tool. They have not addressed *the child as spectator*. In this chapter I argue that this void signifies the problematic of understanding the elusive concept of *aesthetic distance*. The chapter discusses how aesthetic distance operates in early childhood, opening a wide vista for understanding the child as spectator, territory as yet uncharted in the domain of aesthetic education. Children's theatre is a late–blooming artistic phenomenon. It began to develop in the first decade of the twentieth century, emerged side by side with the development of

139

L. Bresler and C.M. Thompson (eds.), The Arts in Children's Lives, 139–151.
© 2002 *Kluwer Academic Publishers. Printed in the Netherlands.*

children's literature. It is still searching for answers to basic questions about the very essence of its existence, its identity and its place in the framework of the theatrical art which has been well established in our civilization for centuries.

Playing and culture are interwoven. Moreover, as Huizinga shows in his book *Homo Ludens* (Barash, 1984), playing is itself one of the foundations and causes of culture. The proximity of playing to art is obvious. Like art, playing creates an imaginary world detached from reality. When a person plays, he or she wittingly leaves the everyday world. The playing child, like the playing adult, knows that he or she is playing, and this departure from the real world does not detract from the seriousness of the game but turns it into an element of the human being's most sublime activity as a creator of culture (Barash, 1984). A play, like a game, is a free activity conducted willingly, but when it takes place obligatory rules and order reign over it. The starting point of the discussion is the understanding that every person can catch the acting "bug," and in any case every person assumes various roles in daily life and throughout his or her life's course (Goffman, 1973; Harre, 1979).

While acting, children have the chance to be imaginative and expressive in order to develop their social, emotional, physical, and intellectual abilities. In dramatic play they have the opportunity to explore the way their bodies move and how they can interact with others, and to make distinctions between the real and the imaginary world, which involve high–level thinking operations. For example, watching a four–year–old playing with chairs, one often sees that he turns the chair into something else, such as a car or a train, and that the dramatic element is inherent in his playing. In active play children acquire forms of control. In their playing of, which is always active playing, children express their own feelings and interpretations referring to any given context.

The Israeli Context

Israel is a tense and sensitive society in which drama is an immanent and unavoidable component. It is a society in which war is a constant possibility. Yet looking at the early childhood theatre repertoire in Israel, one finds few traces of this tension. Moreover, Israeli society has always been characterized by its multi–ethnicity and, as such, has to deal with problems of acceptance and tolerance among diverse cultural groups. But none of these conflicts has been found in its children's repertoire. I would add that there are other components, described below, that may shed some light on theatrical habits in Israeli society, components that may affect the early childhood theatre repertoire.

Several surveys conducted by the Israeli Ministry of Education and by other bodies constantly show that Israel, along with Finland, is a society where one can find the highest percentage of native theatre–goers. This remarkable finding becomes even more significant if we take into consideration the fact that, throughout its history, Jewish culture rejected the theatre on religious grounds. Only in the late 1960s did the theatre become a prominent cultural phenomenon in Israeli society. Another interesting fact is that nowadays, along with teenagers' lack of interest in theatre, we witness an opposing trend, of parents and educators showing great interest in children's theatre. This phenomenon has never been examined. Nevertheless, it is possible to assert that when speaking of theatre in early childhood education in Israel, we refer to a rather extensive phenomenon that has no parallel in any other country I can think of. Each month at least twenty new theatrical productions come out and compete for the attention of young children. On holidays such as Hanukkah or Purim, it becomes even more noticeable that there are many new productions running simultaneously. A special allowance is granted each year by the Ministry of Education to theatrical companies, encouraging production for children. A National Committee for Children's and Youth Theatre in Israel is operating as well. The task of the committee is to ensure that these productions maintain a high level of theatrical expertise. Having examined the "Sal Tarbut Repertoire Book" for 1997–98, based on the Committee's decisions ("Sal Tarbut," in rough translation, is a culture–package subsidized by the Ministry of Education to be distributed among Israeli schools). More than five hundred theatrical productions for children were offered to the public in 1998.

In the eight repertory theatres in Israel, most of which produce plays for young people, unfortunately few productions are made for young children. Therefore most of the early childhood theatre repertoire is presented by private companies, by young actors, and by unknown artists who take advantage of this situation. Many of them wish to please the Ministry of Education; they therefore produce didactic performances on themes such as: "road safety" and "habits of hygiene." Another popular source is the adaptation of children's stories into plays. Only a few texts were originally written as theatrical texts.

Performances for children are usually presented in kindergartens or small theatres in community centers. The vast majority of performances take place indoors, but outdoor performances are also common. Sometimes, there is no theatre but a temporary space on a street or a hillside (Fingerhut, 1995). Although the differences between indoor theatre and outdoor theatre are critical, both maintain the fundamental separation of actor and audience, and are built on the notion of willing suspension of disbelief.

METHODOLOGY

The study was designed as long–term observational research conducted over a period of three years, as a specific type of applied research whose results are directly relevant to educational practice. My choice of methodology depended on the research problems, which were: *how to obtain direct information from very young children (infants to eight years old); how to gain an understanding about their ways of perceiving theatrical performance; what behaviors to observe.* Children watching a play, their reactions to it, and their ways of explaining their understanding of the play were the phenomena studied, and my question was: *How do the children's behaviors (verbal and non–verbal) reflect aesthetic distance?*

I held short personal exchanges with the children during and after watching a play. The research was conducted in a natural setting, namely children watching a play at a theatre in real time. I wanted to study their behavior as it occurred naturally. There was no control of their behavior nor of any elements of the external setting. The situational context was the important element for data analysis.

I took the qualitative approach, which is "much less controlled, allowing observers' hunches and judgments to determine the content and sequence of what is recorded" (McMillan, 1996, p. 150). My goal was to understand the ways young children react, behave, accept, and enjoy theatre performances. The emphasis was on their ability to view a play within a mode of theatrical understanding that maintains aesthetic distance. I wanted to study the children's appreciation of a theatrical event and their ability to enjoy it. In other words, the methodological approach was based on my observations and their interpretations within a particular interpretative paradigm. The fragile boundary between imagination and reality was studied from the viewpoint of the child viewing a theatre performance. In this pioneering research I examined if and how children aged 5–8 live the aesthetic experience of the performance and how the involvement of the audience of children in the performance affects the reduction of aesthetic distance.

My way of dealing with the data conformed to Elliot Eisner's position; years ago he called for an artistic attitude to educational research (1979). I worked within the hermeneutics approach, a way of interpreting a text (either the original or a script of the performance) which takes into consideration the stance of the interpreter toward the phenomena under inquiry. We are challenged, as Smith (1991) argues, to ask what makes it possible for us to speak, think, and act in the ways we do. The aim of such an inquiry is not merely to find another interpretation to the subject being investigated, but to release the imagination to enjoy a new understanding. In my case, I am looking for a new understanding in the world of the theatre. I have tried to trace the inherent creativity of interpretation while a child is watching a play via the process of creating parameters for aesthetic distance in early childhood. The underlying assumption is that within everything said or done by the children there is something unsaid; therefore the interpretive activity of the children's behavior involves what Schleiermacher has referred to as "commonsense endeavor," to understand the texture of their behavior. Research using hermeneutics clarifies the link between social phenomena and the need for interpretation.

As chairperson of the National Committee for Children's and Youth Theatre in Israel, I have access to all children's theatres around the country. I observe at least three performances every month. This chapter is based on these observations as well as monthly discussions in the National Committee in which twenty–five members (actors, directors, teachers and school principals) discuss the plays they had watched that month.

The Child as Actor versus the Child as Spectator
The Child when Acting

The child when acting operates in the area between make–believe and reality, the same area in which the dramatic act is performed. This is the basic principle needed to understand the art of theatre. The child has to be able to say, "This is happening to me now" and "I am in a drama," but "I know it is imaginary;" that is, the playing child has to sense and understand the paradox of the experience. Small children cannot always separate from reality. One example is a child hauling a bucketful of water to fill the moat in the sand she has dug to defend the castle she has built. We watch her, but cannot say with certainty whether she is playing or working (Wheeler, 1995). Nor can the child. In her playing she evades boundaries.

For children younger than school age, the word *drama* is a synonym for *playing* and the activity is a natural part of their learning process. For older children, playing stimulated by drama expands their experience in the direction of learning activities involving cooperation; in such instances drama enables children to know and to feel.

A dramatic act is always concrete, a physical expression of a role. In fact, it gives form to thoughts and feelings; thus it is significant and symbolic. It can be spontaneous, improvised or elaborated through much rehearsal and planning but, by nature, it is expressive and communicative.

Social Games, Drama Games, Theatre Games

Development of skills for social games is a necessary stage on the way to the dramatic game which, in turn, is an indispensable step on the way to theatre games which themselves are essential in the process of presenting a performance.

Game/play activity, at every stage, is based on two tenets:

1. The starting point of the game/play is always known to the participants, and it obviously has the potential to develop in the next stage.
2. In play/game, as distinct from reality, there is always a way out. Here lies the educational strength of the game/play situation.

Dramatic activity in all its variations, from the social game through drama games to theatre games, is closely connected with social nature and exists in every society. In their earliest years children begin to act, to develop a sense of humor, to pretend, and to play roles. This identity is the basis of the dramatic process, whether the child turns out to be a lion or a cat, or whether at a later age she is a cowboy (Courtney, 1982). The human ability to imagine, to distinguish between truth and fantasy, and to create drama situations in which fantasy is truth may be developed, honed and trained; and in some situations it may attain the status of art.

One of the many questions yet to be explored in this context is: *Do these characteristics of the playing child, based on understanding the nature of a dramatic act, exist for the child as spectator?*

The Child as Spectator

In watching a play the child is given the chance to differentiate between reality and fiction. Theatre involves stepping into an imagined world. To make this imaginary world meaningful, the child must be skilled in "reading" what is happening on the stage. Dimming the lights and raising and lowering the curtain at the beginning and end of an act are both part of the "a highly complex, rule–based principles of the dramatic text, established through the generic and stylistic evaluations of theatre and performance conditions" (Aston & Savona, 1991, p. 17). The theatre as a sign –system is based on conventions which are learnt. The child can gain insight into the nature of the theatre art by being trained to "read" dramatic elements such as light/dark, movement/stillness, sound/silence. These and other elements are integrated by the director into the play and are essential for a real understanding of dramatic action. The child moves through a range of moods he/she is attuned to. He/She can hear, see, and be involved in the three main aspects of drama: the sights, the sounds and the action. Each child as a member of the audience becomes involved in watching the performance "by assimilating the actor's characterization into his or her own preexisting set of ideas, ideals, and emotional nature" (Boyce, 1987, p. 4). Observing the child as "receiver" we should be aware that the total communication of the play is transmitted through many channels that the child may not yet have recognized.

From the audience's perspective, the art of the theatre is a dynamic phenomenon which includes the immediate interaction between audience and artists. The child's involvement in the fiction should therefore be suited to his/her stage of mental development as well as his/her experience in watching theatrical performance.

Infants will usually work productively with a partner from their peer group in a play but, as spectators, children will more often require an adult partner. Watching a play, children often require an adult partner to sit beside them to provide security and warmth. Presumably, viewing a play requires an ability that is different from the act of playing; it is linked to the child's capacity to cope with the tension between fiction and reality. Viewing and doing are separate activities, and require different abilities..

In **playing**, children are given a chance to explore their own potential; in **viewing**, they are given the chance to gain the feeling of physical and mental equilibrium as a general sense. In viewing, the child must acquire or maintain a level of self–control. If he/she cannot control herself he/she is no longer a spectator. Watching a play allows flexibility to respond positively or negatively. The response is intuitive.

Approaching the dramatic play from the angle of *the child as spectator* alerts us to contextual aspects affecting the child's experiences, and to the emotional encounter the child may face as he/she undergoes transcendental experience in viewing a play. In order to be theatrically literate, the child should be trained early to decipher theatrical signs.

Along with Hobgood (1987), I argue that, just as it is necessary to train the ear to listen to music and to distinguish the sounds produced by different instruments, so the child should be trained to distinguish between actions that are dramatic/theatrical and those that are not. Here we face one of the controversial issues in understanding theatre, and in defining dramatic talent. What are these distinctions? According to Laurence Olivier (1986), for example, even without a definition of distinctions it is possible to state of dramatic talent that: "You know it when you see it." On the other hand, we can learn from Fergusson's (1949) *idea of theatre,* in which he speaks of "histrionic sensibility" as a form of perceiving dramatic art: "The trained ear perceives and discriminates sound; the histrionic sensibility (which may also be trained) perceives and discriminates actions"(p. 236). Fergusson is thus declaring that action is central to drama, and is also capable of being developed and observed. Children "must learn that bodies on a stage make a statement" (Bolton, 1992, p. 25). However, I argued (Schonmann, 1997) that it is necessary to gain an understanding of aesthetic distance in drama/theatre education in order to understand dramatic actions because aesthetic distance makes it possible to work on feelings and to act in both the real and the imaginary world. The sense of aesthetic distance should be cultivated because it has the ability to make feeling function on a cognitive basis, and it has the potential of discriminating between actions that are dramatic/theatrical and those that are not. When the distance has disappeared there is no art; the actions are merely those of a mundane nature.

One of the many questions yet to be explored in this context is: *How do distancing effects (physical distance, emotional distance, aesthetic distance) impinge on the child as audience, and how do they affect his/her ability to enjoy the performance?*

Aesthetic Distance in Early Childhood

Aesthetic distance is a term implied by Aristotle and developed by early psychologists four hundred years ago. Bullough's essay (written in 1912) on the concept of psychical distance was a central intertext in the theatrical situation (Bennett, 1990). Aesthetic distance is a kind of detachment on the part of the spectator, a gap between the work of art and its audience. When the distance disappears, there is no art. Through aesthetic distance we can watch a play not as a scene from real life but as an representation of life. Vaughn (1978) argued that:

> Our detachment allows us to enjoy on a fictional level, stories that if they occurred in real life, could be unpleasant or even horrifying. "Distance" should not be taken to mean disinterest. In fact, by divorcing one's personal needs and one's practical self from the work, one is able to appreciate a play with even greater and more vigorous interest at the level of art. (p. 6)

Theatre of Brecht vs. that of Stanislavsky is a good example for separation of *player/role*, as opposed to *possession* in ritual drama, and for separation of *audience/player* (Courtney, 1987).

Entering the theatre one must accept and participate in the major theatrical convention, that is, "willing suspension of disbelief." The child, like the adult, knows that the play is only a play — an imitation of something in real life — yet the young child cannot always be aware of the convention, at least not for the entire duration of the play. Here lies the main difficulty in the participation of young children in a theatrical performance. For the play to succeed, the spectator must accept the deception: He/she must be willing to believe in the action of the play but at the same time must acknowledge that it is fiction. The convention of the theatre holds that the spectator be willing to suspend that disbelief for a while. Boyce (1987) argues that, "Suspension of disbelief is a mental exercise that becomes easier with practice and experience" (p. 21). Young children, inexperienced in the world of the theatre, tend to become immersed in the world of make–believe; for them, illusion of reality is understood *as* reality and not as illusion. When distance disappears art does too; it is therefore essential to envisage the audience's reactions in such a way so that the aesthetic distance will be always maintained. Children who are unable to perceive the distance between real and fictional worlds will be unable to enjoy theatre performance as an experience of art.

The Sign System of the Theatre

The sign system of the theatre involves the transmission of meaning through symbols and conventions; and it expresses multiple realities, experiences, and cultures (Elam, 1980). The child has to understand the symbolic nature of the theatrical performance: it includes the words themselves, intonation, facial and bodily expressions, gestures, the actor's use of space, make–up, costumes, and properties, the lighting, and the music. This does not mean that the child should be able to decipher all the symbolic elements and their uses, but he/she has to be aware of certain symbolic elements that are directed at audience members' perceptive ability, for example, the use of objects representing something else, such as, a tail for an animal, a wooden frame for a window, a lamp for the sun). Moreover, the children have to "tune into" the atmosphere created by the music, the lights, and the scenery; they have to know that the music heard in the hall while the soldier is fighting on stage cannot be the sounds that soldier hears on the battlefield.

The Situation of Viewing a Play

Going to the theatre involves preparation, beginning with elementary behavioral codes (such as don't eat, and don't speak, during the performance) through understanding theatrical conventions and modes of presentation. Preparing children to see a play is one of the main concerns in theatre/drama education now being addressed through special curricula plans.

The following is a typical example of children seeing a play, as described by a kindergarten teacher:

The children's behavior in my kindergarten (ages 5–6) is usually like this: when the auditorium goes dark they immediately settle down: they all become quiet, extremely concentrated, waiting for the play to start. Then one hears their enthusiastic reactions to the scenery, the play of light, and the sound effects. My children love to cooperate with the actors: they join in the songs, answer their questions loudly, and clap their hands when invited to do so. They are so involved in the event that they seem to forget themselves; they are lost in the fiction. They love to offer all sorts of advice to the characters who are in "real" trouble in the play. At some moments of tension, they hide their faces, or leave their places, moving to the far side of the hall. Then, when the stress is over, I see them running back to their seats.

Sometimes, the children sit on the floor, on carpets. On these occasions they like to sit huddled together, very close. Some of them become immersed in the fiction, some test the situation all the time and make comments such as: "It's not real," "It's only a play," "It's for fun."

For certain shows younger children (ages 3–4) join us. Then the situation is completely different. Some of the small children cry even before entering the hall. The nearer they get to the hall, the more they cry. Some of them simply do not want to go in. After a while, and only after many attempts to persuade them to enter, some of them agree to watch the show, but some prefer to stay outside (being looked after, of course). The very young children usually are mesmerized by the performance and are glued to their seats. Very slowly you see their body language coming back to them, and afterwards some of them are even willing to take an active part in the situation.

Observing children as they watch a play, one sees that they sometimes have difficulty believing situations and events, but sometimes they are drawn into the fiction and lose themselves in it. This double–edged situation was precisely what I sought in attempting to understand modes of behavior (verbal and non–verbal) and the signs which indicated enjoyment (or otherwise) of the performance.

Here are two more examples to understand the children watching a play:

The Case of Noa (age 7):
We could see that at the beginning of the play, when the lights were turned off, Noa was sitting on the edge of her chair; during the performance she changed her position a few times. In the scene where Don Quixote was fighting with the windmills, she said, "What a noise!." She did not realize that a musician was on the stage creating the noisy sounds until her friend told her to pay attention to him. Then she laughed and enjoyed it, and from time to time she said, "It's beautiful." When she saw the woman from the Inn, she said, "Look, she is walking on her knees. That's why she's so short." She asked, "Is Don Quixote his real name?" After a while she lost interest in the play and asked to leave.

Noa's reactions to the play were a mixture of "belief "and "suspension of disbelief." She entered the theatre with the intention of enjoying the play, and she got herself ready for viewing by sitting on the edge of the chair, so that she would be able to see more clearly. At some points she could not understand how the fiction was created, and asked for explanations. Yet, at other points she reacted by willing a complete suspension of disbelief. Noa showed her understanding that "a play is only a play" by realizing that the woman from the Inn was walking on her knees and explaining why she was so short. The spectator has to maintain the convention that a play is an imitation of life, until the very end of the performance. Noa was swinging between "belief "and "suspension of disbelief" until she lost interest. My claim, along with Boyce (1987), is that willing one's suspension of disbelief is a mental exercise that becomes easier with practice and experience.

The Case of Avi (age 6):
Avi sat on the edge of the chair most of the time. His eyes were wide open. From time to time he turned to his father to see if he was still there. He laughed several times when nobody else did; when the narrator told the audience that Don Quixote liked

chocolates, he imitated enjoying eating chocolate, and he did so a number of times. In the scene where Don Quixote was fighting with windmills, he became tense, and had to be reassured by his father that it was only a play. At the end of the scene he relaxed, and lay back in his chair. At a certain point he asked why they did not bring a real horse onto the stage, and laughed out loud as he asked the question.

In a way, Avi's reactions were very similar to Noa's. He also was swinging between "belief "and "suspension of disbelief. Yet from his reactions we can learn something about expressions of tension and ways of seeking relief. Along with Scheff (1979), I maintain that tension is a necessary condition to experience dramatic action. Yet this must occur in a context which provides a measure of emotional safety. In Avi's case, his father's presence provided this condition. Laughing, crying and other emotional reactions all belong to the idea of catharsis. Children, like adults, seek stimuli which provoke fear or grief, and catharsis can explain the paradoxical behavior of "thrill–seeking".

We can observe how different are the reactions, how differently individuals respond to the theatrical performance. Not all spectators react alike: different connections develop between the stage and each member of the audience. Children's involvement in and reaction to a play is an ongoing communication from the beginning of a play to the end. Sometimes children are encouraged to participate in the theatrical event and to voice aloud their ideas or feelings. But most of the time they are asked to sit quietly and watch. Yet even without speaking the child sends messages to the stage such as crying or laughing or applauding, and, in turn, gets feedback from the actors who are alert to every sign.

Parameters for Aesthetic Distance in Early Childhood

In the absence of any theory on children's becoming involved in fictional worlds as audiences, we decided to look at four parameters for distance:

1. The children's body language: e.g. how they sit, stand, jump up and down, or wander from one place to another; how they use their hands — waving, holding hands, putting the hand on/in the mouth; how the body is held; how their faces express tension, fear, joy.
2. Explicit expressions of emotions such as: crying, shouting, laughing, happy sounds, fear utterances, boredom.
3. Every word the child says: this reveals what he/she is thinking at that very moment.
4. Reacting to other children, adults or the surroundings in the auditorium: this reveals or conceals his/her awareness of the theatrical event.

These parameters serve as criteria to organize, describe and interpret the children's behavior at a live theatrical performance. They help to determine three levels of engagement:

1. "Low" distance, in which the child is so immersed in the fiction that he/she cannot separate the imaginary world created from the real world she lives in.
2. "High" distance, in which the child is completely detached from the performance and is not involved in the fictional world created.
3. "Optimal" distance, in which the child shows that his/her involvement is of the appropriate measure that results in artistic–aesthetic pleasure.

Throughout the performance the children move from one level to another. The relationship between them and the stage is determined by the actors' ability to hold their attention as long as possible and to help them to maintain optimal distance.

Since drama depends on its audiences, the various levels of engagement are essential to understand the ways of perceiving theatrical art. People differ in their ability to react and one person may have varying levels of distance in the presence of objects of art. Therefore it is fundamental to understand, as Bullough (1912) argued, the variable essence of psychical distance as an aesthetic principle. He identified two critical limits: *underdistance*, namely intense involvement with the art object, versus *overdistance*, in which one is completely detached from the art object: "All art requires a distance — a limit beyond which, and a distance within which only aesthetic appreciation become possible" (p. 98).

The following instances exemplify the three levels of behavioral involvement based on the four parameters mentioned above:

'Low' distance signs were expressed by:

1. Beckoning to the actor to "come to me"; going toward the stage: "I want to go and help Don Quixote to….”; hiding under the chair: "I don't want to see, he will kill him..."

2. Hysterical crying, loud laughter, or shouting out of proportion: losing control over one's feelings.

3. Calling out to the actors on stage: "The witch is cruel! run away..." "The thief is behind you..." "Look at the clock! Cinderella, it's almost 12 o'clock."

4. Sitting on the adult's lap, saying: "I'm scared that the lion will jump out of the cage"; hugging the adult lightly at different times during the performance.

'High' distance signs were expressed by:

1. Walking up and down the sides of the auditorium, kneeling on the chair, with their backs to the stage.

2. No emotions at all were expressed

3. "I want some popcorn," "Where is my doll?" The child could not "escape" the darkness and the special atmosphere of the theatrical event and asked to leave: "Mommy I want to go home."

4. Hitting children sitting nearby, pushing the adult, talking to someone about things unconnected with the play: "I don't like you," "Go away," "Do you want to play with me?"

Optimal distance signs were expressed by:

1. Sitting on the chair and watching the play with a very concentrated expression.
2. Crying or laughing as the occasion demanded.
3. Saying, "What a beautiful dress, I want one like that," "I also have a superman."
4. "Father, is that the real King David?" "Mommy, look, you see the legs of the donkey? They are Tami's legs," "Look at this, the snow is made out of paper."

It is reasonable to say that aesthetic pleasure is a complex emotional and intellectual experience, embracing a combination of parameters of aesthetic distance. This is a multi–layered flexible construct which changes according to the development of the fiction on stage; it does not seek to achieve any scientific or utilitarian target but it is the thing itself. Only when one maintains an equilibrium between the two limits of the distance can one derive pleasure from the performance.

CONCLUSION

Usually the goal of a children's theatre production is to absorb the audience in the illusion of the world on stage. Yet it is important that the child as a spectator will be aware that it is a play and will be able to live both the fictional world and the real world. As a spectator the young child may be influenced and changed in some way, simply by having experienced the theatre production. The optimal distance can guarantee an aesthetic pleasure needed to control the experience. I agree with Eisner (1998) who claims that:

> The common function of the aesthetic is to modulate form so that it can, in turn, modulate our experience. The moving patterns of sound created by composers, in turn, create their counterparts in the competent listener. The physically static forms produced by visual artists create in the competent viewer a quality of life analogous to those in the forms beheld. In sum, the form of the work **informs** us. Our internal life is shaped by the forms we are able to experience. (p.34)

My intention was to open one more path in our understanding the "aesthetic mode of knowing," a phrase coined by Eisner (1985) who insisted that we have "to free the aesthetic from the province of the arts alone to recognize its presence in all human formative activity"(p.28). My intention was also to emphasize that despite the problem of defining aesthetic distance, and despite the elusiveness of the concept, there is no doubt that in the eyes of many, this distance is an essential component of children's theatre. The child as spectator should be nurtured from early childhood. Along with Bresler (1992), I argue that as we listen to teachers' beliefs about the arts, most of them highlight its uniqueness for the children; yet most teachers do their work intuitively, and this is not enough. More comprehensive pedagogical and aesthetic ways of thinking and working, need to be elaborated on the basis of children's reactions to a play.

REFERENCES

Aston, E. & Savona, G. (1991). *Theatre as sign–system.* London: Routledge.

Barash, M. (1984). Johann Huizinga and his thought. In J. Huizinga, *Homo ludens* (pp.9–31), Jerusalem: Mosad Bialik (in Hebrew).

Bennett, S. (1990). *Theatre audiences theory of production and reception.* London: Routledge.

Bolton, G. (1984). *Drama as education.*London, Longman.

Bolton, G. (1992). *New perspectives on classroom drama.* London: Simon & Schuster.

Boyce, N. S. (1987). *Welcome to the theatre.* Chicago: Nelson–Hall.

Bresler, L. (1992). Visual art in primary grades: A portrait and analysis. *Early Childhood Research Quarterly,7,397–414*

Bullough, E. (1912) "Psychical distance" as a factor in art and an aesthetic principle. *British Journal of Psychology, 5*, 87–118.

Courtney, R. (1982) *Re–play: Studies of human drama in education.* Toronto: OISE Press.

Courtney, R. (1987) *Dictionary of developmental drama.* Springfield, IL: Charles C. Thomas.

Eisner, E. W. (1979) *The educational imagination: On the design and evaluation of school programs.* New York: Macmillan.

Eisner, E. W. (1985) Aesthetic modes of knowing in : Eisner, E. W. (Ed.), *Learning and teaching: the ways of knowing* (pp. 23–36). Chicago: NSSE

Eisner, W. E. (1998) *The kind of schools we need.* Portsmouth: Heinemann.

Elam, K. (1980) *The semiotic of theatre and drama.* London: Methuen.

Fergusson, F. (1949) *The idea of theatre.* Princeton: Princeton University Press.

Fingerhut, A. (1995) *Theatre: Choice in action.* New York: Harpercollins College Publishers.

Goffman, E. (1973). *The presentation of self in everyday life.* Woodstock, NY: Overlook Press. (First edition published 1959)

Harre, R. (1979). *Social being: A theory for social psychology.* Oxford: Basil Blackwell.

Hobgood, M. B. (1987). The mission of the theatre teacher. *Journal of Aesthetic Education, 21*(1), 57–73.

McMillan, H. J. (1996). *Educational research: Fundamentals for the consumer.* New York: Harper Collins Publishing Company.

Olivier, L. (1986). *On acting.* London: Wheelchase Ltd.

Scheff, J. T. (1979). *Catharsis in healing, ritual, and drama.* Berkeley: University of California Press.

Schonmann, S. (1997) How to recognize dramatic talent when you see it: and then what? *Journal of Aesthetic Education, 31*(4), 7–21.

Smith, G. D. (1991). Hermeneutic inquiry: The hermeneutic imagination and the pedagogic text. In C. E. Short (Ed.), *Forms of Curriculum Inquiry* (pp.187–209). New York: SUNY Press.

Vaughn, A. J. (1978). *Drama A to Z.* New York: Frederich Ungar Publication.

Wheeler, S. (1995). Drama and relationship play in early years of education. *The Journal of National Drama, 4*(1), 5–7.

AUTHOR'S NOTE

I thank H. Kochavi, my student, for her part in the research

An early version of this chapter were published in *Visual Arts Research, 25* (2), 1999, 79–80.

Curriculum Interlude

The chapters in the section center on arts curriculum in educational settings, on the provisions made for teaching dance, visual art , video, music, poetry and literature, to young children in preschools, primary schools, and, through electronic media, in their homes. In a post–modern era, we are keenly aware of the many different ways in which curriculum can be conceived, the distinct perspectives from which it can be conceptualized and experienced. John Goodlad (1979) distinguished among the ideal, the formal, the operational, the perceived, and the experienced curriculum. The ideal curriculum represents our best intentions, that which we desire, know, and believe we ought to teach. The formal curriculum is that ideal transformed into textbooks and instructional materials: the songs, stories, images and ideas we present, ready made, to children. The operational curriculum unfolds in our daily interactions with children in classrooms, The perceived curriculum refers to the teacher's sense of what is being taught and learned. Finally, the experienced curriculum represents the students' point of view.

Frequently, tensions exist among these levels of curricular thought and practice. It is possible, for example, that the materials a teacher may choose to convey a particular concept to students do not represent that concept as well as they might. It is possible that children may experience the curriculum in ways the teacher never intended. As case studies of arts education reported in Stake, Bresler, and Mabry (1991) indicate, advocacy for excellence in arts education is often a more accurate reflection of ideological yearning than of the reality of schools and classrooms. We agree with Michael Fullan (1982) that effective reform is seldom accomplished by raising standards or setting goals: Change is more likely to occur when problems are analyzed carefully and areas of policy and practice susceptible to improvement clearly identified. It is equally crucial to take all possible perspectives on curriculum into account, acknowledging the day–to–day realities of teachers and learners as we remain focused on the visions and aspirations that inform our best practice.

Just as theories of development have evolved toward greater sensitivity to individual children and particular circumstances, our understanding of the contexts in which learning occurs, and the mediating role that teachers play in helping children to decipher and reconcile often conflicting messages, has also grown in recent years. We recognize that, at least where the arts are concerned, all institutions, schools and preschools as they are, permit and facilitate some practices and prohibit others. Schools are where children learn routines and rituals, where they confront the necessity of sharing space and materials, working within prescribed periods of time and cleaning up and putting away when they are told to do so. (See Tarr, 1995, for a description of the ways in which very young preschool children are inducted into the social structures of schooling through art experiences). While it is possible to view the imposition of any form of external structure on young children's exploratory play with materials, movements, sounds or stories as dictatorial and Scrooge–like, an alternative perspective

L. Bresler and C.M. Thompson (eds.), The Arts in Children's Lives, 153–156.
© 2002 *Kluwer Academic Publishers. Printed in the Netherlands.*

suggests that something valuable is gained by facilitating play in ways that help children forge connections to other more experienced players (Jones & Reynolds, 1992; Thompson, 1990). Moreover, hard–boiled realism suggests that parents and teachers do influence children's art even when we have no intention of doing so. The materials—art media, props, instruments, costumes, objects—we choose to make available, the ways in which they are presented or withheld from children, and the response we make to the works that result are powerful ways in which we encourage and support—or discourage and dissuade—continued explorations in the arts.

Although those who teach the arts in schools are often called upon to articulate (and defend) their understanding of art and its contribution to human experience, the everyday culture of the schools does not always encourage deep reflection on the nature of one's teaching. Too frequently, any activity involving work with media associated with one art form or another passes as art: Any type of singing is thought of as music; any project involving colored pencils or paints is considered an art experience. Stinson reminds us to look beyond more superficial similarities to discern and preserve the essence of artistic activity, the "how," the concentration and awareness, that distinguishes dance from mere movement, for example. Following John Dewey, Stinson identifies experience and engagement, combined with a sense of form, as central to the meaning of dance. As she does so, she reflects on the balance between individualism and connection to others that are critical to education in the arts.

The chapters that follow take up the interrelated issues of content—what we teach—and pedagogy—how we teach it. Susan Stinson shares a personal reflection on the nature of curriculum and the teacher's role in determining it. Stinson invites teachers to draw upon their beliefs, values, passions, and commitments, as well as their professional knowledge of artistic skills and pedagogical strategies. She also encourages teachers to reflect critically on their practice, to question the beliefs, the values, and the habits that underlie and shape their work with children. Stinson suggests something of the power that arts educators have enjoyed and valued to design curriculum that is specific to individuals and situations, and not merely responsive to external mandates.

The second chapter, by Liora Bresler, centers on the operational curriculum, framing it within an institutional context. The chapter is based on a three year study of arts specialists in elementary school settings, including data sources of observations and interviews with teachers. Bresler examines the nature of elementary visual art curriculum, identifying four types of art that are employed in the primary grades: child art, child craft, fine art, and art *for* children. Using Goodlad's ideas as an interpretive frame, she addresses the tension between the operational and the ideal arts curriculum, as they unfold institutional contexts characterized by particular notions of space and time, specific communities of practice, and inclusive goals which are not always compatible with goals appropriate to the arts. Although she recognizes that the arts are peripheral to the academic or core curriculum of most American schools, Bresler points to the continuing importance of the arts on those occasions when the school community comes together to celebrate special events. These performances and decorations, produced in arts classrooms for the benefit of the school and its community, are in many ways unique to schooling, unparalleled by any professional or cultural practice beyond the schools.

In the next chapter, Dan Thompson, describes the close connections between literary education and the teaching of the arts. Literacy is seldom considered in discussions of arts education. Moreover, literacy education enjoys privileged status in the schools, in comparison to the arts which are frequently dismissed as peripheral to the central missions of schooling. Thompson suggests, however, that the arts provide a model for the teaching of the subjects considered "basic" in most schools. He offers an intriguing inversion of the perspectives and priorities which have lead some arts teachers to imitate the academic disciplines in their goals, pedagogical approaches and evaluation practices. Thompson describes the benefits that accrue to the arts by virtue of their marginal position in the schools: Freed of formal requirements, standardized testing, and community expectations, the arts can emphasize experience and interpretation, the exploration of personal meanings, and immersion in forms of engagement that are potentially transformative. As Thompson point out, the arts—and literacy taught as an art—emphasize processes that other school subjects do not, encouraging children to conceive meaning for themselves rather than to merely perceive meanings created by others.

Thompson's focus on the significance of awareness and expression in poetry and other forms of writing apply, as Stinson's conclusions do, to all art forms. Just as teachers of young writers must guide, structure, and facilitate meaningful experiences for their students, leading them through stages of competence and confidence within a functional community of writers and readers, teachers who work with children in other art forms must strive to create a community of meaningful practice in which children originate and pursue projects of value to them.

The last two chapters in this section focus on [art forms that are expanded by technology. Tina, can you think of better way to frame this? It seems awkward] Video production has the potential to change narrative and literacy education in a fundamental way, the electronic media shapes students' interactions with music. The close associations of technology with popular media (so different from the traditional "school art") can change the traditional boundaries of schooling. Donna Grace and Joe Tobin explore the issues and tensions that emerged during a three–year project in which the informal, unofficial, and everyday interests of children were brought into the curriculum through the medium of video production. Drawing on Mikhail Bakhtin's writings on the carnivalesque (1968), and Roland Barthes' (1975) concepts of *plaisir* and *jouissance*, they argue that video production opens up a space where students can play with the boundaries of language and ideology and enjoy transgressive collective pleasures. The influence of popular culture on video production is clear. This boundary–crossing and pleasure–getting by the children in the midst of the curriculum pushes teachers to think about their authority in new ways

Peter Webster describes the relatively new context for music education, created by the forms of electronic technology that daily become more accessible to teachers and students. Just as the availability of wax crayons radically transformed the range of activity that occurred in children's art classes, contemporary advances in computer technology, both in the complexity of graphic capabilities and synthesized sound, may reconfigure arts education profoundly. Webster notes the speed of the progress that has taken the classroom computer beyond the "traditional drill–and–practice techniques that. . . made computers nothing more than expensive and flexible flashcards." He traces the evolution of educational software from the earliest forms of programmed instruction to the more sophisticated and educationally relevant musical learning software available today, and reviews nine of the best programs for young children.

Webster notes that very little research exists to confirm or dispute the impact of computer technology on early musical education. Research from general education indicates, not surprisingly, that children's enjoy the light, the sound, the motion and immediate feedback that computers provide and demonstrate positive effects from their interactions with computers. Music teachers and researchers (very much like their peers in other arts disciplines) have been slow to embrace electronic technologies. Many remain unconvinced that computer assistance is necessary, or even possible, in early education, in settings in which even such "basic" arts materials as a set of rhythm instruments or a full complement of tempera paint are often nowhere to be found. Such reservations about the practical and educational priority of computer technologies will debated in the years to come. What is certain, as Webster indicates, is that the available technology becomes increasingly relevant as teachers and children use and critique it, as they discover ways in which it contributes to teaching and learning, and as they recognize areas in which it fails to support the goals they value. As Webster suggests, this still–new technology both creates and suggests new contexts for music teaching, for computers may be best used in exploratory ways, by individuals or small groups of children working independently at stations or centers, rather than in the large group, "teacher–directed and rule–governed" contexts which music education traditionally favors. Thus new forms of pedagogy may arise in response to new tools, a response that is predictable when teaching and learning are recognized as sociocultural activities.

REFERENCES

Bakhtin, M. (1981) *Discourse in the Novel*, Austin: University of Texas Press.

Barthes, R. (1975) *The Pleasure of the Text*, New York: Hill and Wang.

Eisner, E. (1979). *The educational imagination.* New York: Macmillan.

Fullan, M. (1982). *The meaning of educational change.* New York: Teachers College Press.

Goodlad, J. (1979). *Curriculum inquiry: The study of curriculum practice.* New York: McGraw–Hill.

Jones, E. & Reynolds, G. (1992). The play's the thing (Teachers'roles in children's play). New York: Teachers College Press.

Peshkin, A. (1994). The presence of self: Subjectivity in the conduct of qualitative research. *Bulletin of the Council For Research in Music Education, 122,* 45–57.

Stake, R. L., Bresler, L., & Mabry, L. (1991). *Custom and cherishing: The arts in elementary schools.* Urbana, IL: Council for Research in Music Education.

Tarr, P. (1995). Preschool children's socialization through art experiences. In C. M. Thompson (Ed.), *The visual arts and the early childhood learning* (pp. 23-27). Reston, VA: National Art Education Association.

Thompson, C. (1990). "I make a mark:" The significance of young children's talk about their art. *Early Childhood Research Quarterly, 5,* 215-232.

SUSAN STINSON

11. WHAT WE TEACH IS WHO WE ARE: THE STORIES OF OUR LIVES

Teacher education students in methods courses learn to teach according to rules provided by other people. Once in their own classrooms, however, teachers sort through those rules, deciding which ones to keep and which to discard or replace with their own. While most teachers are still subject to guidelines and curricula provided by their employers, I find a lot of validity in the truism, "What we teach is who we are." Who we are incorporates how we see the world (including those parts of it we call the curriculum), what we know of children, what we think about teaching and learning. These visions come through a filter of our values—what we believe in, how we want to live our lives in relation to children. One way to become aware of our values is to look at the stories we tell. Just as myths and legends embody cultural understandings, and treasured family stories give evidence of what a family values, we each as teachers have stories that exemplify our beliefs. When we look at our stories, we come to recognize what we know and value.

But recognizing our values and visions is not enough if we are to go beyond the habitual to the intentional in teaching. We also need to question our beliefs, to recognize their limitations as well as their possibilities. In other words, I believe that we should teach who we are only if we are willing to engage in ongoing questioning, reflection, and self growth. Without such questioning, teaching who we are can mean ignoring the needs of our children and the context of our communities.

To exemplify this process, in this paper I will share stories that reveal some of my own visions—of dance, of young children, of the world and people in it—and how these visions have given rise to what and how I teach. Many of the stories about children are about those I know best, my own children. (This, of course, presents its own limitation, which I shall discuss later.) I will also raise issues or questions with each piece of my vision. In this process, I am using myself only as an example; my visions are no more important than anyone else's. What is important is not my personal vision, but the reflective process that brings to consciousness our values and how they translate into what and how we do and do not teach.

VISION OF DANCE

One definition of dance is rhythmic movement, usually done to music. Certainly the impulse to move rhythmically is a powerful one; most of us have a strong urge to tap a foot or clap our hands when we hear rhythmic music. I remember how surprised I was when I had my first job working with day care mothers and their infant charges, to discover that babies only a few months old may bounce to music with a strong beat. I am still charmed

L. Bresler and C.M. Thompson (eds.), The Arts in Children's Lives, 157–168.

at outdoor concerts to see toddlers get up and unselfconsciously bounce and sway. As noted in the recent guide on *Developmentally Appropriate Practice in Movement Programs for Young Children* (1995) by the Council on Physical Education for Children (COPEC), good movement programs give young children opportunities to move rhythmically, finding their own ways to do so.

Conscious Awareness

However, my vision of dance, now informed by many years of varied experiences, goes further than rhythmic movement. I remember my first teaching experience, when my supervisor came to observe after I had been working with a group of rather unruly youngsters for several sessions. Following the lesson, she told me as gently as possible about her mentor, renowned dance educator Virginia Tanner, who was able to get even very young children to not only move creatively, but also dance. That sent me on a journey of many years, trying to figure out what makes the difference between dancing and just moving.

One key insight I found in study with dancer and choreographer Murray Louis. I ask the reader to do the following activity, adapted from Louis, rather than just read it:

> *First reach up and scratch your head; then return your arm to your lap. Next, choose a part of your arm that can initiate a reach; it could be fingertips, wrist, elbow, or shoulder. Starting with that part, begin extending your arm. Continue to a full extension, then past the point where your arm is straight, so that it is stretched, and the stretching energy comes out your fingertips. Now redirect that energy back toward your head, and condense the space between your hand and head, until your fingertips are just barely resting on your scalp.*

You have just done a dance.

As this example reveals, dance is not what we do, but how we do it. It is a state of consciousness involving full engagement and awareness, attending to the inside.

When I reflect upon this definition of dance, I sometimes question whether it is appropriate for young children. Often, when I observe movement and dance activities for young children led by other teachers, they seem to be primarily about getting the children to move and to make their own movement choices. I value both of these goals, but by themselves they do not make dance. In my definition, the aesthetic experience of dancing can only come when we move with concentration and awareness; it is this which transforms everyday movement into dancing. But I sometimes question whether I may be allowing my own personal desire for aesthetic experience to take priority over the needs of children. In a later section of this paper, I will reflect further upon this issue as part of my vision of young children.

While listening to my concerns, I have worked to find ways to enhance the ability of young children and older ones to go beyond just doing the movement. This has involved "teaching to the inside," helping students become aware of what movement and stillness in different positions feel like on the inside. I can teach children by age eight or so about their kinesthetic sense, and how it works to tell them what their body is doing without their looking. With preschoolers, very simple experiences can help develop this awareness. For example, we shake our hands for about 10 seconds, then freeze them, noticing how they still tingle on the inside. A young child once told me this feeling was "magic," and I often use this description in teaching others. I teach the children that our dance magic lives in a calm, quiet place deep inside us; most seem not only to understand, but to already know this. We make a ritual of sorts at the beginning of the class, finding our "dance magic," and I try to use language and images throughout the class to help children not only move, but feel the movement. When we start to lose the concentration this takes, we take a break and intentionally do something that is "not magical," so that children will develop their awareness of when they are dancing and when they are just moving.

Form

One other piece of my vision of dance that I share with young children has to do with what adults call form. Just as humans have an impulse to move rhythmically, we also have an impulse to give form and order to our perceptions and experiences. For example, adults have organized perceptions of differences throughout the age span into what we call stages of development. Similarly, we organize movement into games and dances.

Story form, with its beginning, middle, and end, is often used for organizing our experiences. I recently spent a week at the beach, all too close to where hurricane Bertha (the main character of this story) was also in residence. Bertha's presence ensured that we spent less time on the beach and more time watching the Weather Channel, and many nearby attractions were closed for part of the week. However, our vacation was not a complete loss. Bertha gave our week a sense of high drama, and offered us an opportunity to tell an exciting story upon our return. The story began as we were carefree and ignorant of Bertha's presence. Tension rose with our discovery that we were under a warning. The peak of the crisis came at 11 pm one night, when Bertha suddenly changed course and headed toward us; we packed our bags to prepare for what appeared to be an imminent mandatory evacuation. The tension resolved when Bertha shifted still again, and the story ended in relieved sunshine.

While some dances have very complex form, the most basic concept of dance form is understandable to preschoolers: A dance, like a story, has a beginning, a middle, and an end. Usually in preschool, we begin and end dances with a freeze (stillness), so that the dance is set off from movement that is not part of the dance. This reinforces John Dewey's (1934) concept of art as experience—he describes "*an* experience" as being set off in some way from the stream of the rest of the world going by.

Dewey's definition of "an experience" goes far beyond the simple perception of beginning, middle and end; his description of aesthetic form includes many aspects beyond the cognitive level of preschoolers. We do not expect a dance made by a preschooler to be complete in and of itself, with parts that flow together to make a whole; we do not expect both unity and variety, internal tension and fulfillment. But many of these conditions which make a good work of art also make a good dance class, even for preschoolers.

Just as many stories begin with "Once upon a time," a beginning class ritual focuses children's attention and prepares them for what is to follow. In my preschool classes, we do focusing activities to begin. A class gets unity from a theme; I use something from the real or imaginary world of young children, such as thunderstorms or toys, or a story, to provide the theme. Within the theme, I take different ideas, such as clouds, thunder, and lightning, or bouncing balls, floppy dolls, and wind–up toys, to provide variety. We translate each of these ideas into movement, finding, for example, which body parts can bounce, and how to "throw" oneself to a new spot by jumping.

Making parts of a class flow together is always part of my plan. For example, in a class on autumn leaves, I might ask the children to let the wind blow them back to the circle so that we can continue with what comes next. I also plan for a real ending to each class, something that brings closure and also leads into a transition to the next activity of the day.

I admit that lessons with preschoolers do not often go exactly as planned, and there are many opportunities for improvisation, another skill I learned as a dancer. But in many ways, planning and teaching my classes feels to me like a form of art–making, an idea for which Elliot Eisner (1985, 1987) is well known. He encourages us to think of evaluating teaching much as we do works of art, and encourages educational "connoisseurship" and criticism.

Sometimes when I finish teaching a class, there is that wonderful satisfaction of knowing that all the parts have come together seamlessly to create a real whole, and a shared transcendent experience has taken place. Even though such experiences occur less often for me with younger children, they are ones to cherish. As Madeline Grumet (1989) points out, it is all too easy to become seduced by a "beautiful class." We need also to maintain our critical faculties, and consider both the gains and losses of thinking about such classes as the peak experience of teaching. I have to ask myself whether the transcendent experiences mean anything in the long run, or whether they are just feel good moments that keep us engaged so we can persevere to what is really important. And what is really important is often as messy as a preschooler's play area, leaving considerable ends that are not neatly tied up into an aesthetic whole.

VISION OF YOUNG CHILDREN

Adults used to think that children were simply miniature adults. Now prospective teachers of young children are taught about distinct developmental differences. These are most often framed in terms of those things young children cannot do (and should not be expected to do), when compared with older children and adults. For example, we do not ask them to sit still for very long or to learn multiplication tables. We assume that young children will get "better," i.e., more like us, as they develop. I have reflected elsewhere (Stinson, 1988) on my concerns over how a developmental model limits our thinking about important qualities that young children possess that all too often disappear as they grow up in our culture.

In this section, I will discuss three aspects of early childhood that are not always mentioned in early childhood texts but have made significant contribution to my choices of content and methodology: their capacity for engagement, their impulse toward creativity, and their drive to develop skills and become competent.

The Capacity for Engagement

Many of my undergraduate students have a vision of young children that I used to share: the idea that young children have a short attention span. My experiences with young children have taught me that sometimes their attention span far exceeds that of an adult. (I certainly tired of reading the classic children's story *Madeline* every night long before my daughter did.) While they are usually less willing than adults to stay with an activity in which they are not engaged, most young children have the capacity for significant engagement. For example, one day I was talking with a friend and colleague about her dissertation (on creativity in children) while our children, then 4 and 5, played in a back room. When we finished we went back to the playroom, but stopped at the door. Ben and Sarah were engaged in pretend play, in fact, so engaged that they did not notice when we came to the door. My friend and I stood there for several moments before we tiptoed away. It was as though our children had created something sacred; we were not part of it, and we could hardly have walked in at that moment and said "It's time to stop now" any more than we could have walked into a religious service or any other sacred activity. This story exemplifies for me how children can engage so fully that they seem to be in another world.

I also remember my daughter at age 2 1/2, when I took her into a partially lighted theater on my way to what was then my office; she looked around at the collection of stage sets and props, and whispered, "Does Santa Claus live here?" How many times children notice the extraordinary moments that we miss: the rainbow in the puddle, the trail of ants, the sound of grass growing. It may require great patience for us as adults to allow children to be engaged.

I think this capacity is worth cultivating. If we are always disengaging young children from what calls them, is it any wonder when they learn not to get too involved, and then we eventually berate them for their lack of concentration?

An appreciation for the capacity for engagement has had a great impact on my teaching, particularly as it has come together with my previously discussed vision of dance. COPEC's guide to developmentally appropriate practice notes that teachers of young children should serve as guides and facilitators, not dictators; this implies a child–centered curriculum, which I think facilitates engagement. We need to make sure that children have choices, and have opportunities to move and dance during free play, not just during instructional time. We need to follow as much as lead, help them discover their interests, appreciate their creations, and give them the respect of our full attention. Young children also give us very clear signals regarding when to stay with an activity and when it is time to move on; we need to attend and respond to them.

Eventually, of course, schoolchildren will be asked to concentrate on the things that interest teachers, not only the things that interest themselves. This presents many dilemmas to those of us who see how engaged young children are in their own learning and how disengaged most adolescents are. How much of this change reflects normal development, and how much comes from asking students to leave their interests behind for those things adults consider worth learning? How much should teachers prepare young children for the teacher–and subject–centered schooling that will come, and how much should they allow learning to be child–centered? If school were entirely student–centered, would this only encourage self centeredness? I know too many adults who only want to do the chores they find interesting, leaving the boring work to partners or colleagues.

Even more troubling in regard to this part of my vision for young children is my recognition that deep engagement does not come readily to all young children. I remember my daughter's 5–year–old friend, who was so hyperactive that he entered our house by attacking it, and within minutes something was broken. Eventually I decided that this child would need to be an "outside friend," and I planned visits to a nearby park in order to allow the friendship to continue. While he was the most extreme example I have encountered, I have met many other children in my classes who had difficulty finding their "calm quiet place inside," and certainly could not remain there for very long. They are readily identifiable as "zoomers," who would spend an entire dance class running through space if that were possible. These children remind me to include vigorous, challenging movement throughout the class, with quiet moments as contrast. A freeze after sudden shape changes or shaking a body part allows us to notice ourselves in stillness. I try to start "where the children are," and gradually move with them from frenzied activity toward calm engagement. But I still question whether my cherishing of the calm center is a reflection of my own need, and my carefully developed techniques to facilitate engagement and inner sensing of the movement a way to manipulate children.

The Importance of Creativity: "I Made It Myself"

When children tell me, "I made it myself," or "I thought of it myself," I am reminded how important it is for young children to see themselves as creators, as makers, as inventors. My son was a sculptor; he pulled all the toilet paper tubes, cereal boxes, scraps of wood, rubber bands, string, and everything else out of the trash can for his constructions before I learned from him, and started not only saving everything but also soliciting from my friends. One year his Christmas stocking held eight rolls of masking tape, a supply which did not even last a year. When we ran out of room to store his constructions, I took pictures of them to save. I wanted him to know how much I valued his original creations.

I try to give young children many opportunities to be creators: to make their own shapes (not just imitate mine), to find new ways to travel without using their feet, to invent a surprise movement in the middle of a backwards dance. As they become more skilled, they take on greater responsibility for creation. At this point, children are not only making choices within structures I provide, but actually creating the structures.

Martin Buber called this impulse toward creativity the "originator instinct," and wrote, "Man [sic}, the child of man, wants to make things....What the child desires is its own share in this becoming of things" (1965, p. 85). But Buber's questioning of the creative powers of the child as the primary focus of education led me to do the same. Buber concluded that "as an originator man is solitary....an education based only on the training of the instinct of origination would prepare a new human solitariness which would be the most painful of all" (p. 87). He reminds me that creativity alone does not lead to "the building of a true human life"; for such a goal, we must experience "sharing in an undertaking and...entering into mutuality" (p. 87). As I will discuss shortly, I find it challenging to try to find ways to educate young children, who often have great difficulty understanding even the concept of sharing, into mutuality.

I am also aware of the current focus of arts education in areas other than creativity. The Getty Center, in a work entitled *Beyond Creating* (1985) and in many others since, has informed arts educators that too much emphasis had been placed upon creativity and production, and too little upon history, criticism, and production. Elliot Eisner (1987) emphasized that art should be thought of as a cognitive activity, rather than an emotional one, and even some early childhood arts educators are writing that young children should spend more time looking at and responding to art made by adults, which implies less time making their own. Anna Kindler (1996) criticizes any "hands off" curriculum that just allows children to create, believing that just creating is not enough stimulus for children to develop cognitive skills.

I continually question whether my vision of the young child's impulse toward creativity is some mere romantic notion that is hopelessly out of date. I also know that I gave up the idea that children needed only opportunities to dance, and no instruction, when I decided to become a dance *educator*. My career has been spent developing ways to help children go beyond where they might be "naturally," without dance education. But my vision of the young child's impulse to create is still strong.

The Importance of Competence: "I Did It"

A third piece of my vision has to do with the importance of competence, of being skillful, in young children's self esteem. My son at the roller skating rink gave me one of many stories that exemplify this perception. His style of learning to skate involved leaning way forward, then going as fast as he could to get as far as possible before falling down. Etched forever in my memory is the first day he made it all the way around the skating rink without falling, and how he crowed, "I did it!!" We need to give young children many opportunities to say, "I did it," and gain the pride that comes with such achievements. To me, this means opportunities to go beyond what they can already do—not too far beyond, of course, because that generates the kind of frustration that can make children give up. But those of us who appreciate children so much *as they are* need to remember that no one shouts "I did it" when the task has not been a challenge.

It took me a fairly long time to recognize the importance of movement skill, what dancers refer to as "technique," for young children. Like many other teachers enamored of creative dance, I wanted to preserve what I saw as the "purity" of children's natural expressiveness in movement, and not spoil it by teaching them technique. Eventually I realized that children are learning from adults, and imitating us, from a very early age; this learning includes movement skills. We have to choose not whether to teach children skills, but what and how we will teach them. I know that children can still feel good about themselves when they learn by imitation; this is how they learn to tie their shoes, which they always seem to view as a great accomplishment. I have also seen the pride felt by a three year old in demonstrating a ballet step, no matter how poorly.

Yet I still find myself led toward exploration more than imitation, finding that a sequence of exploring/forming/performing is useful in developing movement skills as well as creative work. For dance technique, exploring possibilities (such as the differences between a bent, curved, straight, and stretched arm) is important in building the kinesthetic awareness necessary if performance of movement is to be not only correct but expressive.

I also find myself interested in basic movement skills more than codified dance steps. These skills are the kind that children will use in all dance forms and other movement activities. These include how to run or jump or fall without making a sound, how to move close to another person without touching, how to stop oneself (which is hard if one has been moving fast), how to swing oneself around in a turn, how to make points and curves with an elbow. Exploring these kinds of activities will help children become more skillful movers in any dance form they may choose when they become older, and will help them become people who say "I did it!" in the present.

Back in my reflective mode, I look through my first born's baby book and see more dates of achievements than stories: crawling, pulling up to standing, first steps, shinnying up a flagpole, going hand–over–hand on the horizontal ladder, tying her shoes, riding a two wheeler. Sometimes I could not sort out her pride from my own, thinking that I proved I was a good mother by my child's accomplishments. I think sometimes teachers make the same error, seeing a child's accomplishments mostly as a reflection of our own competence as teachers. It is humbling to realize how many skills young children will develop without formal instruction, as long as they have opportunities that include safe and appropriate space and equipment, time to explore, and an adult who notices and encourages.

When I reflect now, I have to ask the same question my daughter asked me at age 3, when I told her I was going to teach a dance class: "Why do you have to TEACH people to dance?" Another time, when someone asked her if she planned to be a dancer when she grew up, she replied, "I already am." Dance educators are fond of saying that everyone is a dancer, whether they know it or not. I wonder whether dance teachers would be needed for young children if our culture were one in which everybody danced, and knew they were dancers. In such a culture, at what level might a need for instruction be felt by a child?

As I continue to reflect upon issues raised in my previous discussion of creativity, I am aware that the only skills I have mentioned are psychomotor ones. What about the cognitive skills that the Getty Center and others are so concerned about developing? Certainly an inability to read or write is likely to be more damaging to a seven year old's self-esteem than an inability to ride a bicycle or to dance. I do think we should be expanding young children's vocabularies for describing dance, and I took my own children as preschoolers to every dance performance suitable for them, encouraging them to name and respond to what they saw. But there were not many of these, and there are very few dance videos that can hold the attention of most young children for very long. There seem to be far more adult created works in visual art, theater, and music that are appropriate for young children.

I am also convinced that children learn dance concepts better through movement than through looking at other people dance, especially in early childhood and in students of all ages who are kinesthetic learners. Even when I ask young children to watch me demonstrate, for example the difference between low and high levels, most of them automatically move along with me while they are watching. But I wish there were more opportunities for young children to see people other than their peers perform, and I continue to encourage those few choreographers who make performances for children to consider making videos as well. I wonder what kind of aesthetic education in dance might be possible if more suitable materials were available.

Reflections On My Vision of Children

For a number of years, I have taught developmental stages to my students through stories, theirs and mine. While the students have voiced appreciation for this approach, I have realized its potential limitation: Whose stories do we tell? Because my students are, like myself, primarily white middle class women, if we only collect our own stories, we are simply reinforcing what I have heard called the prison of our own experience. I continue to seek experiences for myself and my students that will allow us to expand our prisons, knowing that we can never escape them completely.

VISION OF THE WORLD AND PEOPLE IN IT

I remember a Sesame Street book one of my children had, about Grover and the Everything in the Whole Wide World Museum. Each room in the museum was different: Imagine a room filled with tall things, another with small things, another with red things, or scary things. After going through room after room, one finally came to the last door, which led to "Everything Else in the Whole Wide World," and Grover left the museum. My vision of the world is filled not with things but with ideas or principles; I will share two of them.

Individuality

The first piece is about individuality: Each person is unique and special. I often begin teaching dance to a new group of young children by showing a collection of geodes. On the outside, they look plain and ordinary. But on the inside, each one is different and special and magical. As I tell children, so are *they*. This kind of appreciation of differences is an essential part of a preschool dance class. My belief in the importance of individuality is another reason to encourage each child to find her own way, his own shape. Because young children often imitate each other as well as adults, we usually have to give additional encouragement to generate differences. But children in any creative dance class learn early on that the teacher values invention more than imitation.

I have already raised Martin Buber's concern about the temptation to place too much emphasis on individualism in education when we think about creativity. We also have to remember that images of individuals are constructions deeply imbedded within our own culture. (See Martin, 1992, for a particularly thoughtful discussion of these images in American literature.) But there are other concerns as well about an overemphasis on individuals doing their own thing. I recall an incident when I first offered creative dance classes for preschoolers at what was primarily a ballet studio. One parent who had come to sign up her three year old told me angrily that her daughter needed to develop discipline, not creativity; her child apparently climbed on the dining room table to perform, an act the mother did not appreciate.

But I think that another part of individuality that I want to cultivate in the world and in dance is the responsibility for self management. I remember one particularly challenging second grade class that I taught. After two sessions that came close to bordering on chaos, I devoted an entire lesson to "controlling your own energy." This class was held the week after a major hurricane had occurred, and I was able to use this as an example of how destructive energy can be when it gets out of control. Bordering on desperation, I even told them that children who could not control their own energy get sent to the principal's office, while adults without control get sent to jail. Since the positive side of the message was that controlling our own energy allowed us to make things instead of destroying them, we then spent the rest of the class exploring three kinds of energy—strong and sharp, soft and sustained, and exploding—in order to make a dance about a storm. I concluded that this was probably the most important lesson I taught them.

The concept of the "inner teacher," which I absorbed from two years of teaching in a Quaker school, has also encouraged me to think of self management as an aspect of individuality. Even with preschool children, I give opportunities to "be your own teacher, tell yourself what to do" during a class. If all children could find their inner teacher, think how different schools would be.

Connectedness

Another part of my vision has to do with the connectedness of all these diverse individuals, what some feminist theorists refer to as a web of relations. Our experience of connectedness begins at birth; we are born connected to another person. Beyond ties of birth, however, we usually think of connections as something we must create, with an assumption that things and people are basically separate; we have to find ways to bring them together like pieces of a child's construction set.

But my experience in dance has taught me that a great many connections exist outside our awareness of them. We do not have to create these connections, but simply become aware of them and use them in moving and thinking. For example, I have spent many hours in dance classes lying spread–eagled on my back, finding the diagonals that exist in my body, so that movement initiated by the right hand and arm results in movement by the left leg and foot, conveyed through the center of the body.

I am convinced that, just as our bodies are held together by internal connections, we are connected to others by ties that are sometimes as difficult to see as our own ligaments buried beneath layers of skin, muscle, and fat. I have also been moved by Buber's (1958) consideration of connection: When we recognize our connectedness, we become responsible for that to which we are connected. If we recognize our connections with others, we become responsible for them; this is critical in a world in which peoples are fragmented and at war. It is also critical to recognize our relationship with, and responsibility for, the earth.

Originally spurred by Buber's call toward community, I have spent many years seeking ways to enhance community building among my students. For me, this gets far easier beyond early childhood. I find it challenging to teach relationship skills to young children; their egocentrism means that they are not ready for most partner and group work that could facilitate dance relationships. With preschoolers, I find it easier to teach lessons that deal with relationships between themselves and the environment and/or human–made objects in the world. Ideas for classes come from the imaginary and real worlds, not just from movement words like rise, turn, and sink, and abstract concepts such as high, low, fast, and slow.

For example, imagine for a moment some of the things from the everyday world that go up, turn, and come down. For the most part, when I construct dance classes with children, it is about things they care about which have shapes and/or move. My first thoughts usually go to the natural world, because I feel such a strong connection with the earth, and I want to share that with children. So autumn leaves might get picked up by the wind, turn, and fall back down. Or a bird might go into the air, circle a tree, and come back to the nest. The sun rises, shines over all the earth, sinks. The largest number of my class themes came from nature until one time I was asked following a conference presentation, "What about those urban children who do not have much opportunity to experience nature?" That question led me to expand my themes; airplanes and helicopters, as well as helium balloons, can also go up, turn, and come down.

I must note that, despite the use of themes that can easily be personified, I do not ask children to pretend to be anything other than who they are: dancers. Instead, I ask them to try on the qualities they share with whatever we are dancing about. Although some will transform themselves into leaves or birds or helicopters, I prefer to let a child's pretendings belong to them.

In my reflective mode, I still feel concerned that I do little to facilitate the development of community among preschoolers. While I do this more with primary grade children, I have little success even getting children to work successfully in partners until the third or fourth grades. At one point I smugly thought I was merely being developmentally appropriate. Now, I read of others teaching cooperative learning techniques to young children, and I wonder why I am so rarely successful in having young children sensitively mirror a partner, unless that partner is an older child or adult.

CONCLUSIONS

Taking the opportunity to think about meaningful moments in our lives, those that come to exemplify something we believe, helps us become more conscious of our visions and values. Asking ourselves questions about our values and visions gives us the opportunity for professional growth. Sometimes reflection affirms our current practice and its underlying beliefs, and sometimes it challenges them. Even when challenged, it may take a while before we know how to change what and how we teach.

Yet teachers of young children are busy people, with far fewer opportunities than college professors have to reflect on their values and visions. My hope is that professional development for early childhood educators might provide not only workshops for teachers to learn new skills (such as teaching movement and dance), but also opportunities to share and to question the stories of their lives that guide their professional practice.

REFERENCES

Buber, M. (1958). *I and thou* (2ⁿᵈ ed.) (R.G. Smith, Trans.). New York: Harper.
Buber, M. (1965). *Between man and man* (M. Friedman, Trans.). New York: Macmillan.
Council on Physical Education for Children. (1995). *Developmentally appropriate practice in movement programs for young children, ages 3–5.* Reston, VA: American Alliance for Health, Physical Education, Recreation & Dance.
Dewey, J. (1934). *Art as experience.* New York: Minton Balch.

LIORA BRESLER

12. SCHOOL ART AS A HYBRID GENRE: INSTITUTIONAL CONTEXTS FOR ART CURRICULUM

INTRODUCTION

The complexity of the arts is recognized in contemporary society, where art is seen not as a monolithic idea or practice, but as filled with conflicting values and perspectives. We see art as a means for self–expression and personal interpretation. We note its service to politics and propaganda, its function as a commodity. We used to speak of art as timeless and transcendental. We now construct it as multiple. Multiple constructions assume, implicitly and often explicitly, that the meaning of any kind of art is inseparable from the conditions under which it is generated and experienced. Religious art evolved in awe–inspiring churches to communicate, inculcate and inspire. Fine art thrived with the establishment of professional academies and museums striving towards aesthetic goals as well as for the attention of an elite audience. Avant–garde and post–modern art have been connected with social and political movements and issues. Folk art has been promoted alongside political movements and the quest for national identity. Popular art received a boost with modern technology which made it widely accessible to targeted large populations.

Still, the boundaries among the different art genres can be blurred, and there is borrowing across genres. For example, fine art of the late 19th and the early 20th centuries borrowed from "primitive" African art, which was regarded as uninfluenced by socialization, exemplifying the freedom and independence of natural expression. Less ideological but not less important is the interchange between fine art and media which has been on–going since the latter half of the 19th century where artists have learned from advertising and from the illustrated press. In this paper, I examine school art and some of its specific contexts. School art is distinct from other genres, yet draws on them, re–framing and adapting contexts to create a unique genre to its unique goals and structures. I discuss the various art types which school art borrows and adapts, and describe the resulting homogenized genre.

Artistic genres, classical and popular, are discussed extensively in the scholarly literature, examining their distinct contents, formats, purposes, clienteles, and value systems. In contrast, the contents, formats, clienteles and value systems of "school art" are rarely discussed. Among the important exceptions are Arthur Efland who first coined the term in his seminal article (Efland, 1976; see also 1983 and 1990); and Tom Anderson and Melody Milbrandt (1998) with their important discussion of the authenticity of this style.

L. Bresler and C.M. Thompson (eds.), The Arts in Children's Lives, 169–183.

The understanding of "school art" as a genre requires the understanding of the contexts that shape and define it. Context can be defined as "the whole situation, background or environment relevant to some happening" (Grossman and Stodolsky, 1997, p. 181). A context is a "culturally and historically situated place and time, a specific here and now, the unifying link between the analytic categories of macrosociological and microsociological events" (Graue and Walsh, 1999).

In this paper, I focus on the meso, the institutional contexts for art specialists—the structures for art education and the communities of practice of the school. Meso contexts draw on the tradition of art as a school subject, and are connected to other school subjects, arts as well as academics, and their relationship to visual art. Meso contexts interact with micro level contexts – the individual teachers' and students' beliefs and backgrounds—and the macro level contexts – the larger cultural values. The mutual shaping of these multiple contexts creates and shapes the genre of school art.

Unlike the fine arts, school art functions in contexts that are not artistic nor exclusive. School art evolved in the educational settings of the 19th century with the expansion of public school and mass education. Its incorporation into the general curriculum was a struggle from the very beginning, never quite assuming equal citizenship with the academic disciplines which have constituted the foundations of schooling. During the 150 years of its existence, school art rode different ideological and pedagogical waves, assuming radically different functions: from a highly utilitarian skill, through a humanistic discipline assumed to cultivate the mind and the spirit, to the embodiment of the child's self–expression and emotional outlet. These ideological views aside, the contemporary reality of school arts is tinged with the bare necessities of educational settings: most principals and administrators I talked with said that the arts were there primarily to comply with union requirements of release time for classroom teachers.

However, the role that the arts play in the public schools is more complex than the one acknowledged by principals, a role that is at the same time marginal and central to the ways that schools establish their presence as institutions. Arts disciplines are peripheral to the academic, core curriculum: school art is another disciplinary layer added to the many separate areas of instruction present in today's schools. In this sense, it is a by–product of foundation ideas of curriculum that build from the basics or essential knowledge outwards to the peripheral or less essential knowledge. The three R's are at the center—and art, while more institutionalized than something like an anti–drug program, still exists on the outskirts (Bresler, 1998, December). At the same time, school art surrounds the building, contributing to the everyday "school look" as well as to the festive holidays and special events. This decor, distinct and unique to schools, serves and fits with schools' goals, explicit and implicit messages in its contents and forms of presentation.

This chapter is based on a four–year qualitative study[1], which examined the genre of school arts in American elementary settings as reflected in the operational curricula (Goodlad, et. al., 1979) of visual arts, music, dance, and drama. The focus of this paper is on the visual arts.

In general, art is taught by (i) art specialists; (ii) classroom teachers; or (iii) artists in residence. To complement other studies of school art which focused on classroom

---

[1] The study was sponsored by the Bureau of Educational Research and the Research Board at the University of Illinois (for a methodological discussion, see Wasser & Bresler, 1996).

teachers (e.g., Bresler, 1992; 1994; 1996) and artists in residence (Bresler, 1991; Bresler et al., 1999), this study investigated art specialists.

The genre of school art, I believe, can be understood as a hybrid one, drawing on various types of art. Specifically, school visual art draws on the types of: (1) "child craft"; (2) "child art"; (3) "fine art"; and (4) "art for children". Each of these art types is associated with different contents, pedagogies, and evaluation practices. Each is based on a separate set of ideologies and goals, and is related to different underlying assumptions about the nature of art as well as of art learning (e.g., Smith, 1986; Thompson, 1990). These assumptions are incompatible with each other on both the ontological level (what constitutes art) and the pedagogical level (how to teach it). These four types operate not just in visual art but across the various school arts disciplines – music, drama and dance.

The first part of the paper examines these four art types as they are manifested in the operational curriculum. The second part of the paper describes the institutional contexts in which school art operates, in particular, the contexts of time and space for art instruction, as well as the communities of practice in which school art functions. Each of these components plays a different, though interrelated, role in the resulting "school art" genre.

Rationale, Settings and Methods

The study of the operational school arts has particular significance, for a number of reasons. Whereas the American constitution makes the states responsible for education, curricular decisions are made in each local school district. In the school subjects of arts, more than academic subjects, it is the individual teacher who makes decisions, with relatively few constraints or formal requirements. Although philosophies and agendas for arts education abound, school arts *practice* (consisting of the formal and the operational curricula) has received little attention. This is all the more intriguing in view of the fact that little can be known about arts in the schools without *actively* exploring practice. In theory at least, the arts are among the "core subjects". Yet, they are less accessible to inquiry than other subjects. Factors contributing to this inaccessibility include nonstandardized curricula; the scarce use of formal requirements and materials (e.g., textbooks); the vast diversity of potential arts activities; and the absence of testing. These factors are interrelated. Because arts curricula are not subject to either local or national testing and comparison, they are less likely to be of concern to parents and administrators. Consequently, there are few national, state, and district–level prescriptions, thus leaving more room for diversity and open–endedness.

The study examined visual arts program taught by two itinerant specialists in four mid–size schools (ranging from 400 to 500 students) in a university town school district. The schools housed a range of SES student body, including a lower and middle class minority population.

Data sources included: (1) intensive, non–participant observations of 4 visual art classes a week during two years, (2) observations of in–and out–of–school art exhibitions, as well as meetings of program specialists across arts subjects, (3) semi–structured interviews with teachers and principals, and (4) analysis of materials such as art textbooks, and students' artwork. As a case–study, there is no claim of representativeness or generalizability. Rather, the aim is to capture the richness, complexity and contextuality of art education in its varied manifestations.

School Art

To understand the complex and hybrid nature of school art, I categorized it to the following four types: (1) in "Child craft", I refer to the employment of activities and designs to achieve predetermined ends; (2) in "Child art", I refer to original, open–ended (in at least some aspects) compositions which are intended to reflect students' interpretations and ideas; (3) in "Fine art", I refer to the inclusion of artworks created by established artists; and (4) in "Art for children", I refer to art created by adults specifically for children, often for illustrations of books, or for didactic or entertainment purposes.[2]

Each of these types has its own history and journey in becoming part of the school genre. "Child craft" was introduced to schools in the 19th century, prevailing in the first decades of public schools, and shaped by the industrial revolution. "Child art" entered the school as part of the child study movement and the progressive education at the beginning of the 20th century. The use of "Fine art" in the school sprinkled the curriculum from the mid–19th century, with an added boost from the Getty Center and the Discipline–Based Art Education approach in the 1980's and 90's. "Arts for children" was typically part of language arts throughout the last 200 years with occasional presence in the visual art. In the following sections, I describe each of these types as they are manifested in the arts curriculum in our study.

I. Child Craft

The origins of child craft reflect some similarities to the goals of fine art; both focus on the development of perception, following Pestalozzi's early 19th century writings about the essential role of perception as the foundation of clear concepts. Pestalozzi believed that all perceptions are organized through form or number. He developed systematic method of instruction that would avoid the pitfalls of trial and error (Efland, 1983), a method characterized by efficiency and preordained products. He regarded drawing as facilitating perception because it involved proportion and measurement, and because it registered perceptions of form and number.

By the mid 19th century, industrial drawing, which developed an ideology, goals and activities distinct from those of fine arts, was the norm in the school. Contents of industrial drawing focused on lines and geometric forms rather than the study of the human figure (associated with fine arts and the academy). Later in the 19th century, it was the tradition of handicraft (for men) and decorative arts (for women) that shaped child craft activities (Wygant, 1993). Pedagogies were teacher–centered and rote, consisting of step–by–step dictation and students' copying from workbooks, blackboards, and cards (e.g., Efland, 1990; Logan, 1995; Wygant, 1993). The utilitarian ideology of crafts, contrasted with the "art for art's sake" ideology of fine art and compatible with the demands of an industrial age.

---

[2] For a discussion of three of these genres in the disciplines of the performing arts – music, dance and drama—see Bresler, 1998, Sept/Oct.

The present day version of child craft has maintained the teacher–centered, step–by–step pedagogies, while it offers diluted skills that center on basic coloring, gluing and pasting instead of drawing. Lessons are typically "one shot" activities. Child craft activities are typically conducted by classroom teachers with little expertise in art (Bresler, 1991, 1994), and only rarely by arts specialists. Ideas are derived from general classroom magazines as well as common traditions. Rather than aiming at employable industrial goals, contents revolve around holiday and seasonal themes (e. g., Easter bunny decorations, winter penguins, Valentine cards), the cute rather than the useful.

II. Child art

Like child craft, child art was initially associated with the skill of drawing, but in a free style, rather than geometric drawing. In recent years, child art has expanded to include other media – collage, paint, sculpture, papier mache, occasionally masks and puppets. The 19th century emphasis on drawing in "child art" can be traced to its association as a cultural attainment since the renaissance, and in that sense resembles the aspirations of fine art. In the American colonies, for example, aspiring young men and women learned to draw as part of social advancement (Wygant, 1993). In addition to its practical and social benefits, drawing was associated with moral values, as part of the good, the true, and the beautiful. "Representational drawing was seen to nurture an apperception of beauty as it developed accurate perception, the love of order, harmony, and suitableness in nature, art, literature, and life" (Wygant, 1993, 5).

The *interpretive–expressive* ideologies of child art, which thrived in the early 20th century, were a product of pedagogy imported from Europe. Its educational philosophical foundations can be traced to Rousseauian notions. Its distinct disciplinary aspect was influenced by the 20th century art educators Herbert Read and Victor Lowenfeld, who developed and articulated art–specific goals and pedagogies.

In our observations, child art was usually the territory of arts specialists. Unlike classroom teachers who often presented art as a recreation or enrichment.[3], specialists presented child art as a subject with a particular body of knowledge that was taught in an organized, sequential fashion, similar to other academic school subjects.[4]

The form of both types, however, was similar. Both "child craft" and "child art" typically consisted of relatively quick products, completed within one 30 minute lesson, though "child art" projects did occasionally span 2–3 lessons. Art specialists, unlike classroom teachers, taught sequentially, developing concepts and skills from one lesson to another. Arts vocabulary and techniques established frameworks for arts activities. Specialists typically provided guidance and modeling of their work (rarely using students' artworks as models), yet allowed students' choices. Sometimes, themes and topics were prescribed, whereas at other times they were not. Teaching was typically well planned, systematic, and clear. The curriculum focused on the elements

---

[3] Some early childhood and ESL teachers adopted a non–interventionist open–ended instruction, where teachers provided visual materials for children with no direction, aiming at "child art" and self expression rather than craft.

[4] Though the teaching of concepts and skills is an expected outcome of all academic school subjects, we found that they were rarely part of principals' expectation of the *Arts*.

of art and design—shape, form, balance, and color—and related concepts and art vocabulary to sensitizing children to visual qualities and to the development of specific artistic skills. Materials were basic: construction paper, crayons, less regularly craypas, and occasionally beads and feathers. Even markers were used sparingly, mostly for unusual projects (like masks). Scaffolding was conducted by probing questions and suggestions grounded in artistic rationales. Usually themes were connected to skills that provided the backbone for the lessons, but we also observed activities where both concepts and skills were presented open–endedly, like "Draw your favorite activity" or "Draw your favorite artistic activity." In general, child art was characterized by a highly supportive environment, with ample encouragement available. In contrast to classroom teachers who provided feedback in a more generic way ("I like it"), specialists provided feedback related to a specific quality ("I like the way you use color to make your pattern stand out").

In spite of the interpretive mission of child art and the open–ended aspects of the instruction, visual artwork of the children often looked nondescript, with few indications of individual expression.[5] Part of the lukewarm tone in the exhibits of child art we observed could be attributed to the poor quality of materials that did not lend themselves to artistically rewarding experimentation. Another related factor was the limitation of technical facility that students possessed. Artwork presented, unframed and crowded together in the school or in the local shopping mall, was still another factor. However, I believe that as important as materials, techniques or exhibition style, it was the lack of time to develop and explore, the lack of teachers' and school's expectation that children invest themselves in creating something meaningful, that shaped children's art process and products. Indeed, children's artwork reflected few indications of exploration of ideas, moods or feelings. Thus, child art resembled child craft in its lack of personal expression.

The discrepancy between the ideology of child art as means for self–expression and the lack of expression found in the operational curriculum is an important aspect of school child art. Observations of the operational arts curriculum indicated few invitations to communicate one's feelings through artistic means. Indeed, interviews with art specialists revealed feelings of ambivalence towards the goals of expression in the structured environment of the school. These concerns mirrored the school culture, which regards discipline and management as necessary for emotional and physical safety and is apprehensive of expression in all its messiness and unpredictability.

In our observations, interpretive artwork occurred only when the topic *demanded* personal interpretation, when children could interpret the topic easily (for example, in the kindergarten's assignment to draw a picture of themselves doing their favorite thing), or when students were scaffolded in their interpretation and given more time. On these occasions, students' work reflected a variety of ideas, experiences and ranging levels of sophistication.

Clearly, expression and interpretation in child art are complex processes, involving more than the use of visual materials and the permission for spontaneous creativity. Expression requires attention and involvement as well as sophisticated knowledge of

---

[5] It is intriguing that this relative uniformity of style could be discerned also in the classes of those classroom teachers who adopted an extreme open–ended pedagogical style (Bresler, 1992). There, some students did create artwork that was original and different, but most students produced artwork similar to that made in the highly prescriptive classes.

technical issues and some formal skills. Without knowledge and personal investment, artwork was dutiful at best, sloppy and meaningless at worse, and its expression, to invoke Langer (1957), was symptomatic rather than artistic.

III. Fine art

The incorporation of "fine art" into the school curriculum can be traced to the 19th century view of aesthetics as a corollary to moral education. Grounded in humanistic goals, fine art was based on a pursuit for excellence and the acquisition of cultural knowledge. The teaching of fine arts in the schools revolved around the disciplines of arts history and arts criticism. The highlighting of the aesthetic mission and the focus on art masterpieces were part of the popular configuration of self–culture. Harris, the U.S. Commissioner of Education, was instrumental in promoting the study of the fine arts as great civilizing agencies in the school curriculum, emphasizing history in general and the Greeks in particular as an important part of school art (Efland, 1990; Wygant, 1993).

Traditionally, fine art as adapted to school has placed less emphasis on viewers' personal interpretation and focused on structured perception and the acquisition of transmitted knowledge. Pedagogically, it drew on cognitive, factual and critical approaches. Recently, fine art, like child art, became (to a limited extent) associated with personal interpretation. New approaches like the Visual Thinking Strategies (e. g., Housen, 2000; Housen & Duke, 1998) incorporate the construction of personal meaning by centering the curriculum on open–ended questions eliciting children's interpretations. These, however, are still the exceptions in school art.

In our study, observations revealed that "fine art" existed far less systematically than "child craft" and "child art". Fine arts activities were the exclusive territory of specialists with intensive art background, who sometimes used fine art as an integral, but small, part of their curriculum to present the works of the great masters in reproductions (posters and postcards). The presentation of masterpieces involved 2–3 minutes of looking at artwork, with attention drawn to a concept learned in that lesson. Biographical information about the artist, when provided, consisted of the artist's name, birth dates, country of origin. Focusing on a surface perceptual level, these interactions with fine art rarely involved explorations of the artwork and the construction of personal meanings; discussions and observations about style; reflections on what makes the artwork interesting or innovative; or comparison of different artists in terms of formal, technical or expressive qualities. The brevity of the encounter did not highlight the distinctions between the various works, styles and expressions. Occasionally, it was students who initiated conversations about fine art, sharing with art teachers calendars of famous artists they brought from home.

Arts specialists lamented the fact that children easily get bored with facts, that they are used to doing things actively. Students' low interest in the historical information may have been related to the fact that school–based fine arts was often "close–ended," focusing on the factual and informational, with little attempt to elicit students' interpretation of the artwork and engage them in meaning making. The lack of interpretation and construction of meaning in the "fine art" component paralleled the lack of interpretations in the "child art" activities: both activities feel hurried and rushed.

IV. Art for children

"Art for children" in visual media has been popular at least since the 19th century, mainly in story books.[6] As an art type, art for children claims no lofty—humanistic or scientific—framework: it does not, like "child art," espouse self–expression; nor does it assume, like "fine art,, to be "the best of the culture" (though some "art for children" shares the best qualities of fine and folk art). Instead, it was supported by a developmental perspective, and served practical needs in communicating and illustrating materials that were meant to be developmentally appropriate, accessible and relevant to children's life. Its main medium in visual arts has been illustrated books which were credited with contributing to the rearing of children. Parents accepted the notion that picture books were the best way to cultivate the minds of their children. Diana Korzenik(1995) quotes from *Parents Magazine* in 1841, advising its readers on selecting books for their children:

> The youthful eye is pleased with beautiful forms in nature: the child is gratified with. . . houses, birds, and animals, retard his bounding feet, as he pauses to gaze upon their beauty. A book, also is fascinating, when it comes with the same recommendations. He will search for pictures of castles, mountains, water–falls, forests, lakes, and whatever is capable of pleasing the eye; and express the liveliest gratification in the beauty and perfection of the mechanical execution (p. 74).

In our observations, the presence of visuals was an important part of current early childhood and elementary school level books. Children were often exposed to illustrations in their language art and trade books. Unlike "art for children" in the school subjects of music and drama, which often used didactic songs from textbooks and dramatic school performance written specifically for children, visual arts teachers did not incorporate this type of art as an integral part of the curriculum. On occasion, however, teachers asked children to illustrate stories in the style of the examples in their trade books with open–ended (within the story line) topics, concepts and skills. Thus, although art for children was a more central part of school curriculum than the other art types, it was the type least practiced in formal instruction.

* * *

Much of school art is characterized by inexpensive, poor quality materials. Arts budgets are typically low and are expected to cater to a large number of students. Reproductions of fine art, too, are of low quality[7]. Museum visits are rare, and typically children don't have opportunity to see original works of high quality. This is true even for schools in large cities (e.g., Chicago) that are famous for their rich arts activities and offerings. In the schools we studied, only the most basic materials and resources were afforded.

---

[6] The "music for children" counterpart goes back at least 100 years earlier to pedagogical compositions for children by Bach and other Baroque composers in Germany and France.
[7] Of course, no reproduction is perfect, misrepresenting scale and texture, etc.

Pedagogies varied across art types with a range in the flexibility and the open–endedness of the activities. "Child craft" activities tended to be on the close–ended side of the continuum, with "fine art" following closely. "Child art" and "art for children" activities in the visual arts incorporated open–endedness in several aspects.[8] For both child craft and child art, teachers provided formal demonstrations, focusing on how to use materials, and, in child art, presenting concepts and artistic skills. Fine art activities often presented historical information, only rarely prompting students to observe, reflect and offer personal interpretations.

The instruction of all art types reflected a general low priority for guided exploration of materials and ideas, deep interpretation and meaning making. Creativity, commonly identified by teachers and principals (as well as national guidelines) as the raison d'être of school art, is closely tied to personal connection and expression. In the worlds of child and fine art, creativity often involves problem *setting* as well as problem solving, it requires personal investment and ownership. It comes out of explicit probing into meaningful issues, and exploration of meaningful issues takes time and dedication. It has to be nurtured by active support and recognition of a community of practice. Children, like adults, are quick to discern the explicit and implicit rules of the activity, what is required, what will elicit attention and acknowledgment. The environment of schools supported the "cute" and the superficial. The need to construct meaningful interpretations, to invest and to push oneself and one's boundaries, are not part of the general climate. This is, I believe, why there is no direct relationship between the open–ended aspects of child art curriculum and originality and expressivity in students' artwork. Rather than mere open–endedness, it is the framing of the artistic experience as challenging creative and interpretive, combined with by teachers and other students attention and the recognition of the artwork that nurture an invested, meaningful art making.

A central question in the larger study of which this is part addresses the kinds of *knowledge* presented in school art. To what extent does the operational curriculum reflect the knowledge and ways of thinking of the artist, the *maker*, concentrating on "how to" (e.g., "What happens if I do this?" "How can I use that technique in my work?"). To what extent do we discern the knowledge of the informed *perceiver*, actively interacting with the artwork, concentrating on noticing and understanding (e. g., "What does this artwork say to me?" "What are the formal, technical and expressive qualities in this work?" "How do these qualities shape my experience of it?"). Is there a connection among these two stances, an attempt to relate them to each other? (e.g., "How is this artist's ideas and problem solving relevant to my own work?").

Clearly, these two stances of the maker and the perceiver can and should be interrelated. John Dewey (1934) suggested that both of these stances offer multiple entry–points into the aesthetic experience: when they function together in an integrated way, combining creation and appreciation, they enhance the artistic/aesthetic experience. Research suggests that even as preschoolers, young children can assume this dual stance: artistic development occurs as a result of children's ability to juggle their activities as creators and viewers (Wolf, 1989). Indeed, children's early representational

---

[8] Interestingly, there was no correlation between the openness and the expressivity of the art work.

drawings often emerge as a result of a dialogue between production and perception (Thompson, 1995; Thompson & Bales, 1991).

In view of this research, as well as the wealth of suggestions available regarding the nature of the ideal arts curriculum, the weak emphasis in all four art types on the knowledge of either maker or perceiver is glaring. Observations revealed that students were rarely invited to initiate discussions and to ask questions. Rather, the dominant pattern was for concepts or specific tasks to be presented by the teachers, establishing a fairly substantial structure that did not allow space for reflection and personal interpretation. This seems to be a direct result of the short time allotted to art lessons, resulting in a diminished sense of students' ownership and investment, the absence of inquiry, reflection and interpretation.

The power of school arts to serve expressive and intellectual ends, to facilitate new understanding, redraft vision, and help develop children's' interpretive skills is strongly affected by the general school culture and ways of practice. One way this is achieved is through focusing concern on the technical—concepts and skills—as opposed to more holistic, social, political or expressive concerns. The different types of art become homogeneous in the operational curricula of the school art genre. The resulting school art assumed a safe, surface level style, evasive of meaningful issues, avoiding the wider ends of the emotional and intellectual continuum that could be evoked and expressed, eliminating the problems that art could raise. The potential of art to inform children's lives in this setting and trigger in them deep experiences is diminished. Thus the goals of school art seem to be far more attentive to mainstream educational norms than they are to artistic concerns. Like many school disciplines, school art is tamed within school boundaries, relinquishing its potential for evoking powerful experiences.

INSTITUTIONAL CONTEXT FOR SCHOOL ART:
ROLE AND STRUCTURES FOR ARTS SPECIALISTS

The contexts of elementary art specialists are quite different from those of classroom teachers, in that specialists represent a distinctive subculture within schools: theirs is frequently the only subject that is not taught by classroom teachers. Hence, their position, a marginalized one, as "the other" teacher. Classroom teachers, responsible for the teaching of academics as the central mission, focused (if and when they taught art) only on child craft. They regarded art as a relief from the rigor or tedium of academic contents, rather than an important subject on its own (which, in any case, they typically knew little about).

The reduction of art to "child craft" can be attributed to classroom teachers' lack of knowledge and skills in producing art and analyzing it, their familiarity with craft rather fine arts and aesthetic aims (Bresler, 1992). However, the superficial treatment of art we observed is intriguing when it comes to arts specialists. Specialists are knowledgeable of the qualities that the arts in the real world go by—sophisticated technique, creativity and excellence. And yet it was only in a few of these specialists' classrooms that one could sense the power of any of the art types. I believe that the roles of specialists and the structures in which they operate are central to the understanding of the limitation of school art.

Space

Art teachers represent a distinctive subculture within the school, with special meaning to themselves as insiders and to classroom teachers as outsiders. Consistent with classroom teachers' view of art, art teachers are typically seen by the administration (as well as by other teachers and children) as having less status. One of the places where this is reflected is in the allocation of space. One's room is a highly significant possession in school terms, symbolizing professionalism, autonomy, and self–control. In their room teachers have control over use of materials and rules for comportment, autonomy that is lacking in most other arenas of teacher life. It is indicative of the image of art within the culture of schools that half of the observed schools had no rooms for art teachers. This constituted a marked difference not just from regular classrooms but also from other spaces allocated for specific purposes and programs—libraries, gyms, offices for social workers and counselors. It contributed to the framing of art as a "release time" ("freedom from" the rigid academic subjects, rather than "freedom to" create), rather than an area with its own merit, inspiration, possibilities and opportunities. Those arts teachers that did have a room of their own often operated in a space that was not meant to be for art, but housed computers and other school "stuff."

This state of affairs has implications beyond image and status: space shapes contents and activities of arts instruction. Itinerant visual art teachers, for example, were constrained by the lack of storage space for their art materials, and for partially finished art projects. They sought to avoid the problem of storing uncompleted projects in the regular classroom or on their cart. For their "child art" activities, they opted for projects that could be finished in a short amount of time. For both child and "fine art," they used materials that were not heavy or cumbersome to cart around. When art teachers did not have their own classrooms, the "mess" generated by studio art activities could cause problems for classroom teachers and affect their relationship with specialists. Some classroom teachers monitored art teaching, interfering with instruction in what they felt were *their* "territories." Thus, the ability to negotiate positively with classroom teachers and to create allies among the school's communities of practice was central for specialists.

Time

Arts instruction typically took place within a weekly narrow 30 minute slot. In music and in dance/drama where the activities—singing songs, doing movement exercises—consisted of several short performance "units", arts specialists did not see the limited time as a problem. However, in visual arts which required sustained time for reflection and experimentation with materials, a 30 minute time slot was highly constraining. In most classrooms, visual arts teachers had time for the brief introduction of an art skill (about 12 minutes), a brief practice of that skill (about 15 minutes), and an extremely brief evaluation of the experience (often a minute or less). Art teachers did not always have control over their time: we observed classroom teachers being late to pick up their students from the art room causing delay for the next class. With limited time, discussion, interpretation, and expression were marginalized.

Limited time constrained the curriculum to projects which the children could quickly clean up by themselves. While most art teachers acknowledged that primary grade students need to experiment with paint and color, they are not always able to clean everything up well. Consequently, to fit with the tight schedule, specialists drew on activities of drawing, using crayons and construction paper, or the gluing and pasting, avoiding paints and other messy materials.

The scarcity of time also meant that there was little time for evaluation, for looking over the work that was done in the previous class while still fresh in mind. Within school culture, evaluation represents accountability and accountability is central to the system. (Conversations with teachers invoked an additional, ideological aspect of evaluation in the arts. Evaluation was often regarded as incompatible with the function of art which was perceived, in spite of the fact that it did not function that way, to be a *"self–expressive"* activity. Evaluation, then, was often regarded as a criticism of the child, rather than a means to expand students' skills and sensitivities and facilitate teaching. A related issue concerned teachers' belief that students' self esteem is tied to the absence of criticism, rather than to the active encouragement and challenge of students to develop a sense of accomplishment.) The view and expectations of school arts are reflected in both formal and informal evaluations, where grading is based on mere participation and good will, rather than on mastery of skills, the pursuit of excellence, or the expression of feeling and ideas. In a culture where evaluation is central and symbolizes achievement, the lack of real, substantial evaluation contributed to students' lack of investment in art.

There are additional factors which shape the status of art specialists in the school, and, consequently, the status they can lend to their subject in the school. Classroom control is one such factor, where quiet and order frequently become more important than experimentation with materials, and discussion of ideas. The constraints imposed upon behavior in school art shaped all art classes. Constraints of time and space, and the related dynamics of relationships with classroom teachers, create added technical and emotional pressure for arts specialists to fit and conform to school expectations, to simply be "good enough", rather than to assume a leadership position in the building in their area.

Communities of Practice

Arts teachers live within a community of non–arts teachers, with little contact with the larger art world. Within their buildings, they are often the only teacher in their subject. The larger community of the school typically centers around what are regarded as basic subjects and academics, rather than on art, aesthetics and expressivity.

Teachers' autonomy reflects dialogical relationships of the educational priorities and values in the society. Principals' concern with test scores of academic subjects mirrors society's emphasis on industrial competitiveness, material achievement, money and success as symbolizing self and cultural worth.

Instruction has its roots in cultural discourses and folkways of teaching, as well as values of the larger culture. The finding that school subjects differ in their relative status and place comes as no surprise and is well–supported by the scholarly literature on general school subjects (e.g., Grossman & Stodolsky, 1997). The role of the subject in the society and its reward system and status constitute a central context[9]. Sandholtz found that "the importance society placed on certain subject areas provided additional psychic reward for teachers by increasing the value placed on the teacher's work (in Grossman & Stodolsky, 1997, p. 26). The reverse, of course is true as well: teachers of less valued subjects, like visual art and music, often experience fewer psychic rewards (Cox, 1998).

Principals are concerned with test scores of academic subjects and with accountability to parents, as part of the larger public relations with the community. In that latter public relation role, administrative expectations of arts education highlight school performances in social functions, perceived as a good representation of the school. For visual art, expectations may include putting up bulletin boards and decorating the schools with student work. The emphasis is on the presence of art partly as decoration, partly as a sign of productiveness. The artwork needs to be accessible and acceptable to all factions of their communities. School culture does not strive towards expanded ways of seeing. It is more important to avoid areas of controversy and conflict than to convey original and aesthetic statements.

Furthermore, in the schools, emotion, creativity and expression are often considered loose cannons that could fire off with disastrous results. Management is a primary concern for school practitioners. Keeping school art nice, teachers believe, makes art manageable within school confines. The performance and expression of art, then, has to be tightly controlled. In a culture where intensity, passion and ownership are marginalized, the arts assume a decorative and entertaining role.

The educational context of the United States provides another macro context for school art. In a country whose education system is de–centralized, curriculum reform has different dynamics than it does in more centralized systems. The autonomy allowed to teachers, especially in the arts, permits them to teach what they care about and what they feel most comfortable with, as long as it does not conflict with school values. At the same time, that autonomy means that teachers are not required to push themselves beyond their "comfort zone".

However, in districts with an organized group of art specialists, teachers sometimes gain support from each other, informally, or formally. In the district we studied, arts specialists regularly sought to build a unified curriculum that would make arts terminology generic across various fields (music, dance/drama, visual art), as well as change existing structures for arts education. These meetings, sometimes nurturing, sometimes stressful, were forums for discussing shared concerns and frustrations, as well as initiating changes in contents and formats.

IDEAL VERSUS CONTEXTUAL GOALS OF SCHOOL ART

Each of the original goals of the four types of art implies socialization towards different values and roles. The ideology of "child art" places children in the role of the artist, emphasizing children's engagement, exploration and personal meaning–making,

---

[9] In another study I conducted in a high school arts academy, it was those teachers who did *not* teach in arts subjects who felt marginalized and "looked down"upon by students (Bresler, 1997).

assuming their inner wisdom and natural curiosity. "Fine art" in the schools aspires to connect children to the conversation of great cultural heritage, focusing on transmission of the "best of our culture", and highlighting exposure to masterpieces, which represent excellence in ideas and skills. "Child craft" intends to transmit drawing and craft skills for utilitarian, practical artifacts. "Art for children" aims to facilitate the acquisition of ideas and comprehension of texts. I argue in this paper that all four sets of goals were overruled by the school's existing structures of time, space, and technical priorities. All types ended up emphasizing socialization into following directions and routinized processes and products, rather than leading towards moments of insight and intensification. With a few exceptions, none of the school art types exemplified creativity, ownership and caring.

Clearly, institutional structures and operation carry considerable power in shaping the experience of its members. School art is the site for complicated interplay between artistic notions and pluralistic school values and desires. The exploration of how various artistic forms and practices are transformed or created as they enter the embrace of the institution exemplifies the inherent tensions between the school worlds and the diverse heterogeneous art worlds. The authentic worlds of "fine art" and "child art", from which the ideal curriculum for school art borrows, are based on experience, interpretation and communication, conveying different sets of values and perspectives but also some commonalities. In these out–of–school worlds, art is an autonomous and free activity, aiming at exploration and transformation. Accordingly, the ideal curriculum borrows from these ideals, but the operational curriculum is constrained by its practical, urgent goals as well as by its structures. School art differs in significant ways from art as it is found in non–school locations that provide different circumstances and conditions for the production and appreciation of art. Thus, school art is a blend of educational and artistic expectations, where the agenda of schools and their expectations seems to be dominant.

The experience of school art is interpretive of the school experience itself, infused with the values, norms, and conventions of schooling. The larger issue at stake concerns the kind of contribution that art could make to the school curriculum, whether it accommodates to its current values, or whether it can be used in an Archimedian sense to expand, deepen and recharge the curriculum.

REFERENCES

Anderson, T. and Milbrandt, M. (1998). Authentic instruction in art: Why and how to dump the school art style. *Visual Arts Research*, 24(1), 13–20.
Bresler, L.(1998). The genre of school music and its shaping by meso, micro and macro contexts. *Research Studies in Music Education*, 11, December, 2–18.
Bresler, L. (1998). "Child art," "fine art," and "art for children": The shaping of school practice and implications for change. *Arts Education Policy Review*, 100(1), Sept/Oct, 3–10.
Bresler, L. (1997). *General issues across sites: The role of the arts in unifying high school curriculum.* A Report for the College Board/Getty Center for the Arts.
Bresler, L. (1996) Curricular orientations in elementary school art: Roles, pedagogies and values. *Council of Research in Art Education*, 127, 22–28.
Bresler, L. (1994). Imitative, complementary and expansive: The three roles of visual arts curricula. *Studies in Arts Education*, 35, Winter, 90–104.
Bresler, L. (1992). Visual art in primary grades: A portrait and analysis. *Early Childhood Research Quarterly*, 7, 397–414.

Bresler, L. (1991). Washington and Prairie Schools, Danville, Illinois (ch. 3), & Armstrong Elementary School, Chicago, Illinois (ch. 4). In Stake, R., Bresler, L. & Mabry, L. *Custom and cherishing: The arts in elementary school* (pp. 55–93 & 95–136). Council for Research in Art Education, Urbana, IL: University of Illinois.

Bresler, L., DeStefano, L., Feldman, R., and Garg, S. (1999). "The kids look forward to Tuesday". End of year report for the evaluation of A.R.T. program. Unpublished report.

Cox, G. (1998). Teaching music in the UK secondary schools: Some life history perspectives. A paper presented in the American Education Research Association, San Diego (April, 1998)

Dewey, J. (1934). *Art as experience.* New York: Perigee Books.

Efland, A.D. (1990). *A history of art education.* New York: Teachers College Press.

Efland, A.D. (1983). School art and its social origin. *Studies in Art Education,* 24, 49–57.

Efland, A.D. (1976). School art style: A functional analysis. *Studies in Art Education,* 17(2)

Goodlad, et. al., (1979). *Curriculum Inquiry: The study of curriculum practice.* New York: McGraw–Hill.

Graue, M.E. and Walsh, D.J. (1998). *Studying children in context: Theories, methods, and ethics.* Thousand Oaks, CA: Sage Publications.

Grossman, P. and Stodolsky, S. (1997). Considerations of content and the circumstances of secondary school teaching. *Review of research in education,* 20, 179–221.

Housen, A. (2000). *Voices of viewers: Interactive research, theory, and practice.* A paper presented in American Education Research Association. New Orleans, April 2000.

Housen, A. and Duke, L. (1998). Responding to Alper: Representing the MoMA studies on visual literacy and aesthetic development. *Visual Arts Research,* 24(1), 91–102.

Korzenik, D. (1985). *Drawn to art.* Hanover and London: University Press of New England.

Langer, S. K. (1957). *Problems of art.* New York: Charles Scribner's Sons.

Logan, F. (1955). *Growth of art in American schools.* New York: Harper and Brothers.

Smith, R. (1986). *Excellence in art education.* Reston, VA: National Art Education Association.

Thompson, C. M.(ed.) (1995). *The visual arts and early childhood learning.* Reston, VA: National Art Education Association.

Thompson, C. M. (1990) "I make a mark": The significance of young children's talk about their art. *Early Childhood Research Quarterly,* 5, 215–232.

Thompson, C. M., and Bales, S. (1991). "Michael doesn't like my dinosaurs": Conversation in a preschool art class. *Studies in Arts Education,* 43–55.

Wasser, J. and Bresler, L. (1996). Working in the interpretive zone: Conceptualizing collaboration in qualitative research teams. *Educational Researcher,* 25(5), 5–15.

Wolf, D. (1989). Artistic learning as conversation. In D. J. Hargreaves (Ed.), *Children and the arts* (pp. 22–40). Philadelphia, PA: Open University Press.

Wygant, F.(1993). *School art in American culture 1820–1970.* Cincinnati, Ohio Interwood Press.

ACKNOWLEDGMENT

I am indebted to Judy Davidson Wasser, Deb Ceglowski, Nelson Fertig, Jane Zander, Mary Lemons, Nancy Hertzog and Hsueh–yin Ting for their important contributions to the study. Many thanks to Tina Thompson, Julie Basu and Francois Tochon for reading this paper and for their helpful comments, and to Eunju Yun for excellent editorial help.

An early version of this chapter was published in *Visual Arts Research, 25* (2), 1999, 25–37.

DANIEL K. THOMPSON

13. EARLY CHILDHOOD LITERACY EDUCATION, WAKEFULNESS, AND THE ARTS

> The arts are a field in which we place our own dreams, thoughts, and desires
> alongside those of others, so that solitudes can meet to their joy sometimes, or to their
> surprise, and sometimes to their disgust. When you boil it all down, that is the social
> purpose of art: the creation of mutuality, the passage from feeling into shared
> meaning (Hughes, 1996, p. 32).

It is difficult to find the exact place where early childhood literacy instruction and instruction in the arts connect. Perhaps it is difficult because most of us in literacy education do not speak often or effectively about art. Perhaps too this reluctance springs from our sense of a concern that we know too little about art to speak intelligently about a subject too often marginalized in our schools. Partially responsibile, no doubt, is the fact that these connections have gone largely undocumented (Albers, 1997, p. 338). I am certain we are not as aware of the works of art often found in young people's literacy processes and products as we could be. I have, however, come across an example of a teacher who has found the place where art and literacy connect. I found this example beautifully described by Lisa Siemens (1995), an elementary teacher in Manitoba. She tells of taking her second grade class to a park to write poetry toward the end of the school year. The trip was a culminating experience for a group of students who had become poets—young writers who had come to know writing as an art rather than a literary skill, and who had lived through a school year's worth of exposure to poetry, and of living the lives of poets. The following excerpts describe this experience:

> Each year on the first May morning, when the sun shines strongly and the sky is blue,
> we pick up our pencils and notebooks and make our way to the nearest park.... (p.
> 220)

> By the time we visited the park in May, we had already been so many places with
> poetry that I should not have been surprised that the children would find poetry in the
> park as well.... They had also turned into writers and poets who knew that writing was
> one way to slow down, to stop and notice the world, to save the wonders they were
> discovering (Siemens, 1966, p. 240).

Through Siemens' description I am reminded of Jardine's use of the term *ecopedagogy* (1994, p. 509). "Ecopedagogy in the area of language–arts practices inevitably centres the 'continuity and devotion' that a generative and deep understanding of writing and reading texts requires of me and of the life I actually live (in language)." As Jardine suggests, a proper pedagogy is an intermediary between the life of children and the world. Ecopedagogy becomes, then, an authentic pedagogy, allowing for stopping and noticing the world in all of its complexity and mystery.

L. Bresler and C.M. Thompson (eds.), The Arts in Children's Lives, 185–194.

Poetry, in this instance, becomes an art form available to the beginning writer to "save the wonders."

For the schools to allow young people to use poetry to describe what they see and feel when they stop and notice, requires a belief in two   pedagogical understandings that have received much attention recently. The first of these understandings is that young people are fully capable of making significant discoveries about the real world through observation and reflection. The second of these understandings is that a conventional literary form, such as poetry, can be used by young children as a medium to convey these new–found meanings.

Recently, those of us in early childhood literacy education have experienced an upheaval in our understanding of how children learn to read and write. We have come to know that fostering literacy growth means to build on the formidable understandings children have acquired about language before they enter our schools rather than to assume literacy skills begin with the acquisition of an inscribed set of skills children master in a prescribed sequence and at a time proscribed by mental age (Clay, 1982, Durkin, 1966). The research of Bissex (1980), Dyson (1982), and Purcell–Gates (1986) among many others have given us many convincing examples of the heretofore unknown linguistic and literacy competencies children have at their disposal to interpret the world in which they live. Commonly referred to as *emergent literacy*, this understanding directs early literary teachers to adjust their teaching to the language abilities of the young learner rather than to require the student to enter an alien world characterized by visual and auditory discrimination tasks which are often as mindless and distant as circling objects on worksheets.

Until the 1980's it was a common belief that our students should first learn the skills of reading and writing and then use their newly acquired reading and writing skills to learn. This scientific, logical approach makes perfect sense if the curriculum designer looks only at the most obvious characteristics of language; the graphemes (letters) and phonemes (sounds) of printed language. Under this general approach of thinking many of our beginning readers, at first eager to learn to read and write, get separated from meaningful language as they are kept in a holding pattern memorizing sight word lists and phoneme–grapheme correspondences. Societal, familial, and school pressures were enough for many students to learn to read despite this joyless, mechanistic approach. But for many children confusion was followed by failure; and this failure followed by resentment. Intense pressure to succeed in reading meant that failing to learn to read was failing in school in general. We witnessed a special education boom that chose to neglect the product of uninspired teaching as the source of the problem. The schools attempted to mollify the crisis by shuffling reluctant readers off to Chapter One, Reading Recovery, Learning Disabilities, and other programs that often repeated the same mechanistic approaches that had turned the students off to reading in the first place. Many schools found it easier to blame the students for the problem, rather than seriously consider the effects of their instructional methods. Parents, naturally concerned about their children's success with reading and writing, were often the first to cry out for special classes. Unaware of the potential of a different approach, they helped to feed the seemingly insatiable appetite for a solution through special education.

Fortunately, most of the leaders in literacy education, from those in higher education to those in the elementary schools, understood that blaming large numbers of students for their difficulties in coming to literacy undermined any hope of real progress. By exposing children to a variety of good literature instead of the intellectually vacuous, vocabulary controlled, basal readers of the past (Goodman, 1986), whole language teachers have encouraged a relationship with literature that is stimulating and meaningful. By rooting literacy instruction in the composition and comprehension of meaning, our young readers and writers edge closer to the transfer of personal meaning that is central to all authentic arts activities. By de–emphasizing the requirements for the conventions of writing (correct spelling, formal sentence and passage structure) we have freed up children to use their rich language skills to convey meaning in print unhampered by those conventions of print that lie beyond the student's zone of concern. The work of Bissex (1980) revealed that invented spelling, and other initial attempts to convey meaning in print, did not result in longstanding errors in spelling or the other conventions of writing. This has given teachers license to free beginning writers from the shackles of copy writing concerns as they focus on creating meaningful language.

The issue of concern for the young reader or writer confronted with a print composition or print comprehension task has now become "What does the writer mean?" rather than, "What did the writer say?" This difference is critical. Print has become something that requires personal interpretation. Meaning is not simply ideas transferred from page to mind, or mind to page, but ideas filtered through the mind of each student as they make meaning. This distinction was illustrated in Oliver Sacks' study of the autistic child artist Stephen (1995). Stephen, who could make incredibly detailed drawings of buildings of which he had only had a few moments to view, had, as Sacks described, "An unusual capacity to render the object as perceived" (p. 47). Unfortunately, as Sacks went on to say, Stephen "did not possess this ability to reconstruct." (p. 51). Stephen could *perceive*, but not *conceive*. How different this is from the poetic response of Siemens' students. Her students were recording their thoughts about the place, not merely recreating the place. Sacks summarized his impressions of Stephen: "I found myself thinking of him as a sort of train himself, a perceptual missile, traveling through life, noting, recording, but never appropriating, a sort of transmitter of all that rushed past—but himself unchanged, unfed by the experience" (p. 56). It is the proper goal of literacy instruction as well as arts instruction to teach children to conceive the world, not merely render those outward properties available to the senses.

As a way of introducing this new place of literature in the lives of children, I developed a lesson for my elementary teacher certification course in reading instruction. I open the first day of class by having the class engage in small groups discussions that has each student consider the question, *Has a book changed your life?* The answers vary considerably, but a few patterns emerge. Some students say that no, they can't think of a book that fundamentally changed their life. Some students mention books that changed their relationship to the act of reading, such as an intense reading of *Little Women,* or, *The Secret Garden.* Some mention the Bible.

By the end of our discussion they have discovered some significant facts about their own elementary experience. First, very few of the books that brought about change were read as part of a school assignment. Secondly, even those who could not name a book that had changed their life believed that it was possible for a book to do so. Thirdly, more often than not, their own experiences with reading class in elementary school actually turned them off to reading. Whether it was the relentless answering of questions at the end of the chapter; the assigning of irrelevant reading selections; or the absence of reading caused by a preponderance of workbooks and worksheets, these students often described how disconnected reading lessons had soured them to all reading. (I can't help but wonder how much worse it was for those students who were not as successful in school as my high achieving students were.) My take on what these students experienced in school was an unintentional reduction of the reading act to *perceive* what they read, rather than attempt to *conceive* meaning.

The shift from perception to conception that coincides with this emphasis on meaning making could not be a more fundamental change in the way our schools view learning. This is truly a revolution in how schools operate. To understand the significance of this change we can go back to what Walker Percy called "the sovereignty of the knower over the known" (1954/1980). The change is from expropriation to *appropriation*. That is, not to take someone else's learning, but to make the learning one's own. This can be done only if the life of the student is allowed to enter the learning situation.

Historically our schools have been predicated on the belief that it is the outsider's knowledge that is *sovereign*. Local, state, and national curriculum guidelines are examples of knowledge that is handed down, not created *by* the mind of the learner, *in* the mind of the learner. An emphasis on test scores, where students are pitted against each other, oftentimes compared to students of other nations, suggests a universality to the knowledge of an "educated" person, that belies what we know about how learning actually occurs with children. The mainstream approach to curriculum is a focus on ends, not means. Because such a curriculum negates the place of the child in his/her learning, learning becomes indoctrination. Curriculum guidelines and testing items may or may not reflect what teachers are capable of teaching to their students. Teachers are faced with a frightening and impossible conflict of interest over whether to teach what their students want to learn and are ready to learn on one hand, and what the curriculum designers deem appropriate for a larger society on the other. As Moffett told us, "Life...surely runs on an individualized curriculum" (1994, p. 238). To expect the schools to teach in a way that ignores the individual is antithetical to the needs of children and teachers and is doomed to failure. Moffett explained, "Teachers make a mash of schooling by trying to please others and do things they do not believe in because they are not free to make many decisions about methods and materials" (p. 53). Both teachers and students become strangers in their schools in the sense that Greene described: "I think that many, many people are moving through their life as strangers.... They are not reflecting; they are not choosing; they are not judging; in some sense they have nothing to say" (1978, p. 151).

The way to reintroduce the sovereignty of the learner into the school is to create environments for authentic inquiry. Students should not be asked to surrender their own curiosities to the demands of the school's curriculum. Student curiosity itself should be the force that defines the school's curriculum. Student inquiry not only answers to the student's desire to learn, but to the way in which language is learned. Echoing the findings of Vygotsky, Moffett tells us language learning occurs "through inner agendas acted on through communal means" (1994).

This rotation of the source of curriculum from expert to individual student redefines the role of the arts throughout the schools. The arts become a system, a pathway, a vehicle, or, as Hughes called it, a "field." Taught in a developmentally appropriate way, and intended as a means to further communication, the arts, whether they be the language arts, the visual arts, or the performing arts, assume the place of what Short (1990) called a "sign system." For Ms. Siemens' second graders, poetry was such a system. Poetry was a tool for understanding the world. Poetry entered the world of the student as a way of conceiving it, appropriating it. Poetry was not only the message; it was the form, the *sign system* of the message.

Where traditional elementary literacy methods have failed, they have often failed because they did not recognize the relationship between the message and the understanding of the sign system. Traditional literacy classes for young children have emphasized an understanding of the formal properties of the sign system, leaving students behind, grasping for a connection between the ideas in their head, and the topic at hand. Our schools often ignore the fact that the students will seek a sign system if it provides an opportunity to enter their thoughts to "the field." When the whole language approach de–emphasized the formal conventions of writing, we learned of the rich messages children were bursting to share. Writing, shed of what young writers would naturally see as unnecessary convention, demystified the writing act. Astute teachers in turn took advantage of this enthusiasm to support the ways specific sign systems assisted in the child's desire to communicate. As students became more fluent, the sign system itself can become a topic of study. As Csikszentmihalyi (1990, p. 125) tells us:

> When a person realizes that a symbol system has an autonomous existence, related to but not homologous with the "paramount reality" of the everyday world, then a whole new set of rewards becomes available, the rewards of operating within the system itself. Intrigued by the opportunities of the domain, most students will make sure to develop the skills they need to operate within it. (p. 126)

A reciprocal relationship between the message maker and the sign system develops. The message maker masters the sign system to better convey the message, and, in turn, the students who have mastered the sign system engage in more sophisticated messages. Familiarity with the tools result in alternative as well as improved art forms.

As "we place our own dreams, thoughts, and desires alongside those of others," we do so within the framework provided by the arts. Art, as a tool, becomes both enabling and debilitating. One aspect of the arts is that they are a discipline. They direct ideas, at the same time they allow for their expression. The arts provide a place for new ideas. But not all ideas will conform to the prescribed discipline of the arts. The arts structure experience, but in the wrong hands, can smother authentic learning.

The art of teaching the arts is to know when the various disciplines of the arts themselves hinder personal involvement and when they encourage the scaffolding of student understanding. This knowing is a product of knowing the students well, and knowing the forms of art the students will use to add voice to their learning. This knowing depends, as Jardine (1994) tells us, "(upon) a living response to the living, deeply dependent interactions that pertain in the classroom" (p. 512).

The whole language movement is a movement away from an education that has been more concerned with the form of expression than the expression itself. The previous bottom–up approaches to reading and writing instruction that concentrated on the teaching of abstracted sub–skills such as phonics and grammar left students cold, unable to detect where all this was leading. The curriculum designers knew. But the message was inaccessible to the learners. Whole language teachers (and many teachers who were teaching in this manner long before the term "whole language" was coined) never lost sight of the fact that the language arts are a vehicle for expression, not an end in itself. With one eye on the psychological needs of the child, and the other eye on ways the language arts clarify student thought, whole language teachers empower students to express their ideas in ways unimaginable to the unassisted mind of the child. Siemens' second graders would not have come to learn poetry or consider themselves to be poets if she (1) had not directed them to poetry, and (2) had directed them in such a way that the students could not compose their own poetry or comprehend poetry in their own way. Siemens' students learned to stop and notice the world because their teacher wanted them to discover the world on their own. She provided the tool—poetry—so that they could see on their own. Had she *told* them what they were seeing, they would have remained strangers to their world with nothing to say. Siemens succeeded because she knew her art form, and she knew her students. Nothing short of this knowledge would suffice.

Siemens took her students through the stages of learning Hawkins tells us is necessary for an authentic understanding of poetry (1990, p. 10). Her students first achieved *competence*. Through exposure to examples to the act of poetry, and through discussions of the meanings and conveyances of meanings in poems, her students developed a vocabulary and personal knowledge of the processes and aims of poetry. Secondly, this understanding allowed for a period of *recognition* of their learning and enjoyment in producing their own poetry. Lastly, the students achieved *social recognition* through the sharing of their poetry with others who cared about what they had to share.

As this understanding develops, and the student progresses from novice, to apprentice, to poet, the act of writing itself becomes *autotelik* (Csikszentmihalyi, 1990, p. 131). A community of writers supports this acquired intrinsic motivation to read and write by providing assistance, audience, and a purpose to convey ideas. A poetry writing expedition answers to the need for a complex environment. Without this level of complexity, the need to communicate newfound understandings would not exist. Optimal educational experiences come about through "a synthesis of integration and differentiation—self and other, unity and diversity, affect and thought" (Csikszentmihalyi, 1993, p. 47). The students become engaged in a satisfying experience. We are drawn to theorists such as Csikszentmihalyi, who discover and detail the underlying principles of intrinsic motivation, because we believe authentic learning is fueled by an inner passion. The trick to all teaching is to connect the student with a motivation to learn. When the object of the learning provides its own motivation, teachers are free to allow their expertise to direct students where they may go to sustain their passion, rather than expend time and energy entertaining or cajoling. We are drawn to theories of intrinsic motivation too because we believe they are connected to how people should live in the world. A desire to learn is a desire for self–realization—the act of becoming truly human.

When self–realization becomes the goal of schools, the process of education becomes one of creating venues that push children outside of themselves, while, at the same time, allowing students to connect new learning to old. When Csikszentmihalyi tells us motivation requires a proper balance of challenge to skills, he tells us that the proper learning environment is both *of* and *outside of* the student. A way of understanding all teaching methods is to consider how educational movements have addressed the relative importance of child–centered versus content–centered approaches. To give too much attention in either of these directions is to ignore the source of motivation to learn. Jardine (1994) calls these two extremes *gericentrisim* and *pedocentrism*: two apt terms that suggest the need for educational programs to be personable and challenging:

> The child at the centre will always have to confront what is basic in curriculum if it is truly basic to the course of human life; what is basic in curriculum will always have to be understandable to the child, invigorating of the child's life and invigorated by their taking it up anew. Out of relation, both of these extremities become monstrous (Jardine, p. 511).

The arts, all the arts, answer to the task of self–realization, because it is through our means of expression we enter into what Hughes called "our mutuality." The entrance is not just a telling of our coming to self–realization but an act of self–realization itself. "A life without speech and without action... is literally dead to the world; it has ceased to be a human life because it is no longer lived among men" (Arendt, 1958, p. 176). Self–realization is impossible without an entry point, and the entrance cannot happen without an ability to *have* a voice and *hear* the voice of others. In this way the arts, which provide the structuring form to that voice, become instrumental to becoming human. "Speech corresponds to the fact of distinctiveness and is the actualization of the human condition of plurality, that is, of living as a distinct and unique being among equals" (Arendt, 1958, p. 178).

One can feel the connectedness between self–realization and speech when entering a school where the children's voices have been turned off in an attempt to control students by limiting behaviors. Whether the children are passing silently down a hallway, or sitting quietly for long periods in classrooms, often seated inches away from their classmates—a feeling of unease chills the room. To deny a child's voice in such a way is to deny the child's place and to assume that talking in the hallway or to a classmate is "mere talk." Schools comfortable with silence are most often schools comfortable with placing what is to be learned outside the voice of the student. Good teachers allow a lot of talking in their classrooms not only because opportunities to talk result in improved language learning, but because talk is one way students disclose themselves as human beings. A student without a voice is unknown and unknowable. No one can be fully human and anonymous. Speaking to others reveals us in our ambitions and humility. As Berry reminds us, language is not only "clothes for thought or imagination" but "there should be a fittingness of sound to subject" in the words we use (Berry, 1983, p. 103). The product of this art is the sound. The process of this fitting is the stuff of good teaching. The quality of this fit determines whether the acts become central to the life of the student, or remain an academic exercise disconnected to the tenor of one's own living.

The whole language movement, with its emphasis on the practice of using language in meaningful units, has forced a different kind of expertise on teachers. No longer satisfied to convey information piecemeal in incremental, bottom–up, sub–skill by sub–skill ways, teachers needed a new structuring process that allows for the complexity of language that "whole" language involves. Whole language teachers are not comfortable breaking down poetry into parts, and then teaching these parts in a linear progression until the topic has been covered. Instead, the teacher focuses her energies on conveying to students the wonder and purpose of poetry. Once that is accomplished, the nuances, terminologies, and other academic artifacts of poetry will be taught when, and to whom, the need arises. Although the students throughout the poetry unit expressed themselves in many ways in their responses, a familiarity with poetry was Siemens' goal. *Poetry* was taught because it is a form of expression recognized by adults.

This is where the adult world and the child's world meet—at the point of commonly understood, academically viable, modes of thinking and knowing. Applebee (1996) accurately describes this coming to know poetry through participation rather than as an observer as *knowledge–in–action*. Poetry is, as Applebee explains, "a recognizable paradigm that fits the definition of a culturally significant domain" (p. 3). The teacher's place is to help students participate in the conversations that occur within those domains. We avoid gericentrism by encouraging the expressions of children. We avoid pedocentrism by encouraging expression in ways a larger world can interpret and become involved. Knowledge becomes a product of negotiations, socially constructed through these conversations (Applebee, 1996, p. 40). In Siemens' class, poetry became both the *means* of conversation, and the *topic* of conversation. The student becomes armed not only with the knowledge of an art form that is the source of understanding and enjoyment, but has developed a new way to enter new conversations. I am reminded of an outstanding elementary certification student who wrote a response paper in verse for my reading methods course. Of the hundreds of such papers I read that semester, this was the first and only I received in a format that defied the syllabus requirements. It was a clever, delightfully concocted response that said what he wanted to say, in the way he wanted it said. His knowledge of poetry allowed him to enter a dialogue in a way he would have struggled with through more conventional means.

This band of activity between what Jardine called gericentrism and pedocentrism, within what Applebee calls knowledge–in–action, is the swatch cut by good literacy teachers. Because it helps to define the proper role of the teacher, it is safe to say it is neither child–centered nor is it content centered, but is *teacher*–centered. Only the teacher is in positions to know both the students and the particular knowledge domain well enough to find a suitable match. Teaching, as Ayers tells us, "is fundamentally about leadership... To choose teaching is to choose to enable the choice of others" (1993, p. 5).

Whole language encourages the development of the language arts by never losing sight of the need for each student's day to be focused on meaningful units of composition and comprehension. By creating a community of young poets, Siemens connects learning to life. Siemens, like all good teachers, put the life of her students ahead of, but not beyond, the discipline of poetry. The teacher's agenda is a daily agenda, with any long term goals corrected and altered because of the complexity of the student, whose understanding can never be accurately predetermined. Good teachers, like good farmers, as Berry (1983) reminds us, focus on *atonement* and *renewal* and *quality*. Educators outside the classroom, particularly those who harbor ideas of what students they can't personally know should learn, concern themselves with *training, newness,* and *quantity*.

Perhaps unwittingly, whole–language has borrowed its most consequential features from the longstanding principles of good art education. Art educators have long known that a student's motivation to learn to draw or paint or sculpt comes about largely through the practice of drawing and painting and sculpting. The proper scaffolding of art making presumes an environment where the majority of time is devoted to practice, and a carefully curtailed, but essential amount of time devoted to idea inception and technique. It has been art educators who have modeled to the rest of us outside art education the importance of valuing the process and products of our students' efforts. Art education has taught us (1) that the young student's art is every bit as much *art* as the art of adults because it reflects an authentic attempt to make art; and (2) that it is this authentic art making that encourages the young child to continue to create.

When you walk into a whole language classroom you see students reading to others, students writing on the walls, and classroom libraries that actually look like they are being used. The products of the work of the children is encouraged, highly valued and displayed prominently. As in an art galley it is displayed carefully and placed in a situation that invites response. Students in whole language classrooms are taught that reading and writing are not only mean to learning about something else, but part of what is learned. Whole language has adopted this understanding of the relationship between making and learning.

As a result of the strange and peculiar workings of our schools, art has in a way led a charmed existence. Because art education has been so marginalized, while literacy, math and science have taken center stage, art has been freed from some of the unfortunate obligations of which these other subjects have had to contend. Art education, because it is not as often viewed as central to the life of our schools has not suffered as much from the debilitating, regimenting effects of standardized testing, which serves to reduce learning to the mastery of lists of generic outcomes. Because school and state agencies have often treated art education as a somehow *nonacademic,* and often frivolous luxury, art classrooms have often shown more concern for the interests of its students who have been freed from the scrutiny of outsiders. Innovative teaching methods have been not so much accepted as condoned. I'm confident the state boards of education will eventually try to stick their hands in art education too in their misguided attempts to make schools accountable. But until then art classrooms, under the guidance of sensitive teachers, will remain places where teachers and students can create something meaningful despite the fact that art teachers often reside in the dankest classroom (indeed, if they even have a room to call their own in the school), suffer the worst of schedules, and can rely on the most fickle administrative support. Many of us regular classroom teachers are envious of the freedom to invent a curriculum that our art teaching colleagues take for granted. When my students would return from the art classroom, with faces swelled with pride, their hands carefully cradling half–wet paintings, it was clear that something special had been going on.

Whole language teachers have often captured the excitement for learning commonplace in many art classrooms. I don't think they perceive art education as a model, but they certainly are doing many of the same things. Moffett (1994) told us, "If we consider literacy holistically we realize that it grows out of non–verbal contexts out of play, out of sociality, and out of the physical activities that include the arts" (Moffett, p. 239).

Art as source of language learning completes its mission for literacy. It has been argued here that art can be both the means of expression and the topic of discussion. Adding art as a source of literacy learning suggests that the schools should reverse the place of art. Its centrality to language learning does not match its present marginal position. Rarely acknowledged, the whole language movement's most fundamental tenets rest on the longstanding practice of good art education. But this past leads both ways. Art educations can benefit from the widespread belief in the fundamental utilitarian nature of becoming literate. If those involved in creating and developing school curriculums will recognize that the arts offer both the methods and the content fundamental to becoming fully literate, then an aesthetic education will emerge as a definition of basic education. I am convinced, that wakefulness to experience, which is the most fundamental of education goals, depends on our schools' willingness to see art education as the model for teaching in all of our disciplines.

REFERENCES

Albers, P. Art as literacy. *Language Arts, 74,* 338–350, 1997.
Arendt, H. *The human condition.* Chicago: University of Chicago Press, 1958.
Applebee, A. *Curriculum as conversation.* Chicago: University of Chicago Press, 1996.
Ayers, W. *To teach: The journey of a teacher.* New York: Teachers College Press, 1993.
Berry, W. *Standing by words.* San Francisco: North Point Press, 1983.
Bissex, G. *Gnys at wrk: A child learns to write and read.* Cambridge: Harvard University Press, 1980.
Clay, M. *Observing young readers.* Exeter, N.H.: Heinemann Press, 1982.
Csikszentmihalyi, M. Literacy and intrinsic motivation. *Daedalus, 119,* 115–140, 1990.
Csikszentmihalyi, M. Contexts of optimal growth in childhood. *Daedalus, 122,* 31–56, 1993.
Durkin, D. *Children who ready early.* New York: Teachers College Press, 1966.
Dyson, A. H. Reading, writing, and language: Young children solving the written language puzzle. *Language Arts, 59,* 204–214, 1982.
Goodman, K. *What's whole in whole language?* Portsmouth, N.H.: Heinemann Press, 1986.
Greene, M. *Landscapes of learning.* New York: Teachers college press, 1978.
Hawkins, D. The roots of literacy. *Daedalus, 119,* 1–14, 1990.
Hughes, R. The case for the elitist do–gooders. *The New Yorker, 72,* 32, 1996, May 27.
Jardine, D. W. 'Littered with literacy': An ecopedagogical reflection on whole language, pedocentrism and the necessity of refusal. *Journal of Curriculum Studies, 26,* 509–524, 1994.
Moffett, J. *The universal schoolhouse: Spiritual awakening through education.* San Francisco: Jossey–Bass, 1994.
Percy, W. *The message in the bottle.* New York: Farrar, Straus & Giroux, 1954/1980.
Purcell–Gates, V. Three levels of understanding about written language acquired by young children prior to formal instruction. In J. Niles and R. Lalik, eds. *Solving problems in literacy: Learners, teachers, and researchers.* Rochester, N.Y.: National Reading Conference, 1986.
Sack, O. A neurologists notebook: Prodigies. *The New Yorker, 65,* 44–51, 1995.
Short, K. *Learning: Making connections across sign systems.* Paper presented at the National Reading conference, Miami Beach, FL, 1990 December.
Siemens, L. "Walking through the time of kids": Going places with poetry. *Language Arts, 73,* 234–240, 1996.

An early version of this chapter was published in *Visual Arts Research, 25* (2), 1999, 90–98.

DONNA J. GRACE AND JOSEPH TOBIN

14. PLEASURE, CREATIVITY, AND THE CARNIVALESQUE IN CHILDREN'S VIDEO PRODUCTION

It is a sunny October morning in Pearl City, Hawaii. The third–graders at Waiau Elementary School are seated on the floor, ready to watch the videos they have made. As the room is darkened and the monitor lights up, the students' eyes widen, and grins appear. The children giggle, squirm, and nudge one another as they recognize faces on the screen.

The first video, *The Dog Who Knew How to Play Tricks*, is about a dog and a cat who enter a talent show. Enjoying seeing their peers pretend to be animals, the children chuckle at the silly antics performed before the camera. Next, there is *The Planet Knick–Knack*, a musical about a dog named Beethoven, who runs away from home and gets lost. The video closes with the cast singing the familiar childhood song "This Old Man." The audience spontaneously joins in a chorus of slightly off–key voices. The third piece is called *Chase Master Monster*. The video opens with three boys playing the parts of little monsters who live on the very hot sun. They wake up one morning, put on their air–conditioned shoes, and begin playing the game "Chase Master Monster." The narrator then informs the viewers that the little monsters "fall on their butts" and burn them on the hot sun. On screen, the actors are running around in imaginary agony, swatting at their buttocks and shouting, "Ooh! Ouch! Ooh! Ouch! My buns are burning! My buns are burning!" They keep running until they find some ice, which they rub on their burning rear ends. In the next shot, their eyes roll upward and they sigh with deep relief. Their expressions are those of pure bliss.

The class finds this scene hilarious. Performers and audience are fused in a surge of camaraderie, a spirit of oneness joined by laughter. The adults in the room exchange uneasy smiles. This festive moment is formed in relation to us, the authority figures, and fueled by the knowledge that classroom norms have been transgressed. The moment passes, and the next video begins. The children are quiet, focused on the new images appearing before them. The adults, however, are left with lingering doubts and questions. The equilibrium of the classroom has been unsettled. Taken for granted boundaries have blurred before our eyes.

Video production in the Waiau classrooms provided an opportunity for students to incorporate their own interests, experiences, and desires into schoolwork. A space was located where they could explore the limits of speech, behavior, and humor allowed in the classroom. In our three years of doing video

L. Bresler and C.M. Thompson (eds.), The Arts in Children's Lives, 195–214.
© 2002 *Kluwer Academic Publishers. Printed in the Netherlands.*

work with children at Waiau, we found many examples of students pushing the boundaries and transgressing the norms of everyday life in school. Alongside the many entirely acceptable and nonproblematic scripts the children wrote, a number of more questionable scenes and storylines emerged. These pieces contained words, actions, and situations that challenged classroom norms and decorum. For the children, these moments of curricular slippage and excess provided the opportunity to produce their own pleasures, on their own terms, in the classroom. Yet, these same moments posed questions and gave rise to tensions for the teachers.

That children are frequently fascinated with things that adults consider to be rude, uncouth, or gross comes as no surprise. Alison Lurie (1990) traces the subversive nature of many popular children's stories, rhymes, and verses from the Grimm brothers on through the present day, and Tom Newkirk (1992) writes of children's predisposition for poop jokes, farts, and insect mutilation. Peter McLaren (1986) and Paul Willis (1981), among others, have documented ways students have found to subvert school control and authority. However, these behaviors usually occur outside of the school agenda. Significantly, the transgressions that emerged in the Waiau video project were organized and authorized *within* the curriculum rather than apart from it.

This chapter explores the issues and tensions that emerged during a three–year project in which the informal, unofficial, and everyday interests of children were brought into the curriculum through the medium of video production. Drawing on Mikhail Bakhtin's writings on the carnivalesque (1968), and Roland Barthes' (1975) concepts of *plaisir* and *jouissance*, we argue that video production opens up a space where students can play with the boundaries of language and ideology and enjoy transgressive collective pleasures. This boundary–crossing and pleasure–getting by the children in the midst of the curriculum pushes teachers to think about their authority in new ways.

The Study

A great deal is known about children as readers and writers in classrooms. Little, in contrast, is known about children as producers of video texts. Video production is a new form of literacy that integrates art, language skills, problem solving, technical proficiency, and performance. Although there are manuals available on the technical skills involved, there has yet to be a critical, theoretically informed study of video production with young students. The small body of work that examines the process of production comes largely out of the United Kingdom and has involved older students (Buckingham, 1990; Buckingham & Sefton–Green, 1994; Buckingham, Graheme, & Sefton–Green, 1995). With the use of video technology rapidly increasing in school systems worldwide, research is needed that can help us understand what happens to students and teachers when cameras are put in students' hands.

In light of these facts, we developed a video curriculum project with a group of teachers at an elementary school in Hawaii. In meetings with the teachers, it was decided to begin integrating video production into the curriculum, building upon the children's interests in and prior knowledge of television and movies. This was viewed as a unique opportunity to enhance the elementary language and literacy curriculum while increasing our understanding of children as communicators and meaning makers.

The video curriculum was tested in two third–grade classes during the spring of 1992. It was then introduced to grades 1–6 in the fall and continued for the next two school years. In all, eight classes of approximately 25 children actively participated in the video curriculum. This chapter focuses on work that emerged in grades 1–3.

Our role throughout the project was that of participant–observers, with the emphasis shifting over time from the former to the latter. During the pilot study and the first phase of video production, we were actively involved in developing and teaching the curriculum to both the teachers and the students. As the teachers and children grew more comfortable and confident with the process, we settled into the role of observers.

Our research method is an ethnographically informed case–study of children as videographers. We do not view children as a distinct cultural group separate from adults, but as an interpretive community, a subgroup within the larger culture, with shared interests, experiences, and understandings, reflecting their age, generation, and situation as students. As Anne Dyson (1993) writes, school children operate in a peer social world framed by a sense of "being in this together" (p.3). Their responses to school authority often include attempts to claim a space for themselves in the classroom and to assert their collective identity as children. Bringing the unofficial into the official is one way of establishing territory of their own and forming networks of peer relationships in the process.

Child–centered Pedagogy

During the pilot phase of the student video production project, we spent two to three days a week working with the children in Waiau classrooms on scripting, storyboarding, using video equipment, and the production process. The children in each classroom were then placed in groups and asked to retell, script, storyboard, and tape a familiar story. The resulting productions included such favorites as *Chicken Licken, Snow White, Jack and the Beanstalk, Henny Penny,* and *The Princess and the Pea.* From an adult standpoint, these productions tended to lack creativity. However, they functioned as good entry points into video production. The retellings seemed to offer the children some safety, security, and predictability while they were working in this new medium with unfamiliar technology. In the second phase of the project, we decided to give the children free choice in content and genre, putting many of our teacherly beliefs about classroom control and the curriculum to the test.

Progressive educators speak of "giving children choice," "building on their interests, background knowledge, and experiences," and "making learning fun." These pedagogical assumptions underlie student–centered, inquiry–based, whole–language, and constructivist approaches to curriculum and instruction. Most often, when teachers tell students, "You can write on anything you want to," the students interpret this invitation to mean "anything you want to that I, a teacher and an adult, will consider appropriate for a school assignment." Yet occasionally, moments arise in the classroom when students do work that ignores, transgresses, or exceeds teacherly, adult notions of appropriateness. Such moments may occur in a writing assignment, a literature circle, an art project, or a science experiment. At Waiau we learned that there is something about video production that produces an outpouring of transgressive, excessive moments, which push us to question how comfortable we are when the curriculum becomes child–centered.

Giving Children Choice

Our intent was to give the students considerable latitude in the content of their videos. The teachers, however, had a hard time relinquishing their right and inclination to guide, shape, and influence these choices. In order to see what would happen if students' unrestrained choices were authorized in the classroom, we asked the teachers to give the children as much leeway as they felt they could. As video production got underway, it became apparent that the scripts created by the children were strongly influenced by popular culture. They included X–Men, ninjas, and characters from the television shows *Saved by the Bell, The Simpsons, Full House,* and *Ghostwriter*, and from such movies as *Cop and a Half, Airborne,* and *Jurassic Park*. Themes and characters were also occasionally drawn from more controversial television programs and movies including *Beavis and Butthead, Studs, Child's Play,* and *Friday the 13th*. Tensions arose. Although the children were reading, writing, storyboarding, editing, and gaining technical proficiency in their video work, notions of normalcy in school were being challenged. As popular culture entered the classrooms, the unofficial interests of the children shifted from the periphery of classroom life to center stage.

Fear of the Interests and Knowledge of Children

Although child–centered curricula emphasize connecting the world of school to the lives of the children, many of their everyday pleasures and interests lie untouched and untapped in the classroom. Movies, television, videos, popular magazines, fiction, and video games contribute to the shaping of student experiences and subjectivities. However, these interests must typically be left on the doorstep when arriving at school each day.

As Buckingham (1990) and Buckingham and Sefton–Green (1994) point out, there are many reasons for the failure to incorporate the popular culture of children into the curriculum. Perhaps foremost is the danger of contagion.

Television, movies, comics, videos, and electronic games have commonly been associated with such negative effects as passivity, immorality, poor health, delinquency, a decline in literacy skills, acts of aggression, the loss of innocence, and desensitization to crime and violence. Although adults consider themselves immune to such effects, children are believed to be hopelessly and helplessly vulnerable to them. Such concerns and fears have resulted in a growing body of articles and studies on the relationship between children and the media. Although studies by such media education scholars as Hodge and Tripp (1986) and Buckingham (1990) have shown that children are sophisticated media viewers, a narrow, often distorted, and limiting view of children's interest in and knowledge about the media persists. The political left and right meet in curious agreement on the debilitating effects of media on children. Where the right faults the media for undermining the morals and values of the dominant society, the left blames the media for perpetuating them. Children are seen as passive and powerless mini–consumers duped by the "culture industry." Gemma Moss (1989, p. 2) writes that teachers tend to accept this view and "assume a wholesale swallowing of popular culture by their pupils." The children's video work in our project provided evidence to the contrary. We found that they used this medium to play with the meanings and messages of the media, rather than absorbing them uncritically.

A second reason for the exclusion of popular culture from the curriculum is the threat to teacher supremacy. Teachers like to feel that they are standing on secure ground when it comes to curriculum. Students often know more than their teachers do about popular television shows, movies, and video games. In this domain, the children are the experts.

A third reason relates to the fear of erasure of boundaries. When popular culture is brought into the curriculum, lines are crossed between the high and the low, the official and the unofficial, the authoritative discourses of the school and the internally persuasive discourses of the children. The canon is compromised.

In the face of these concerns, we nevertheless insist that popular culture should be brought into the primary school curriculum. Because school privileges the written word, the knowledge children bring to school about plots, characters, genre is often underestimated in the classroom. Including children's knowledge of popular culture in the curriculum provides another avenue for children to enter school literacy, especially for those who have had limited experiences with reading in the home. We also support teaching about movies and television in the primary grades because the role of pleasure has long been overlooked and neglected in schooling. Most children find great pleasures in popular culture. Making a place for such pleasures in the classroom can enrich the school lives of children.

We are aware, however, that by bringing popular culture into the official curriculum, there is the danger that adults will colonize one of the last outposts of children's culture. Bringing popular culture into the school curriculum may serve to rationalize and regulate it. Once transported into the domain of the classroom, these outside interests are in jeopardy of being purified, homogenized, and reconstituted as curriculum or motivational strategies. When popular culture is co–opted by the teacher, aspects of pleasure associated with it may be destroyed. Our goal, therefore, should be to validate the popular cultural interests of children without appropriating them. Student video production provides an arena for this to occur.

Popular Culture and Video Production

The children's videos produced in our study were greatly influenced by the media and popular culture. But the videos do far more than mimic and imitate. Rather than simply replicate remembered plots and themes, children play with aspects of the familiar and conjoin them in imaginative and pleasing ways. In the children's videos, the world of popular culture is interwoven with the world of school. In *Zip and the Ninja Turtles*, for instance, a group of first–graders turned a favorite classroom book about a lost dog into a tale involving a runaway worm that is eventually rescued by three Ninja Turtles. Another group of children from the same class created a story entitled *The Nine Astronauts and the Revenge of the Slimy Earthlings*. This tale involves a shootout with drool–covered, earthling–eating aliens and ends with the cast singing a song they had learned in school about the planets. A third–grade group did a take–off on the *Wizard of Oz* called *Dorothy Goes to Candyland,* in which Dorothy visits a land where candy grows abundantly on trees. There she is threatened by a slime–breathing, rock–spewing blob that she eventually destroys with a magic candy gun. These are but a few examples of how children imaginatively combined their interests in movies and television with classroom literacy and knowledge.

These videos were not unlike the stories children might write when given free choice of content in a language arts assignment. However, the medium of video, along with the dynamics of the collaborative group process, worked to enhance children's sense of freedom to explore and transgress. The extra–linguistic elements of gesture, facial expression, sound effects, and performativity carried the written words into a new and sometimes forbidden realm. As the students incorporated their own interests and pleasures into the videos, they pushed at the borders of propriety, reminding us of the fragility of classroom equilibrium.

Clearly, the children's sense of audience influenced the type of videos they produced. When the intended viewers included parents, relatives, or other community members, their videos took on quite different forms. This was demonstrated in videos the students created for the school's Open House, the sixth grade graduation, and for competition in a video festival, all of which were very well received. However, when produced with their peers as the anticipated audience, the content noticeably strayed from adult–pleasing fare. Fueled by the desire to surprise, amuse, and entertain, the content of some of these videos was of questionable taste, including depictions of drool, burps, blood, dripping mucus, butt jokes, aggression, violence, and occasional severed body parts. These scenes were enormously appealing to the children and the source of a good deal of transgressive excitement. What was most popular with the children, tended to be unpopular with the teachers.

Video Production and the Carnivalesque

In analyzing the children's videos, it became apparent that they did not fit neatly into traditional categories. They hovered in sort of a literary homelessness in the classroom. Genres were collapsed and borders erased. Their videos, to use Bakhtin's term, were "carnivalesque." In *Rabelais and His World* (1968), Bakhtin described the world of the carnival as one of laughter, bodily pleasures, hierarchical inversions, and bad taste. Bakhtin categorized the manifestations of carnival humor into three forms: ritual spectacles (feasts, pageants, and marketplace festivals), comic verbal compositions (oral and written parodies), and billingsgate (curses, oaths, slang, profanity). The laughter provoked by such humor was bawdy, crude, and irreverent. Rank and privilege were temporarily overturned. The people portrayed kings as fools and peasants as royalty. It was the official world as seen from below.

Over time, the carnival of the Middle Ages was gradually suppressed. It became licensed, regulated, and tamed. Its remnants survive today in Mardi Gras, the Carnival of Brazil, and Germany's *Fasching*. Elements of the ancient carnivals, Bakhtin reminds us, live on in our everyday life as well. These carnivalesque moments foreground freedom, pleasure, and desire. They unsettle the existing order of things. They use satire and laughter to imagine how things might be otherwise. Mary Russo (1986) writes, "the masks and voices of carnival resist, exaggerate, and destabilize the distinctions and boundaries that mark and maintain high culture and organized society. . . .They suggest a counter production of culture, knowledge, and pleasure" (p. 218).

Like the carnivals, fairs, and marketplaces Bakhtin wrote about, the classroom may be viewed as a site of conflicting agendas and desires where the high (teachers and the curriculum) and the low (children and their interests and desires) meet. Carnival offered peasants opportunities to symbolically invert the usual hierarchies and imagine different roles and relationships. Video production at Waiau offered many such opportunities. With the click of a button, students could become rock stars, royalty, or superheroes. Tiny children might portray giants or all–powerful rulers. The academically marginalized had the opportunity to choose roles as scholars, teachers, or wizards. Serious children could play parts in comedies and parodies, and the quiet and shy could blossom under the guise of fantasy. Through the medium of video, the students were able to momentarily acquire the power of the represented.

The children's video productions often featured the parodic, the fantastic and horrific, the grotesque, and the forbidden. These scenarios enabled the children to locate a space where collective pleasures were produced. As with carnival, however, there were also darker sides to the merriment. Without this darker side, carnival would lose much of its potency and seductive power. In our project, the darker side emerged when students discussed making videos involving cruelty and hurtful stereotypes. Topics in this category included portrayals of animal cruelty, racial caricatures, a stuttering singer, and a blind man who stumbles into various objects around him. In some cases, the groups themselves dismissed these ideas, and in others the teachers exercised their veto.[1]

Laughter and Parody

For Bakhtin (1981), parody, the "laughing word," is a corrective of reality. Embodying dual intentions, it contains both the meanings of the author and the refracted meanings of the parodied text or situation (p. 324). Parody can bolster cultural barriers as well as break them down. In some situations, parody functions to release tension, thereby preserving the status quo. In others, it offers opportunities for opposition tempered by humor. Regardless of the outcome, parody provides a space for critique and change. It may pose questions, challenge assumptions, and offer new possibilities.

Our students well appreciated the pleasures derived from humor and parody. In the wink of an eye, the serious became comical in their videos. The driving force in the children's scriptwriting was the desire to make the audience laugh. Several of the student groups incorporated parody in their videos. They produced ridiculing and humorous versions of television shows, movies, books, classrooms, and field trips. Two videos parodied marriage (*The Three Stooges Get Married* and *The Rock and Roll Marriage*). A second grade group, which began quite seriously to script their research report on the Gila monster, wound up with the lizard eating the reporter. The third–grade production of *The Magic School Bus Visits Plant Quarantine* parodies a class field trip. The video begins with students sitting in a row, frowning and slumped over, with their heads in their hands. In a dreary, singsong monotone, they say in unison that school is boring and they want to go on a field trip. Miss Frizzle, played by a boy wearing an outlandish wig, agrees. They go to Plant Quarantine, where animals are held on their arrival in Hawaii. There, scenes such as a student getting his hand sliced off by a man–eating piranha alternate with very scholarly reports on toucans, flowers, and fire ants. In other videos, laughter is produced through humorous depictions of tyrannical teachers, ridiculous rules, and rebellious students.

The very ambiguity of parody is the source of the power and pleasure associated with it. Initially, the teachers wondered how such parodies should be taken. However, rather than view these scenes as threatening or subversive, the teachers eventually came to perceive them in a generally pro–social light. They were able to overcome their initial fears and join in the pleasures of the carnivalesque. The teachers eventually realized that the children were not attacking them or their school routines and practices—these teachers did not have deadly boring classes, nor had they sent children to sit in the corner; it was the stereotype, the comic–book representation of school, that was the object of ridicule.[2]

The Fantastic and Horrific

The students' videos demonstrated their fascination with these genres. They overwhelmingly wanted to make videos that were scary, funny, or both. Their video plots were full of monsters, ghosts, aliens, beasts, werewolves, and giant scorpions that frightened, threatened, and eventually were conquered by the protagonists. Inevitably, these conquests provided an opportunity for the usually forbidden play–fighting and produced a great deal of transgressive excitement for the children. In portraying such awesome, fear–inspiring creatures and characters, the students experienced power, agency, and control. Neither size nor gender determined who would play these roles. One of the smallest children in a first–grade class portrayed Magnito, a powerful villain and enemy of the X–Men, and girls frequently chose to play fierce Ninjas, creatures from outer space, or mummies and vampires awakened from the dead. Although the hero and monster roles are traditionally figured as masculine (strong, brave, tough, fearless) in the movies and television programs the children see, this was not necessarily the case in their own productions. Traditional masculinity and femininity were frequently muted and blurred in their video stories.

The horrific beings in these scripts usually wound up being more humorous than terrifying, more like the "gay monsters" of the Rabelaisian world and less like the terrifying creatures typical in films of this genre. They tended to be inserted into very childlike plots and in a context of play, providing the children the opportunity to explore their fears and fantasies in the safety of the group, surrounded by laughter.

The Grotesque Body

A central concern of carnival is the body. According to Bakhtin (1984), the grotesque carnival body represents a lowering of all that is that is high, privileged, sacred, or ideal. In this oppositional form, the body serves as a site of resistance to regulation, social control, and definitions of normalcy. The grotesque body is ugly and monstrous in comparison to the classical body, as represented in Renaissance statuary. Where the classical body is pure, clean, finished, beautifully formed, and with no evident openings or orifices, the sensual, earthy, grotesque body is protuberant, excessive, impure, unfinished. It emphasizes the parts of the body that open up to the world: flared nostrils, gaping mouth, the anus, and what Bakhtin termed "the lower bodily strata" (belly, legs, feet, buttocks, genitals). The grotesque body is overflowing and transgresses its own limits. Bakhtin (p. 24) writes that these images, over time, have lost their positive dimension. However, in the Renaissance, they represented becoming and growth, a phenomenon in transformation, an unfinished metamorphosis. In this sense, the grotesque body has much in common with childhood. Not yet fully formed nor matured, children typically do not share the repulsion adults feel with sweat, runny noses, dirty bodies, or germ–spewing sneezes and coughs. Rather, they are full of interest and curiosity about their bodily orifices and functions, as their videos make clear.

Images of the grotesque body were prominent in the students' videos. Their works provided many examples of the gaping, oversized, overflowing body. Some scripts also contained suggestions of cannibalism, or the swallowing up of bodies by other bodies. Stam (1989) refers to this as the ultimate act in dissolving the boundaries between self and other (p. 126). In a first–grade production of *Chicken Licken Goes to Jupiter*, for example, the story ends with Chicken Licken getting eaten up by a mean space creature before she is able to complete her journey to reach the king. In *The Nine Astronauts and the Revenge of the Slimy Earthlings*, another group of first–graders created a script involving a confrontation between several astronauts and the aliens they encounter on the planet Saturn. Upon sight of the astronauts, the aliens begin rubbing their tummies, licking their lips, and trying to capture the astronauts to feed to their babies. In enacting this script, the aliens worked up a healthy supply of saliva, which oozed profusely from their chomping, hungry mouths. Like all other examples of the grotesque body, such scenes produced the intended surprise, delight and carnivalesque laughter in their viewing peers.

The Forbidden

Scatological, parodic, and grotesque elements in children's videos have the power to offend adult sensibilities, but they can be dismissed as typical amusements of childhood. We shake our heads and convey our disapproval but assume that with increased maturity such interests will fade. Fighting, aggression, and suggestions of violence in children are more disturbing to adults. In many homes and schools, play–fighting is forbidden, on grounds of safety. Yet, more children are injured by falling off playground equipment or participating in sports than in play–fighting. The fact that monkey bars, jungle gyms, and ballgames are rarely banned suggests that something other than safety underlies adults' concerns about play–fighting. Aggressive behavior in children taps into much deeper fears about crime, violence, and moral decline in society as a whole. Something about children's delight in mock violence threatens adult authority and disrupts culturally constructed notions about childhood innocence. Thus, we impose rules and prohibitions and attempt to socialize children away from such behaviors. Nancy King (1992) writes that in education the goal has been to create environments and situations in which children will produce only "good" play, consisting of socially approved behaviors such as rule–following, cooperation, turn–taking, inclusion, socially approved uses of imagination and conversation, and good sportsmanship. In other words, "good" play has little in common with the everyday, nonrestricted play of children. As any parent or teacher of young children knows, toy guns may be banned, but fingers can be used as pretend gun barrels; play–fighting may be prohibited, but rough and tumble activities rarely disappear.

A predisposition to play–fighting was clearly evident in the children's video stories. Group after group incorporated such scenes, usually involving some form of martial arts. These usually forbidden behaviors produced high levels of transgressive excitement in both the performers and their child audience. In a third–grade production of *The Four Ninjas* these scenes turned out to be the story's driving force. This tale began with fighting practice for the ninjas (three boys and one girl). Soon they discover that their father has mysteriously died, and their mother has been kidnapped. Preparing to avenge their father's death and rescue their mother, they go back to fighting practice. The next day, the enemy ninjas, played by two girls, invade the classroom, and the big battle begins. It goes on until the evil ninjas are eventually conquered. The four victorious ninjas end the night with a celebration at Pizza Hut.

In this video, as well as in others with similar themes, the fighting scenes were greatly elaborated. In each of these scenes, good triumphed over evil, and there was no intent to harm. Enacted in a spirit of play, these scenes have a comic character and begin and end with laughter. Bakhtin (1984) writes that in the carnivalesque, "ruthless slaughter" and death are "transformed into a merry banquet," and "bloodshed, dismemberment, burning, death, beatings, blows, curses, and abuses – all these elements are steeped in 'merry time'" (p. 211). In neither classroom nor carnival are such scenes meant to represent or transfer to the real. That children find pleasure in these mock battles does not mean that they enjoy violence in real life. As with the grotesque body, they find power, pleasure and opportunities for resistance in portraying these strong, bold, and courageous characters.

In acting out hand–to–hand combat, the children were also able to engage in a physical closeness with one another that they are otherwise denied. The body–to–body contact characteristic of the carnivalesque crowd appeared to be a source of pleasure for the children in their video fighting scenes, allowing for bodily contact typically repressed by social codes in school. Once past the preschool hand–holding stage, students have few opportunities for touch. Yet such sensations are still needed, desired, and enjoyed by them. Play–fighting provides a space for this while producing a very intense form of transgressive pleasure.

Another area of the forbidden that surfaced in the video projects was the notion of animal cruelty. This occurred as a third–grade group of two boys and two girls were trying to decide on a topic for their script. Portraying a mad scientist and doing crazy experiments had been suggested, so the group members were flipping through science books looking for ideas. One of the boys asked if they "could do some animal cruelty," adding "or is cruelty not allowed?" The rest of the group did not appear to be surprised, concerned, or even interested in this query. They just shrugged and indicated that they preferred to go ahead with the mad scientist idea. As observers of this scene, we were seized by competing impulses. On the one hand, we wanted to question the boy as to his intentions. On the other hand, we were disturbed by what we had witnessed and wanted to erase ourselves from the scene. The taken–for–granted had been unsettled, and the familiar had suddenly become strange. This overheard bit of conversation had denatured the ordinary and brought us face to face with the tenuousness, contingency, and uncertainty that lie just below the surface of classroom pedagogy and practice. Why had this boy suggested animal cruelty? Why weren't the others surprised by this suggestion?[3]

In contemplating the parodic, horrific, fantastic, and forbidden elements in the students' videos, it is important to remember that they occurred in a playful, carnivalesque context. The video stories were not empty reproductions or mirror reflections of their perceptions of reality. They were more like funhouse mirrors, where all is exaggerated and distorted for comic effect. The very *unreality* of the children's stories contributed to the enthusiasm and enjoyment associated with them. The videos gave students the chance to represent their desires, to work through their fears and concerns, and to play with their identity as children. In the process, collective pleasures were produced. The teachers, however, were less sure about what to do when school became not just fun but pleasurable.

Fun vs. Pleasure in the Classroom

Schooling has traditionally been defined largely in instrumental terms. Along with the explicit goals of imparting knowledge, skills, and information, the school has also been implicitly mandated to transmit the norms, language, styles, and values of the dominant culture. School has typically been a place to learn, work hard, and develop such traits as punctuality, perseverance, conscientiousness, self–discipline, and initiative. In earlier times, fun in school was incidental. Play was considered frivolous, nonproductive, and indulgent. However, discourses surrounding children in school have changed.

Today there is an emphasis on "making learning fun" through child–centered, play–like activities. Play is now considered to be an activity contributing to the cognitive, psychological, and social development of children. Play is utilized to motivate and reward children. Typically play in school is defined, planned, and monitored by teachers. Studies by Nancy King (1979) and Maria Romero (1989) have demonstrated that young children and teachers tend to have very different perspectives on play in school. Teachers define play as being "creative, fun, pleasing, and rather easy" (Romero, 1989, p. 406). Children consider activities play when they are voluntary and self–directed. All activities assigned or directed by the teacher are relegated to the category of work. Teacher talk of "making learning fun" masks play's motivational and disciplinary purpose and its intent of preparing the child for the later world of work. Play is rarely valued by teachers as an end in itself.

For the students, video tended to blur the lines between work and play. In their journals, they wrote repeatedly about the fun of video production, yet they often mentioned how much work was involved. Video production seemed to represent a type of work that was fun and in which the children located spaces to play. In their collaborative groups, they read, wrote, problem–solved, and gained technical skills, yet they also found ways to produce pleasure in exploring the boundaries between rules and freedom. Such pleasure frequently moved beyond what we typically think of as fun in school. Spontaneous and sometimes transgressive, the students' videos privileged community, festivity, and solidarity. The pleasures experienced in the video project existed in and of the moment and had a life of their own.

In *The Pleasure of the Text* (1975), Roland Barthes presents his twofold notion of pleasure as *plaisir* and *jouissance*. *Plaisir* represents conscious enjoyment and is capable of being expressed in language. It is more conservative, accommodating, and conformist than *jouissance*. Where *plaisir* is a particular pleasure, *jouissance* is more diffuse; it is pleasure without separation: bliss, ecstasy, pure affect. *Jouissance* is an intense, heightened form of pleasure, involving a momentary loss of subjectivity. It knows no bounds. Fiske (1989) sees the roots of *plaisir* in the dominant ideology. Where *jouissance* produces the pleasures of evading the social order, *plaisir* produces the pleasures of relating to it (p.54).

In school, fun is much like that described as *plaisir*: conservative, connected to curricular purposes, and usually organized and regulated by adults. The intent is either to provide a momentary release of tension or to induce the students to engage in the activities on the academic agenda. Pleasure, like *jouissance*, is produced by and for the children, in their own way and on their own terms. It exhausts itself in the present: the human interplay is all that matters. Where *plasir* is an everyday pleasure, *jouissance* is that of special moments. At times, in the video work, *jouissance*–like pleasures were created. At these moments, the teacher's presence temporarily ceased to exist, and the children were united in a spirit of camaraderie, a celebration of "otherness" organized around laughter.

Is the Carnivalesque Transformative?

Several colleagues who read earlier versions of this chapter questioned our celebration of the carnivalesque classroom. One commented, "So some kids made butt jokes in a school project. That doesn't mean they've overturned the power structure of the school." Another warned, "I think you need to be careful not to idealize the transformative potential of the carnivalesque." To avoid being misunderstood, we need to clarify our view of the significance of opening spaces for pleasure and the carnivalesque in the curriculum.

Our colleagues' concerns reflect a deep ambivalence and a long debate among progressive educators about the naughty, resistant, and transgressive behaviors of students. Viewing schools as sites where capitalist, patriarchal societies crush and indoctrinate students, some theorists argue that playing with and even flaunting school expectations, norms, and rules represents a meaningful and even desirable form of resistance (Britzman, 1991; D'Amato, 1988; McLaren, 1986). Other Neo–Marxist and feminist theorists are suspicious of such claims that naughtiness accomplishes anything.

In *Learning to Labour* (1981), for example, Paul Willis argues that the anti–authoritarian antics of the "lads" in a British secondary school work to support rather than overturn the anti–egalitarian structure of the school and more generally of the larger society. The scatological humor, sexual banter, and, most disturbingly, the mock and real acts of violence that characterize the everyday lives of the lads in and out of school function in the end to further legitimate the school's authority and to sentence the lads to reproducing their families' position in the economic system as an inexpensive source of labor. By antagonizing their teachers and ignoring their school work, the lads take themselves out of competition, giving their better behaved middle–class peers a less contested path to educational opportunities and better jobs. The lads' transgressive talk and behavior supports not just capitalism's need for a labor pool, but also patriarchy and misogyny, as their sexual banter supports the objectification of the girls in their school.

In a study set in a nursery school, Valerie Walkerdine (1990, p. 4) finds the roots of patriarchal violence against women in the sexual banter of two four–year–olds boys who verbally assault first a female classmate, and then their thirty–year–old female teacher:

> Terry: You're a stupid cunt, Annie.
> Sean: Get out of it Miss Baxter paxter.
> Terry: Get out of it knickers Miss Baxter.
> Sean: Get out of it Miss Baxter paxter.
> Terry: Get out of it Miss Baxter the knickers paxter knickers bum.
> Sean: Knickers, shit, bum.

Walkerdine argues that such talk, though resistant and transgressive, is far from progressive or emancipatory. The boys succeed in resisting the authority of the teacher and the school, but only by reproducing the patriarchal power available to them as a male birthright.

Willis' and Walkderdine's arguments are disturbing and persuasive: There is nothing inherently emancipatory or progressive in students' acts of resistance and transgression. Nevertheless, it is our position that educators in general and media educators in particular have erred in discounting the significance and value of opening up space for transgressive and carnivalesque moments in the curriculum. Our argument is that children's sexual, grotesque, and violent play and expression can be ways of working through rather than just reproducing dominant discourses and undesirable social dynamics, and of building a sense of community in the classroom.

Video projects that include representations of violence, racism, and other objectionable subject matter may merely reproduce, or, through parody, undermine the sources they imitate. As Bakhtin argues (1981), "of all words uttered in everyday life, no less than half belong to someone else" (p. 339). Applied to children's video production, this concept suggests that children's videos necessarily will imitate and cite images, plots, and characterizations borrowed from popular cultural sources. But in the process of remaking a movie or television and imitating previous forms, there is also, always, an element of newness and thus the potential for transformation.

In her reflections on the pornographic memoirs of the gay African–American writer Gary Fisher, Eve Sedgwick (1997) raises the possibility that even sado–masochistic relationships have the potential to be transformative. In a disturbing memoir, Fisher speculates that sexual encounters in which he was hit and called nigger by a white man did not just repeat the dynamics of slavery and racism, but also allowed him a chance to (re)experience these dynamics and potentially to rework them. Performance (sexual as well as video) has the potential to be transformative—a way of coming to understand through doing/acting/reflecting. As Freud argued, the dream dreamt, remembered, and retold simultaneously reproduces and transforms the emotional impact of disturbing life events.

We can use this logic to analyze a take–off on the television show *America's Funniest Videos* produced by a group of third–graders at Waiau. In *Waiau's Funniest Kids*, a sneezing, nose–blowing, mucus–dripping Master of Ceremonies presents segments featuring a blind girl who repeatedly walks into a wall, a stuttering boy who cannot get through his rendition of a popular song, and hula dancers who clumsily bump into one another, knocking off their grass skirts. These segments can be seen as performative attempts to acknowledge, comment on, and work through issues and tensions of everyday life at Waiau. A "full inclusion school," Waiau is home to a great variety of children, including some with physical, cognitive, and emotional disabilities. Some visit the speech therapist to help them with stuttering. There are blind and deaf children, and children in wheel chairs. During the years of our project, Waiau was also home to the Hawaiian Language Immersion "school–within–a–school." The children who made *Waiau's Funniest Kids* were in a classroom next–door to a classroom of immersion children who spent the day speaking Hawaiian and who often performed the hula (although their skirts, to our knowledge, never fell off). The content of *Waiau's Funniest Kids* thus reflects what Bakhtin would call the stratified, heteroglot character of the school. The children's parodic, silly representations of disabled children and of Hawaiian culture are contrary in content and in tone to the authoritative discourse the school imposes on discussions of difference. When given the opportunity to make their own video, these children chose to deal with the variety of Waiau's student body in a satirical, irreverent way. Their representations made the adults who viewed the video uncomfortable. But whether they produced discomfort in their student audience, whether the disabled and Hawaiian children represented in the video felt gratified or abused by being included as characters, and whether the parodies reflect the presence of prejudicial feelings in the children, we do not and perhaps cannot know. The videos produced by the children at Waiau are complex social texts which cannot be tied to the beliefs of their producers or audience in any simple way.

Our sense is that in most cases, the video–making and video–watching brought the children and the school together. *Waiu's Funniest Kids*, and similar videos that lampooned boring teachers, befuddled kindergarteners, and school bullies, while not artistic hits, proved to be great audience favorites. These videos, by subjecting to the same parodic treatment the foibles of everyone from teachers to kindergarteners, worked to reduce, though not erase, distance and hierarchy. In the carnivalesque spirit of the video–making, everyone could be laughed at and everyone could laugh. No disability was too terrible to be lampooned, no difference so great as to be unrepresentable.

These videos addressed the diversity and inequity of life at Waiau not in the modern liberal mode of full inclusion and democratic values under which no one should be laughed at or treated as different but in the Bakhtinian, carnivalesque mode in which everyone is laughed at and differences are to be freely acknowledged. There is a fear in schools, and in society in general, that if differences and inequities are frankly acknowledged, the already frayed social fabric will be torn further apart. In the carnivalesque atmosphere that reigned during the period of our video production project, in contrast, there was a sense of confidence that differences and tensions, even if talked about openly, would not harm the children's and teachers' sense of community.

Another example: in our first round of video–making, as described above, most of the children did remakes of their favorite books and movies. Several of the groups chose to make versions of recent commercial films, with Disney cartoon features the most popular source material. The casting of these Disney remakes often made us uncomfortable, as the children tended to reproduce stereotypical views of race, gender, and physical attractiveness. For instance, during a casting discussion for a second–grade production of *The Little Mermaid*, we overheard the following conversation: "Tina is the prettiest, so she should be Ariel." "Yeah, and you're the fattest, Angela, so you be Ursula." As adults and as teachers, our impulse was to intervene, perhaps by giving a lecture on how everyone is pretty in different ways, or on the importance of not hurting people's feelings by talking about their appearance. But the reality, which the children seemed to accept even if we could not, was that Tina was the prettiest and most petite girl in the group and thus the most like Disney's Ariel, and Angela was the fattest and thus the most like Ursula. The children know, as we do, that such realities govern how real movies are cast, how animated characters are drawn, and how notions of slimness and attractiveness work in our society. Nothing we could say or do could make it otherwise.

In some instances, the children cast their movies against type, with little boys playing giants, girls playing men, Native Hawaiians playing pilgrims, and African–Americans playing Chinese brothers. In these productions, children gave each other latitude to play parts with or against physical, temperamental, and racial type. But whichever way they handled it; the children seemed unafraid to acknowledge their differences, even when those differences are sources of unequal treatment in the larger society.

Marxist, Neo–marxist, feminist, and liberal democratic views of social stratification and inequality share an agenda of reducing difference by making people and the conditions they live and work under more alike. Bakhtin offers a different view of stratification and power, a view which while not inconsistent with an agenda of progress toward social equality, sees stratification and inequality as inevitable but not totalizing. In Bakhtin's worldview, power and status differentials are characteristic of all complex, stratified, heteroglossic societies; societies are better or worse not according to their degree of stratification, but to the quality and quantity of the interactions and the openness to dialogue that exists between high and low, and between diverse sub–cultural groups. Like the marketplace and the carnival, media projects can provide a safe place for satire, parody, and social laughter. Such contexts where high and low meet in a stratified society make life more bearable and meaningful and work as checks and balances on the power of those at the top. Classroom media projects no more erase the power differential separating teachers from students than do carnivals erase the power and wealth differential that separates the rulers from the people. But media projects, like carnivals, have the potential to bring the high and the low together. And in modern societies where the poor are kept not just down but also away from middle class and the rich, increasing interacxtion between the powerful and the powerless is a significant accomplishment. Schools are highly stratified societies. They can be run like totalitarian states, banning satire, parody, and protest, fearing the open discussion of difference, heterodoxy, and inequality, and erecting emotional barriers between students and their teachers. Or they can be more like Bakhtin's vision of feudal societies, in which the rulers did not fear acknowledging their common humanity with the classes below them or creating spaces for dissent, satire, and laughter.

Final Reflections

Over the course of this project, our thinking about children in classrooms was challenged and in many ways changed. As the unseen and unsaid in school life materialized, new questions were posed and alternatives presented. These instances represented a temporary break with the everyday and offered multiple possibilities and outcomes. The laughter of the carnivalesque set both the teachers and the children free and provided an interval in which the terrain of the classroom could be renegotiated. As borders were shifted and redrawn, the unofficial interests, pleasures, and humor of children were acknowledged and given a more equal footing. As Bakhtin (1981) suggests, we are always creating our world, and ourselves moment to moment, in our speech and our actions. It is here that change takes place—not in sweeping waves, movements, or mandates, but in the minute alterations in our day to day lives and relations.

   Like carnival, video production has no essential nature. Classroom video endeavors play out and are interpreted in different ways at different times and places. As video production becomes institutionalized in school curriculums, it is possible that these carnivalesque moments will be tamed, controlled, or stamped out completely. Uncertainty and trepidation accompany the exploration of uncharted territories. However, the possibility for new understandings also exists. As the space is broadened for students to explore, experiment, and construct their own meanings, we stand to learn more about the children, ourselves, and the relationship between us. As we let go of some of our fears about children's behaviors and inclinations, the classroom may become not only a more democratic place but a more pleasurable one as well.

Our point is not to celebrate or romanticize the children's transgressions of classroom norms and values or to suggest that we should write them into our curricula, with, for instance, butt jokes scheduled right after morning recess. Rather, it is to validate the humor and everyday interests of children and to suggest that they have a place in the classroom, in the delicate, fragile, and shifting balance between excess and constraint. Victor Turner's notion of "spontaneous communitas" helps to illuminate this position. Turner (1977) defines this term as freedom coexisting within structure (p. 129). He writes that communitas "transgresses or dissolves the norms that govern structured and institutionalized relationships and is accompanied by unprecedented potency." Yet, the immediacy of communitas gives way to structure in a dialectical fashion. He suggests that "Wisdom is always to find the appropriate relationship between structure and communitas under the given circumstances of time and place, to accept each modality when it is paramount without rejecting the other, and not to cling to one when its present impetus is spent. Spontaneous communitas is a phase, a moment, not a permanent condition. It is nature in dialogue with structure" (1969, p. 140).

Thus, these carnivalesque pleasures are ephemeral. They appear in unexpected places and begin to close at the very instance when they open. As soon as an attempt is made to rationalize and regulate them, they lose their essence and begin to vanish. Yet they will continue to materialize, for these pleasures have value and importance in the school lives of children. They are sites of energy and powerful affect and can be a rejuvenating and creative force for all involved. They can live briefly in the interstices between freedom and structure until their moment is spent, and pleasure can be enjoyed in and of the moment, for itself and nothing more.

ENDNOTES

1.   We do not mean to suggest that there is nothing teachers can do to intervene in the circulation and reproduction of sexism and racism. We believe that the anti–bias curricula that have the most chance of succeeding are those that begin by acknowledging the students' prior knowledge and experience with racial and gender distinctions in the larger society. For sophisticated approaches to this problem, see Gemma Moss (1989), Bronwyn Davies (1989), and Deborah Britzman (1991).

2.   All parodies and satires are not inclusive and harmless. Teachers have to use their intuition and judgment. We intervened, for example, to block the development of a proposal to make a video about "Arnold Schwartzennigger." Perhaps this video would have ended up lampooning racists rather than African–Americans. But we decided to veto it because our intuition suggested that the topic was more likely to turn out badly than well. Teachers must make case by case decisions. In this case, our prior experience at Waiau, a school with only a handful of African–American students, suggested to us that this project was more likely to widen racial divisions than to narrow them. The other project we discouraged, based on our concerns about

the need for separation of church and state, was a proposal to make a video about Jesus. In retrospect, we wish we had allowed this project to go forward.

3. Although the notion of animal cruelty affronts most adult, middle–class sensibilities (ours included), it is not an uncommon feature of games and sport. Cock fighting, dog fighting, rat killing, bull running, and the baiting of wild animals were popular amusements in England well into the 19th century. The inhumane treatment of animals has generally been associated with the lower classes. Harriet Ritvo (1987) points out that during the 19th century the treatment of animals was considered to be an index of the extent to which a person had managed to control his or her lower urges (p.132).

REFERENCES

Bakhtin, M. (1984). *Rabelais and his world*. Trans. H. Iswolsky. Bloomington: Indiana University Press.

Barthes, R. (1975). *The pleasure of the text*. New York: Hill and Wang.

Britzman, D. (1991). Decentering discourses in teacher education: Or, the unleashing of unpopular things, *Journal of Education, 173*(3), pp. 61–80.

Buckingham, D. (1990). *Watching media learning: Making sense of media education*. New York: Falmer.

Buckingham, D., & Sefton–Green, J. (1994). *Cultural studies goes to school: Reading and teaching popular media*. Bristol: Taylor & Francis Ltd.

Buckingham, D., Graheme, J., and Sefton–Green, J. (1995). *Making media: Practical production in media education*. London: English and Media Centre.

D'Amato, J. (1988). 'Acting:' Hawaiian children's resistance to teachers, *The Elementary School Journal. 88* (5), pp. 529–43.

Davies, B. (1989). *Frogs and snails and feminist tales: Preschool children and gender*, Sydney: Allen and Unwin.

Dyson, A. (1993). *Social worlds of children learning to write in an urban primary school*. New York: Teachers College Press.

Fiske, J. (1989). *Understanding popular culture*. London: Routledge.

Hodge, B. & Tripp, D. (1986). *Children and television*. Cambridge: Polity Press.

King, N. (1979). Play: The kindergartners perspective. *The Elementary School Journal 80*, pp. 81–87.

King, N. (1992). The impact of context on the play of young children. In Kessler, S. & Swadener, B. (Eds.) *Reconceptualizing the early childhood curriculum: Beginning the dialogue*. New York: Teacher's College Press.

Lurie, Allison. (1990). *Don't tell the grown–ups: Subversive children's literature*. Boston: Little, Brown.

McLaren, P. (1986). *Schooling as a ritual performance: Towards a political economy of educational symbols and gestures*. London: Routledge & Kegan Paul.

Morson, G. & Emerson, C. (1990). *Mikhail Bakhtin: Creation of a prosaics*. Stanford, CA: Stanford University Press.

Moss, G. (1989). *Unpopular fictions*. London: Virago.

Newkirk, Thomas. (1992). *Listening in: Children talk about books (and other things)*, Portsmouth, NH: Heinemann.

Ritvo, Harriet. (1987). *The animal estate: The English and other creatures in the Victorian age*. Cambridge: Harvard University Press.

Romero, M. (1989). Work and play in the nursery school, *Educational Policy 3* (4), pp. 401–419.

Russo, M. (1986). Female grotesques: Carnival and theory. In de Lauretis (Ed). *Feminist studies/critical studies*. Bloominton: Indiana University Press.

Sedgwick, E. (1997). *Gary Fisher in your pocket*. Durham, NH: Duke University Press.

Stam, R. (1989). *Subversive pleasures: Bakhtin, cultural criticism, and film*. Baltimore: The John Hopkins University Press.

Turner, V. (1977). Frame, flow and reflection: Ritual and drama as public liminality. In Benamou, M. & Caramello, C. *(Eds.) Performance in postmodern culture.* Madison, WI: Coda.
Turner, V. (1969). The ritual process. Chicago: Aldine Press.
Walkerdine, V. (1990/1981). Sex, power, and pedagogy, in *Schoolgirl fictions.* (pp. ___) London: Verso.
Willis, P. (1981). *Learning to labor.* New York: Columbia University Press.

An early version of this chapter was published in *"Making a place for pleasure in early childhood education" 1997 Yale University Press.*

PETER R. WEBSTER

15. MUSIC TECHNOLOGY AND THE YOUNG CHILD

> Technologies, mechanical or otherwise, have a way of fading into the transparent backdrops of our lives. They come to be folded into our beings so seamlessly that some semioticians have suggested that we are all, quite literally, cyborgs.

In the recent book, *Engaging Minds*, Davis, Sumara, and Luce–Kapler argue (2000) for a new way to conceptualize learning and teaching in the complex world that is ours. The authors challenge the educational thinking that has spawned reductive and fragmented collections of formal lesson plans, checklists, evaluation rubrics and prescribed theories in favor of a more fluid conception of teaching and learning that is embedded in the social context of the postmodern world. The book encourages not the abandonment of structure but certainly a loosening of teacher control to encourage the construction of learning (Gardner, 1994). Technology and its ubiquitous quality in children's lives has become a powerful partner in this construction, especially so in the arts where creating things is what lies at the core of the artistic experience.

THE SAME, YET DIFFERENT

Today, children entering formal education settings are unaware of a world without computers, cell phones, personal digital assistants, satellite TV, portable CD and MPEG3 players, and the Internet with its connection to vast worlds of information. Music as art or more often as entertainment is everywhere in these media. To adults who were students some thirty years ago, this may all seem overwhelming and perhaps intimidating. To a child, it is just the way the world is. No big deal.

Interestingly, this kind of setting also existed for these adults and their parents. We can remember how our fathers and mothers suffered with video tape players, push–button phones, fax machines, photo copiers, digital clocks, programmed textbooks, electric typewriters, overhead projectors, and cassette tape recorders—items that to us seemed commonplace in the context of school. We used these devices to help construct OUR understanding just as our children do now.

However, despite this similarity, there are critical differences today in (1) the complexity of knowledge, (2) the best methods to engineer its transmission, and (3) the power of technological support. The world truly is a more complex place today than it was thirty, twenty, or even ten years ago. Multiple cultures and value systems flourish, knowledge is growing at exponential rates, and change occurs faster and with more profound consequences than at any other time in our history.

Not only is the content becoming more complex, but also what we know about how children learn best is a major consideration. Structured ways of rote learning,

L. Bresler and C.M. Thompson (eds.), The Arts in Children's Lives, 215–236.
© 2002 *Kluwer Academic Publishers. Printed in the Netherlands.*

memorization, and patterns of convergent thinking are now more likely to be augmented or even replaced with methods of discovery learning, problem–solving, and divergent thinking. Higher levels of synthetic thinking are seen as a more effective way to teach our youngsters how to cope with complexity. Cooperative learning, peer teaching, and project–centered learning with the teacher as an overseer is much more valued than teacher–dominated interaction (Kafai & Resnick, 1996).

But perhaps the most critical difference for us as observers and as engineers of learning is the extraordinary power of the technological tools at our disposal. For example, traditional drill–and–practice techniques that dominated software for years and made computers nothing more than expensive and flexible flashcards have now been complemented by much more powerful software that use problem–solving and role–playing techniques (Williams & Webster, 1999). Modern hardware and software can create a sense of realism and can offer choices that have consequence. Video, animation, text, and sound can unite to support a symbolically constructed world that represents reality in interesting and meaningful ways for children (Shade & Watson, 1990).

With today's affordable personal computers, even the youngest of children can "play along" with the computer, make increasingly more complex decisions about the composition of the music, or be asked to listen in new and exciting ways. It is not the multiple media alone that is significant, but its use in allowing children to think and feel music experience. When it is used to present children with interesting music problems to solve or to teach important facts and skills in the context of real music experiences, then we begin to see the power of this technology to help music teaching and learning.

As the new century begins, where are we in terms of hardware and software development? What are some current examples of music software for young children that show particular promise? What empirical evidence do we have about music technology and the young child, and where are we headed in the future?[1]

CURRENT STATUS OF MUSIC TECHNOLOGY

It is probably fair to state that the last ten years have seen the greatest historical growth in music software for young children. This is true for nearly all genres of music technology for all age levels, but particularly so for the young child. This is true in large part because of the advances in computer design and affordability, but also because software designers—many of whom are music educators themselves—are becoming more sophisticated in the environments they create.

Perhaps the best way to understand where we currently are is to review a few important historic developments in computer–assisted instruction and music technology. More expanded treatments of this topic exist elsewhere (Higgins, 1992;

---

[1]In answering these questions, this chapter will concentrate on technology associated with personal computers and related digital music instruments. I will not deal with television or other non–computer technologies designed to help teach music. I define "young children" as individuals between the ages of 3–8.

Williams &Webster, 1999; Webster, in press, but a few historic examples here will help to explain the recent advances.

Programmed Instruction and Teaching Machines

The 1950s saw the systematic development of programmed instruction based in large part on the Skinnerian view that instruction could be divided logically and behaviorally into a number of small, linear steps that would lead to mastery. Automated teaching machines were built and branching techniques developed within programmed instruction. Large and cumbersome mainframe computers were used for applying these principles to computer–assisted instruction (CAI) and the famous PLATO system for CAI was created at the University of Illinois. The period from the late 1950s to the 1970s was marked by a number of music instruction programs written for large systems. This software was designed for college–aged students and little or no work was done for younger students. Programmed instruction also influenced the development of audio tapes for music dictation and written materials to accompany them. Music theory skills and historical facts about music were the major instructional foci of this work.

This approach to CAI continued in more recent years as personal computers developed. The early 1980s saw the development of popular machines like the Apple II and the Atari 800. Not only was the style of instruction similar to the earlier mainframe days, so too was the content of instruction. The earliest music software for young children can be traced to the early 1980s, with most of the content centering on music perception skills. The sound used for these programs was low–quality synthetic tones and children used a typewriter keyboard for nearly all responses.[2]

Actually, many of these programs remain available today for more modern computers. For those teachers and researchers interested in straightforward drill–and–practice software for the teaching of very basic skills relating to pitch, rhythm and notational understanding, these programs may have some use.[3]

MIDI, Powerful Computers with Sound Sampling, and Audio CD

Some of the most striking breakthroughs in music technology occurred in the middle to late 1980s. The Music Instrument Digital Interface (MIDI), a protocol for exchanging digital information about sound between digital devices, was finalized by several designers of synthesizers and sound samplers in August, 1983 (Anderton, 1986). This protocol made it possible for music devices like keyboard synthesizers to

---

[2]The one notable exception to this was a fascinating music drawing program developed by Martin Lamb called *MusicLand*. Using an Apple II computer and a music synthesizer called the Alpha Syntauri, the system provided a way to draw musical gestures on the screen and have the synthesizer realize the gestures. The program was years ahead of its time.

[3]Good examples of this kind of software include: *Musicus, Tap–It, Early Music Skills, Music Flash Cards, Note Speller, Tune–It II, and Clef Notes.* Each of these programs is available from Electronic Courseware Systems.

communicate directly with computers and vice versa. For the first time, computer software could be written to record from and play back to these sound devices. MIDI data exchange of this sort helped launch not only whole new categories of software for composition and music printing, but also allowed CAI software to offer students a more musical way to respond to tasks.

MIDI also provided a way for very young children to begin exploring music composition and improvisation without the immediate need of music notation as a symbol system. Using simple sequencing software like *FreeStyle* from Mark of the Unicorn or *Micrologic* from EMagic, young children could enter layers of sound into the computer using music keyboards once they understood the basic operations of the computer and its software. Such software continues to be used in education settings, although most often with older children.

In 1984, Apple Computer sold its first Macintosh—a far faster machine than the Apple II. The Macintosh included built–in, four–voice sound and superior graphic ability. It also used a revolutionary user interface that featured menus, icons and a pointing device called a mouse. Other personal computers would soon adopt this as the computing standard. The Macintosh, the IBM personal computer, and the "cloned" machines based on the IBM hardware model have developed steadily since that time in terms of speed, storage, memory, expandability and software support.

These new machines were developed in tandem with MIDI technology and, by the end of the 1980s, the stage was set for major software development in all phases of music making and music teaching. In addition to MIDI technology, these new machines also began to support *sampled* sound. Early Macintosh computers, for example, had the capability to transform speech, music, or any analog sound into digital information for storage inside the computer. This information could then be converted back to analog sound and played through the computer's speaker.[4] This second major development in music technology has had important implications for children's ability to use the computer to create custom sounds based on their own voice and to use them as part of music composition.

The third important development during this time was laser–based compact disc (CD) technology. Not only was this medium an important step for the distribution of high quality audio sound as a replacement for long–playing vinyl records, but it also served as an excellent medium for text, graphics, and digital movies. The decision by the computer industry to include multi–format compact disc drives as part of each personal computer has had enormous impact on the kind of software that has now become readily available for children. This type of delivery system will only become faster and more powerful in the coming years, moving to newer DVD formats, and will blend with online networks to deliver words, sounds and images from all over the world and beyond.

---

[4]For a more complete description of digital sound sampling and its use in music technology and CAI , see Williams and Webster, 1999.

Modern Era of Software Design

Traditional drill–and–practice software continues today, taking full advantage of increased processing speed and vastly improved sound. However, additional approaches in music software design emerged toward the end of the 1980s and continue today in increasingly elaborate form. These newer approaches, *flexible–practice, guided instruction, games, exploratory,* and *creative,* are important to understand for a well–rounded view of music software for young children. Sampled sound, MIDI–based instruments, and audio CD/DVD are used in all categories with various levels of sophistication and effectiveness. What follows is a brief synopsis of each software category and some examples of real products designed for young children.

EXAMPLES OF SOFTWARE FOR YOUNG CHILDREN

The examples of software that follow are offered as exemplars of the kinds of technology available at the time this paper is being written. Most are available for both Windows and Macintosh computers and all are reasonably priced and readily available. MIDI, together with sampled and audio CD sound sources, are all represented here and I have personally seen each program work effectively with young children. Each program offers instructional content and style that teachers, parents, and researchers might find useful. It is important to keep in mind, however, that the value of a particular piece of software is determined largely by the particular people involved and the purposes for which they use it.

Drill–and–Practice

Because a large part of the music experience is based on skills in aural perception (listening) and psychomotor ability (performance), and because computer software can be written relatively easily to exercise these skills, traditional drill–and–practice remains as a category of CAI. This software is largely *machine–determined,* providing instruction in a manner dictated entirely by the software author and the machine itself. If the student performs a task correctly, the software might provide a new task that is perhaps more challenging. If the response is incorrect, the software might branch off to an easier set. Focus is on small music examples with limited context. There is limited student and teacher choice regarding the kind of music and the order of the tasks. For many, this kind of software provides an efficient and direct means to improve specific skills.

A good example of this kind of software for young children is the MiDisaurus series of programs distributed by Musicware. Figure 1 displays the "Notation" title in this series. A section on articulation is displayed where the task is to drag the bone over the top of the pitches that are tied. When the child does this correctly, a small part of a dinosaur is drawn. The task ends when all the dinosaur is fully drawn. The icons for navigation are learned quickly by the child and all directions are spoken, with little use of text. The drills are presented in a game–like atmosphere but the software is clearly designed to drill skills in notational understanding. The notation is always played and the child begins to develop the relationships between written notation and sounds.

Figure 1 "Notation" from MiDisaurus

Flexible Practice

Software in this category also has the purpose of skill development, but adds many more features. Many of these enhancements are a result of both the increased power of technology and of more creative, and perhaps more musical, thinking by software authors today. Software in this category is student– and teacher–centered in that choices permit individuals to have a hand in engineering their own music education. For instance, students might use their own understanding of pitch direction to design a challenging game for their peers. Flexible practice software typically provides menus and dialog boxes that let students choose the settings for a series of experiences that best suit their needs. In a similar way, teachers can use these features to create a tailor–made curriculum for an individual or class. These flexible options also allow musicians to work with more realistic musical materials, while giving the software more depth of content.

A prime example of flexible practice software in music for young children is *Toney Music Games* (Illinois State University, Office of Research in Arts Technology). It is designed as a set of three programs (Boxes, Puzzles, and Clubhouse) that help develop music memory and tonal perception. The games use movable icons (boxes) that represent either full melodies or melodic fragments that can be heard if clicked upon. The child hears a target melody. Clicking on a box plays either that melody or a few others that sound like it (Figure 2a). The task is to match the right box to the target and, by so doing, help to develop same/different discriminations.

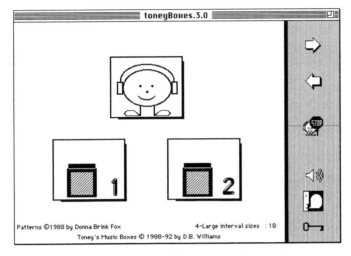

Figure 2a"Toney Boxes" from *Toney Music Games*

In Puzzles, the target exists, but the boxes represent partial fragments of the target arranged in random serial order. The task for the child is to identify the fragments and order them in the correct serial order to match the target. This exercises the ability to hear order and to reconstruct the melody. With Clubhouse (Figure 2b), the target is compared to boxes in the "clubhouse" that have similar music; however, one box is quite different in terms of either its melodic shape or rhythmic design. The task is to identify the odd box and pull it out. Here the child needs to grasp the overall dimensions of music structure. The tasks are based on the Piagetian concept of conservation, as applied to music. In all of the games, enjoyable animation and sound effects support motivation.

Figure 2b "Toney ClubHouse" from *Toney Music Games*

Although these programs may seem to be drill–and–practice, critical attributes below the surface suggest a difference. In addition to allowing the child or supervising adult to set difficulty levels with a library of supplied music examples, the application offers a built–in editor that lets you create your own music patterns. The sound source may be the computer's internal sound or it may be precisely defined clips from an audio CD. This means that teachers can create not only simple music patterns, but full audio examples from any kind of music recorded on compact disc at the local music store.

Guided Instruction

Instead of offering a series of tasks for completion, some music software leads the student through tutorial instruction. An idea is presented through demonstration using text, audio, graphics, animation, movies or some combination of all these. Often the software asks the student to interact with the tutorial in order to verify that the ideas are understood. Material is presented in levels of complexity and may contain related games to test mastery. Guided instruction software can be very imaginative and entertaining. As with drill–and–practice software, music content is nearly always defined by the author of the software.

MusicAce I from Harmonic Vision offers perception experiences but also includes work with note reading, scale structures, piano keyboard design, clefs, dynamics, flats and sharps, and timbre recognition (Figure 3a) . Tutorials are provided by the animated "professor" who guides the children in answering questions about presented content. The levels of instruction are monitored and recorded as the child moves through the program.   A game is provided for each chapter so that skills can be tested.   MIDI sound is supported and children can interact with the program using a music keyboard.

Figure 3a Chapter 16, "Same Pitch, Different Timbres", from *MusicAce I*

Of particular interest is that *MusicAce I* also includes an accompanying "Doodle Pad" option that lets children experiment with composing their own music (Figure 3b). In this part of the program, children can layer notes of different lengths on top of one another to form a composition. Each note's color represents a different timbre. Loudness and tempo are controlled with slider bars, and notes can be tied. The software comes with a few tunes already created, such as the one shown. Having both drill-and-practice and more creative routines in the same software allows children to place skill development in a more holistic context. A second level of the software includes more advanced guided instruction in rhythm, intervals, chords.

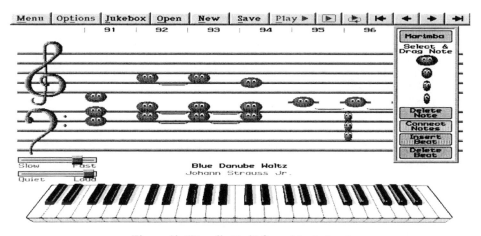

Figure 3b "Doodle Pad" from *MusicAce I*

Games

Some of the most motivational software for music teaching and learning, especially for younger children, is found in this category. Here the emphasis is placed on basic skill development and knowledge of the music elements such as melody or rhythm. This is done in a competitive way, often allowing more than one user to have turns at the correct answers. Sometimes the games are more like adventures in which a single user is asked to solve a puzzle or arrive at some defined plateau. Such adventures often have music tasks to solve on the way to the ending goal. Game software generally makes extensive use of graphics and animation to accompany its many uses of sound. It might also contain elements of the exploration and creative categories.

An excellent example of this category is the *Juilliard Music Adventure* from Theatrix. In this game, the child must solve certain creative tasks such as composing music rhythm patterns and melodies in order to unlock doors in a castle. The goal is to save a trapped queen who is locked away by an evil character called "Noise." Figure 4a provides a view of the entrance into the castle. Clicking on the tablets held by the statue–like figure provide opportunities to practice composing melodies and rhythms (Figure 4b).

Figure 4a "Opening Scene," from *Juilliard Music Adventure*

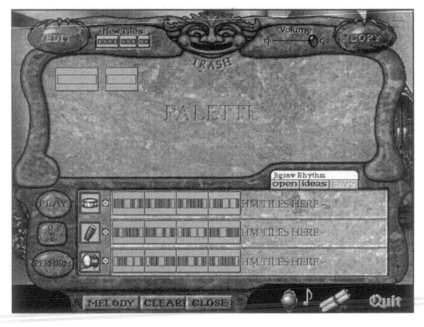

Figure 4b "Rhythm Maker," from *Juilliard Music Adventure*

Exploratory

The software in this category encourages the student to explore resources about a topic in a free way, moving from one topic to another in any approach that makes sense. This is often called "hypermedia."[5] The accent is less on mastering a particular skill or knowledge set but rather in gathering information about a topic through the use of links. Exploratory software does not expect the user to work in a linear fashion from the beginning of the program to the end. Such software often is organized in chapters or units of instruction with content between chapters interrelated. Links to a glossary of terms is common as are connections to relevant content found on the Internet's World Wide Web. The focus of this category of software is on music history and listening experiences. Many titles in this category use audio CDs, CD–ROMs, and DVDs.

Microsoft Musical Instruments from Microsoft features a collection of multimedia experiences organized around information about music instruments from Western culture and from around the world.[6] Figure 5a illustrates a screen that features the French horn, part of a larger set of screens devoted to the brass instrument family. The child may hear digitized sounds of the horn, see the pictures of the different horns, and even hear a voice pronounce the names of the instruments. Children with some reading ability will enjoy reading about the instrument's history. Many links are made to additional material on the CD.

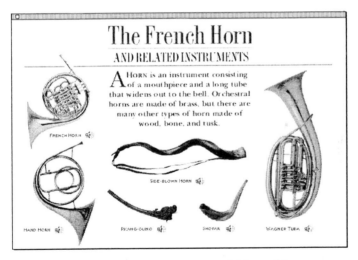

Figure 5a "French Horn," from *Microsoft Musical Instruments*

---

[5]For an excellent description of the history of hypermedia and its implementation as a new model for CAI, see Berz and Bowman, 1994.

[6] At this writing, *Microsoft Musical Instruments* is not in print, but you may find copies still available from distributors.

Figure 5b shows another approach to using the software. Rather than exploring the instrument families, musicians can base their study around an area of the world and the instruments that are likely to be found there. The child is not only offered information about music instruments, but a little geography as well by "zooming in" on countries within continents. This kind of multimedia excursion through cultures is a powerful learning experience not possible in the old days of CAI.

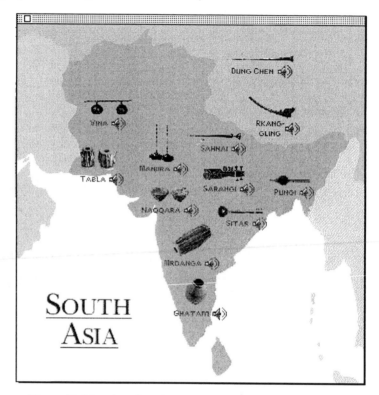

Figure 5b "South Asia," from *Microsoft Musical Instruments*

Creative

The most recent category to emerge in CAI software is what might be called "creative." Here the idea is to encourage students to create music as a way of better understanding the art. For example, creative CAI might provide an opportunity to compose music with graphic representation or improvise original music with accompaniments provided by the software. Still other titles might provide an accompaniment to a traditional solo work. To support listening, creative software might offer a construction kit for creating images and words that demonstrate the organization of the music. The software provides an opportunity to interact with the technology in a way that is as similar as possible to the ways people create music experiences: listening, performing, composing, and improvising. Through this simulation, the student is given a great deal of creative control. MIDI–based sound is often used with this software, as are other multimedia resources (Nelson, 1998).

An example of software that might fall in the "creative" category is *Thinking Things 2* from Edmark. Oranga's Band (Figure 6a) allows children to explore rhythmic patterns by listening to previously composed patterns or composing some of their own. In the Q&A mode, Oranga and his band members play multiple lines of rhythm ranging from very simple to complex and the child has to determine which musician played a particular line of rhythm or which line was played. This helps to teach auditory perception, but without dealing with traditional notation. The patterns are not sophisticated rhythmically, but can get challenging. In the create mode, children can design their own patterns and listen as they are played by the band. Using the microphone of the computer, children can also record their own sampled sound for the band to play.

Figure 6a "Oranga's Band" from *Thinkin' Things 2*

In Toony's Tunes (Figure 6b), children can learn to play a simple melody drawn from a pre–composed set, or ask the animated character to play back an original tune that the child writes. Similar to Oranga Banga's Band, originally composed music can be saved and played back later.

Figure 6b "Toony Tunes," from *Thinkin' Things 2*

Making Music from LTI/Voyager simulates the creative thinking of composers and might be considered another example of creative software (Figure 7). The program allows the child to actually draw music gestures on the screen and manipulate them much like a composer does working without a computer. In Figure 8, we see that two musical lines have been entered, each assigned to a different timbre by using one of the buttons on the left side. Other buttons allow a chosen portion of the musical gesture to be altered for dynamic change, pitch, or tempo. You can ask the program to make global changes like inverting the internals, playing the line backwards (retrograde) or some combination of both. Motives can be "picked up" and moved around to different pitch levels. The child can even alter the underlying scale structures.

Making Music allows the saving of multiple compositions into libraries of creative work and also offers a number of supportive game–like programs for aural skills training. It uses either external MIDI devices or the synthesized sounds that come with the resources of most modern computers. The program is distributed on CD.

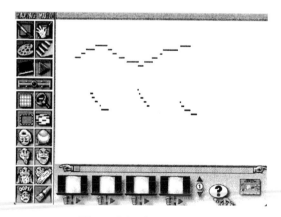

Figure 7 *Making Music*

Rock Rap'n Roll from Silver Burdett Ginn is an interactive simulation program for improvisation and music arranging that uses no notation. The program allows the child to construct a composition from digitized sound excerpts. Several styles of popular music are offered, including blues, techno–pop, rap, and soul. After picking a style, the child is given a screen to construct the composition. Figure 8 shows a screen for the blues. The excerpts listed on the left can be drawn into the circles at the bottom to create a sequence. Once the sequence is chosen, clicking on the start button will play the excerpts in order. As the music is playing, the child can "improvise" by clicking on buttons that play shorter sound fragments designed to go well with the excerpts.

Figure 8 "Blues" from *Rock, Rap'n Roll*

One final point that is quite important: Both exploratory and creative software categories celebrate relationships between broader ideas in context as well as isolated facts. As we begin to better understand the learning process (Papert, 1993) and the many differences that exist within each learner (Gardner, 1991), the strengths of these different software categories and their use in the hands of teachers takes on an important meaning.

RESEARCH ON MUSIC TECHNOLOGY AND THE YOUNG CHILD

These eight titles seem to offer great promise for our work with young children in music. So what empirical evidence do we have about music learning and the young child when it is assisted by technology? The truthful answer is ". . . very little ." This is not because the literature is confused or is supplying contradictory data, but rather because few studies seem to exist at all.

There *is* a growing literature on music and early childhood (Scott–Kassner, 1992), but few studies have used modern computers in a hands–on way as part of the research design. Also, Higgins (1992), Berz and Bowman (1994), and Webster (in press) offer excellent reviews of music education research and computer technology for older students (ages 8 and up), including CAI work at the college–level.

There is also a generous body of research on computers and early childhood *outside* of music as a discipline (Clements & Nastasi, 1993) and I will return to this in due course. What simply does *not* yet exist is an articulated body of work within early childhood music that is devoted to music learning with children working with computers .

Why is this so? Three possible reasons come to mind. First, teachers and researchers are slow to embrace any new technology, especially computer software that is designed on a very different philosophical base. The eight examples of music software described above are, for the most part, recent. Many of the titles in the simulation and multimedia/hypermedia category are designed with paradigms that are far different from computer–assisted instruction in the past. The content and style may challenge even the most adventuresome early childhood music educator. Traditional curricula models are slow to change in order to allow for research to occur. The cycle of experimentation in a curriculum is often so slow and the number of experimenters and experimental settings so small that by the time a teacher or researcher is ready, the technology has changed and the motivation or opportunity is gone.

Secondly, teachers and researchers may still not be comfortable with computer–based instruction. Although the computer has been in use for years as a tool for statistical analysis or as a data–gathering instrument, its use as a focus of instruction with adult supervision is really very new in many schools, research labs, and preschool centers. For many musicians, the idea of computers in the hands of the young child may seem clumsy and unmusical—placing too much between the child and the "natural" music experience. Pre–service curricula at colleges and universities that educate teachers and researchers are only now beginning to include formal courses in music technology. It may take another generation of professional education to yield the kind of understanding that is necessary to sustain technology–focused research agendas.

Thirdly, the amount of equipment available to conduct this kind of research is still not approaching a critical mass. Goodwin, Goodwin and Garel (1986) report that about 25% of licensed preschools had computers in 1984.   Although this changed dramatically in the 1990s, the ratio of computers to children is still only 1 to 22 (Clements &Nastasi, 1993, p. 254). Berz and Bowman (1994, p. 2) offer estimates for public schools that range from 1 to 10 in advantaged systems and 1 to 30 in poorer settings. They are quick to add that the numbers are far worse for school systems with more stringent financial bases. Also, the kind of computers owned by school systems is unspecified in these reports so that what passes for a "computer" might be an older Apple II–type machine—virtually useless for modern work.

Some Studies

Thankfully, there are signs that this is changing. We do have some examples of work completed in the last few years. For example, Bailey completed a study with

4–, 5– and 6–year olds with a curriculum based on the Yamaha Music Education System (Bailey, 1989).   The study used the Yamaha courseware to study the improvement of pitch, rhythm and music keyboard orientation.   Short (15 to 20 minute) lessons with computers and music keyboards were used in an experimental treatment. The study did show greater improvement in skills when compared to more traditional approaches.

Sun (1994) reported results of preschool children composing with icons that matched sounds.   Twenty–three children from a Montessori school were randomly chosen and given exploration experiences with sounds and visual icons that could be used to match with them.   Although some of the results were mixed, Sun reported positive attitudes from the children and acceptance for the use of the computer as a teaching tool by the teachers.

Lee (1994) used a computer learning environment in the study of melody construction.   The computer allowed the child the opportunity to construct melodies freely and the researcher used this environment to study the child's behavior.   Judges were used to study the exploration patterns and to improve the software.

Stauffer (in press) has studied a number of children using Voyager's *Making Music* software in her music laboratory at Arizona State University. She is preparing a formal paper documenting her qualitative study of children working with the software as they created music gestures.   She is using the software not only to provide practical information for the software's developer, but also to study the thought processes and problem–solving skills of these young children.   Results from her work are very promising and may result in some of the most important data we have to date.

From another perspective, it can be noted that computers are growing in popularity as effective ways to actually gather data from the young child.   For instance, Forsythe (1984) used the computer in a creative way to administer an altered version of the Gordon *Primary Measures of Music Audiation* to preschoolers.   White (1989) and Rodriguez (1995) have each used touch–sensitive screens to allow young children a direct method for choosing between objects in perception studies. White was concerned with pitch discrimination and categorization and Rodriguez studied preference for expressive performances. Such work is beginning to demonstrate that the young child is able to perceive musically important events far earlier than was thought because the computer allows a valid response mechanism that is non–verbal.

Finally, it should be noted that a number of authorities have speculated on the importance of computer technology for research with young children, especially as a way to study generative behavior such as is found in composition (Davidson, 1990; Kozerski, 1989; MacGregor, 1992; Moore, 1989; Upitis, 1989; and Webster, 1989). These authors supply little formal data, but rather present a persuasive case for the study of music experience with the support of computer technology as an active agent for the young child.

Inspiration form the General Literature as a Guide for Research in Music

In preparing this paper, I was struck with the body of research that has developed surrounding computer environments for young children outside of music. Dating from the early days of LOGO instruction in mathematics (Papert, 1980) to the present work with computers to help with reading and writing skills, social integration, and the study of higher–level thinking, much information is accumulating—both from qualitative and quantitative paradigms.   Young children seem to really learn from interacting with good technology. They are comfortable with it and seem genuinely excited and motivated by the mergers of symbol systems that are possible.

What follows is a list of the major findings from the general literature, drawn from the excellent review supplied by Clements and Nastasi (1993). I have included some thoughts about what this might mean for research in music.

- Computer technology is not too hard or confusing for children to use. Young children can learn to use the mouse and typewriter keyboard effectively, especially with some adult guidance. Some adult supervision is necessary at key points, but not all the time. Research seems to support the idea that adults are most effective in the ecology of young children and computers when they encourage, question, model and prompt.

  Music education might best occur by allowing young children to discover the complexities of music with technology under such free, but supervised, conditions. Little is know about this kind of style since so much of music teaching is teacher–centered and rule–driven. Good research is needed on how teachers actually do this and how they can make the link from simple exploration to real musical thinking.

- Young children prefer animated, problem–solving software as opposed to more predictable drill–and–practice titles.   Certain applications of drill–and–practice are effective in remediation, however. Language and reading development seem improved by programs that encourage exploration and fantasy.

  The important implication here for music teaching is that software experiences that are based on skill–building and routinized drill will probably not be as effective in most situations as software that is project–based. What do young children think about when they work with this kind of technology? What do they actually learn in music? Is their intrinsic motivation to learn skills and facts necessary for advanced work in music increased?

- Computers can be used in a large setting of children without dominating other activities.   The research seems to support the idea of computer "stations" as a natural part of school settings that include tables and sitting areas devoted to other activities.   Children can spend time with the computer, and then move to other activities.

  Interestingly, this supports some of the recommendations of the curriculum projects in the 1960s like the Manhattanville program (Thomas, 1970). One can easily imagine "music corners" equipped with traditional pre–school musical instruments, recorders and CD players, and a "computer corner" designed to be used by children separately or in small teams. These computers could be self–contained or linked to the Internet. Research on the ways children use this kind of resource and how teachers might use this power is desperately needed.

- Interest in computers seems to begin at around age 4, although there may be many exceptions to this. It is around this time that forms of abstract play develop.

  This finding is based largely on non–music activities and it would be interesting to see if sound exploration using computer–based activities would reveal similar findings. It would be fascinating to see how such interactions develop and how this might relate to our continuing understanding of formal music aptitude.

- LOGO—an object–oriented programming environment designed to help young children experience such skills as sequencing, iteration and structure in terms of mathematics and computer programming—has helped children think more imaginatively when used properly (Papert, 1980). Meta–analyses of LOGO–based research has shown an increase in higher–level thinking, including metacognition. Unfortunately for some, accent on programming as a vital activity for young children to experience higher–level thinking, seems to be on a downward cycle.

  In music, Meckley (1985) experimented with using a music–based LOGO system to encourage creative thinking in music and to allow children to create understanding of music elements. His research was with older children, but such work deserves to be revisited and cast in new ways with contemporary music technology for young children.

- Computers can provide effective "scaffolding" for young children in terms of writing. Based in part on the learning theories of Bruner and Vygotsky, scaffolding allows children to form cognitive structures so that they can operate at high levels of thinking and work more effectively toward their potential.

  The concept of scaffolding in a music context has been suggested by Upitis (1989) and is embedded in the work of Bamberger (1982) and other musician/psychologists who have speculated about music learning. Using programs like *Making Music 1* and *Rock Rap'n Roll* as scaffolding for composition and improvisation, we are likely to learn a great deal. Wonderful opportunities exist in music for the first time because of technology.

- The general literature seems to support the notion that computers, in the hands of young children, increase their creative thinking and encourage risk taking.

  Our understanding of music learning can be increased greatly if we use technology to inspire creative thinking and better record its results (Webster, 1987).

- Finally, children seem to like working in groups with computers. This dispels the myth that computers and technology in the school setting cause isolation and anti–social behavior. Interestingly, Gardner (1991) and other psychologists argue that children learn best by completing projects and solving problems together.

This data is consistent with new trends in general music teaching that encourage group composition, improvisation, analysis and other project–centered work with music. It would be fascinating to study the social interactions in young children that occur in such groups, especially if the quality of the group interaction is enhanced by computers and music technology. Additionally, children might well interact with other children solving interesting music problems, but do so over high speed networks. We already see group music improvisations over the Internet (Williams &Webster, 1999). As each school becomes wired to Internet services like the World Wide Web and video conferencing, the possibilities quickly multiply in richness.[7]

TEACHERS HOLD THE KEY

These many ideas hold promise for future music teachers and scholars interested in the music abilities of the young child. All the pieces are beginning to fall into place for some major advances in our understanding of how children think about music, how they form preferences, and how they develop deeper affective and cognitive understanding.

Of course, the real key to the success of such technology is never in the software or hardware itself but rather in the dynamics of the classroom or studio. The real key is the teacher who understands and applies the research to practice. Our little girl in the television commercial with the trumpet isn't really playing the trumpet. It will take the patience and guidance of a teacher to make the fantasy reality. The small group of six–year old composers creating a small, drawn composition with *Making Music* will need the inspiration and leadership of a teacher to take them further into the composer's craft. The four–year old listener that figures out the order of the pitch boxes in *Toney Music Games* will need the experience of a good music teacher to develop still more sophisticated ways to perceive and enjoy music.

Technology is a powerful tool to aid learning and research, but it is never the point of the experience. That clearly is where the role of the teacher and the supportive research comes into play. Technological tools such as those described in this chapter are enormously exciting, but real improvements in teaching come from people creating the environments in which the greatest music learning experience can exist (Bresler, 1987).

> The child of today will learn about and learn from these ubiquitous technologies, whether or not teachers use them. They can be an essential aspect of a rich educational environment, if and only if a human teacher embraces them into a humanistic and constructivist vision of early childhood education. (Clements &Nastasi, 1993, p. 269)

---

[7]A review of World Wide Web sites designed exclusively for the young child did not reveal many locations as of this writing. As the Web grows, it will be quite natural for this to develop. Affordable video conferencing between educational centers for young children is now a reality.

Well said.

REFERENCES

Anderton, C. (1986). *MIDI for musicians*. New York: Amsco Publications.

Bailey, D. (1989). The effects of computer–based instruction on achievement of four–, five–, and six–year–old children in the Yamaha Music Education System Primary One Course (Doctoral dissertation, University of Illinois at Urbana–Champaign, 1989). *Dissertation Abstracts International, 51*, 777A.

Bamberger, J. (1982). Revisiting children's drawings of simple rhythms: A function of reflection–in–action. In S. Strauss (Ed.), *U–shaped behavioral growth*. New York: Academic Press, 191–226.

Berz, W. & Bowman, J. (1994). *Applications of research in music technology*. Washington, DC: Music Educators National Conference.

Bresler, L. (1987). The role of the computer in a music theory classroom; Integration, barriers, and learning (Doctoral dissertation, Stanford University, 1987). *Dissertation Abstracts International, 48*, 1689A.

Clements, D. & Nastasi, B. (1993). Electronic media and early childhood education. In B. Spodek (Ed.), *Handbook of research on the education of young children*. New York: Macmillan Publishing Company.

Davidson, L. (1990). Tools and environments for musical creativity. *Music Educators Journal, 76* (9), 47–51.

Davis, B., Sumara, D. & Luce–Kapler, R. (2000). *Engaging minds*. Mahwah,NJ: Lawrence Erlbaum.

Forsythe, R. (1984). The development and implementation of a computerized preschool measure of musical audiation (Doctoral dissertation, Case Western Reserve University, 1984). *Dissertation Abstracts International, 45*, 2433A.

Gardner, H. (1991). *The unschooled mind: How children think and how school should teach*. New York: Basic Books.

Gardner, H. (1994). *Arts and human development: A psychological study of the artistic process*. New York: Basic Books.

Goodwin, L., Goodwin, W., & Garel, M. (1986). Use of microcomputers with preschoolers: A review of the literature. *Early Childhood Research Quarterly, 1*, 269–286.

Higgins, W. (1992). Technology. In R. Colwell (Ed.), *Handbook of research on music teaching and learning*. New York: Macmillan Publishing Company, 480–497.

Kafai, Y., & Resnick, M. (Eds.) (1996). *Constructionism in practice: Designing, thinking, and learning in a digital world*. Mahwah, NJ: Lawrence Erlbaum.

Kozerski, R. (1989). Personal computer microworlds for music composition and education (Doctoral dissertation, University of California, San Diego, 1988). *Dissertation Abstracts International, 50*, 17A.

Lee, Y. (1994). Teaching young children music fundamentals in a computer learning environment (Doctoral dissertation, Columbia University Teachers College, New York, 1994). *Dissertation Abstracts International, 55*, 150A.

MacGregor, R. (1992). Learning theories and the design of music compositional software for the young learner. *International Journal of Music Education, 20*, 18–26.

Meckley, W. (1985). The development of individualized music learning sequences for non–handicapped, handicapped and gifted learners using the LOGO Music Version computer language (Doctoral dissertation, University of Rochester, Eastman School of Music, 1985). *Dissertation Abstracts International, 45*, 190A.

Moore, B. (1989). Music thinking and technology. In E. Boardman (Ed.), *Dimensions of musical thinking*. Reston, VA: Music Educators National Conference. 33–34.

Nelson, G. (1998). Who can be a composer: New paradigms for teaching creative process in music. In S. Lipscomb (Ed.), *Fifth International Conference on Technological Directions in Music Learning* (pp. 61–66). San Antonio, TX: IMR Press.

Papert, S. (1980). *Mindstorms: Children, computers, and powerful ideas*. New York: Basic Books.

Papert. S. (1993). *The children's machine: Rethinking schools in the age of the computer*. New York: Basic Books.

Rodriguez, C. (1995). Children's perception, production and description of musical expression. (Doctoral dissertation, Northwestern University, Evanston, IL).

Scott–Kassner, C. (1992). Research on music in early childhood. In R. Colwell, (Ed.), *Handbook of research on music teaching and learning.* New York: Macmillan Publishing Company, 633–650.

Shade, D. & Watson, A., (1990). Computers in early education: Issues put to rest, theoretical links to sound practice, and the potential contributions of microworlds. *Journal of Educational Computing Research, 6* (4), 375–392.

Stauffer, S. (in press). Composing with computers: Meg makes music. *Bulletin of the Council for Research in Music Education.*

Sun, D. (1994). Teaching young children compositional concepts to enhance music learning in a computer learning environment (Doctoral dissertation, The Ohio State University, Columbus, 1994). *Dissertation Abstracts International, 54,* 2941A.

Technology counts: Schools and reform in the information age. *Education Week on the Web,* November 10, 1997. (http://www.edweek.org)

Thomas, R. (1970). Manhattanville music curriculum program: Final report. (Report No. BR6–1999) Purchase,NY: Manhattanville College of the Sacred Heart. (ERIC Document Reproduction Service No. ED 045 865)

Upitis, R. (1989). The craft of composition: Helping children create music with computer tools. *Psychomusicology, 8* (2), 151–162.

Webster, P. (1987). Conceptual bases for creative thinking in music. In J. Peery, I. Peery & T. Draper, (Eds.), *Music and child development,* New York: Springer–Verlag, 158–176.

Webster, P. (1989). Composition software and issues surrounding its use in research settings with children. *Psychomusicology, 8* (2), 163–169.

Webster, P. (in press). Computer–based technology and music teaching and learning. In R. Colwell, (ed.) *Handbook of research in music teaching and learning* (2nd ed). New York Oxford University Press.

White, D. (1989). The discrimination and categorization of pitch direction by the young child (Doctoral dissertation, University of Washington, 1989). *Dissertation Abstracts International, 50,* 3790A.

Williams, D. & Webster, P. (1999). *Experiencing music technology: Software, data, hardware* (2nd ed.). New York: Schirmer/Wadsworth.

An early version of this chapter was published in *Research Studies in Music Education, 11,* 1998, 61–76.

AFTERWORDS

A psychiatrist I know has a wonderful painting framed on his office wall; clearly the work of a young child, the characteristic broad tempera strokes depict a tadpole person—a huge oval head with legs and arms extending wildly from its sides, two dark dots for eyes, and a wobbly smile. The flying head is supported on the page with a decisive dictation: DEAR DR. RUDENTSTEIN, I HATE YOU, I HATE YOU, I HATE YOU. LOVE, AARON. Anyone who works with young children recognizes the sentiment, but how lovely that Aaron could speak up so plainly, and that Dr. Rudentstein could provide the means for that heartfelt expression, that relentless, dynamic and contradictory sense-making.

This book—this interactive conversation between teachers of young children, artists, and researchers—is important, perhaps urgent now, because it points to the possibility of a more robust understanding in practice of the role of the arts in early childhood education. We already know that the arts are universal, that they play a large part in every culture on earth, that they bring pleasure to people, and that children everywhere participate easily in a wide range of art forms. This smart, eclectic collection adds detail and description, arguing that culture and context matter, and that sense-making, the construction of meaning, is at the very heart of the matter.

We teachers begin by seeing our students, looking deeply at children as three-dimensional creatures, knowing them whole and in their complexity in order to teach them. Teachers must know that children are not empty vessels passively waiting to be filled, but are centers of energy-unruly sparks-in search of meaning. Knowing kids, seeing the child, includes inquiring into the contexts of their lives, their cultural surrounds, their family lore, their home arts.

What we want for children we must also recognize and have for ourselves. If we want our students to be readers, for example, we must be readers ourselves; if we want children to engage the arts as a away to interpret and reimagine or remake the world, we should struggle to engage the arts in our own way and at our own level. But we must always address our students as dynamic, in motion and in process, as teachers who are ourselves dynamic and in process as well. We teach our children, and we teach ourselves. We nourish our love of the world, of freedom and engagement, because that is what we want most for the young.

The African novelist Doris Lessing writes that at the age of twelve she knew a huge range of skills:

> how to set a hen,
> look after chickens
> and rabbits, worm dogs and
> cats, pan for gold
> cook, sew... make cream
> cheese and ginger beer, paint
> stenciled patterns on materials,
> make paper mache', walk on
> stilts and a lot else

L. Bresler and C.M. Thompson (eds.), The Arts in Children's Lives, 237–238.
© 2002 *Kluwer Academic Publishers. Printed in the Netherlands.*

Then she says pointedly, "That is real happiness, a child's happiness: being enabled to do and to make, above all to know you are valuable and valued."

That's what we want for every child.

William Ayers
Distinguished Professor of Education
Senior University Scholar
Director, Center for Youth and Society
University of Illinois Chicago

CONTRIBUTING AUTHORS

WILLIAM AYERS is a school reform activist, Distinguished Professor of Education, and Senior University Scholar at the University of Illinois at Chicago where he teaches courses in interpretive research, urban school change, and youth and the modern predicament. He is the founder of the Center for Youth and Society and founder and co-director of the Small Schools Workshop. A graduate of the Bank Street College of Education and Teachers College, Columbia University, he has written extensively about social justice, democracy and education. Author of many journal articles and co-editor of many anthologies on educational issues, his books include *A kind and just parent: The children of juvenile court* (Beacon Press, 1997), *The good preschool teacher* (Teachers College Press, 1989), and *To teach: The journey of a teacher* (Teachers College Press, 1993), A book which was named 1993 Book of the Year by Kappa Delta Pi and received the Witten Award for Distinguished Work in Biography and Autobiography in 1995. His latest book, *Fugitive days: A memoir*, was published by Beacon Press in 2001.

LIORA BRESLER is a Professor in the College of Education at the University of Illinois at Urbana-Champaign where she teaches graduate courses in the arts and aesthetic education and qualitative research methodologies and undergraduate courses in the Campus Honors Program. A graduate of Tel Aviv University and Stanford, Professor Bresler held positions in the Center for Instructional Research and Curriculum Evaluation (CIRCE) from 1987-1990 and The Bureau of Educational Research at the University of Illinois at Urbana-Champaign from 1992-1995, conducting research sponsored by the National Arts Education Research Center (1987-1990) and by the College Board/Getty Center for Education in the Arts (1996-1997). The author of more than fifty articles in scholarly journals, she has also contributed chapters to a number of edited books, including both the first and second volumes of the *Handbook for research in music teaching and learning* and serves on the editorial board of several major journals in the arts and education. With Tom Barone, she is a founding editor of the electronic *International journal for arts and education*. From 1995 - 2000, she served as guest editor for a series of issues of the *Arts education policy review* devoted to international concerns. Professor Bresler has been an invited keynote speaker at conferences on six continents, and has presented papers, seminars, and short courses in universities around the globe.

PATRICIA SHEHAN CAMPBELL is the Donald E. Peterson Professor of Music at the University of Washington, where she teaches courses at the interface of music education and ethnomusicology. She is the author of numerous books on music for children and on world musics in education, including *Songs in their heads*, *Lessons from the world*, *Music in cultural context*, and *Canciones de America Latina: De Su Origen a la Escuela*, and co-author of other music education texts, including a forthcoming series, *Global musics: Experiencing music, expressing culture*, written in collaboration with Bonnie Wade. Professor Campbell has lectured on children's musical involvement and musical cultures throughout the United States, and in Europe, Asia, Australia, New Zealand and South Africa. She directs the American Music Studies initiative and the Music-on-the(Yakama)-Rez project at the University of Washington, and currently serves as editor of the *College music symposium.*

LAURA H. CHAPMAN has taught children and adults in schools, community and museum programs, including undergraduate and graduate instruction at Indiana University, The Ohio State University, the University of Illinois at Urbana-Champaign, and The University of Cincinnati. Her paintings have been exhibited in museums and galleries in the South and Midwest. Among her many publications are a series of texts and resources for students and teachers in grades one through eight, a college text, *Approaches to art in education*, and a policy study, *Instant art, instant culture: The unspoken policy for American schools*, a Book of the Century in Education selection. As a colleague of Manuel Barkan in the 1960s, Dr. Chapman co-authored philosophical, theoretical, and practical guidelines for a federal curriculum development project in aesthetic education, encompassing the visual, literary, and performing arts. She has been an adviser to the National Endowment for the Arts, the National Assessment for Educational Progress, Educational Testing Service, the Research Program in the Arts and Humanities at the Central Midwestern Regional Educational Laboratory, and the J. Paul Getty Trust's Center for Education in the Arts. She has presented lectures, seminars, and workshops throughout the United States, and in Canada, Australia, England, Belgium, Germany and the Netherlands. Her work has been translated into modern Greek, Dutch, Chinese, and Arabic.

KIERAN EGAN was born in Ireland, educated in England and the United States, receiving his Ph.D. from Cornell University in 1972. His first academic position was at Simon Fraser University in British Columbia where he has remained ever since. He received the Graweyer Award in Education in 1991, and was elected to the Royal Society of Canada in 1993, the first person in education to be so honored. In 2000, Professor Egan was elected a Foreign Associate member of the U.S. National Academy of Education. In 2001, he was appointed to a Canada Research Chair in Education and won a Killam Senior Research Fellowship. The author of approximately a dozen books and more than 100 articles, Professor Egan's recent works include *Teaching as storytelling* (1989), *Imagination in teaching and learning* (1992), *The educated mind: How cognitive tools shape our understanding* (1997), *Children's minds, talking rabbits, and clockwork oranges* (1999) and *Building my Zen garden* (2000). A new book, *Getting it wrong from the beginning: Our progressivist inheritance from Herbert Spencer, John Dewey, and Jean Piaget*, will be published in 2002 by Yale University Press.

DONNA J. GRACE is an assistant professor in the College of Education at the University of Hawaii at Manoa where she teaches and conducts research in the areas of early childhood, language and literacy, qualitative research, critical literacy and media literacy. A former elementary school teacher, Professor Grace holds a bachelor's degree in political science from the University of California at Los Angeles, and graduate degrees in education from the Ontario Institute for Studies in Education at the University of Toronto and the University of Hawaii at Manoa. Her recent publications include an article in the journal, *Curriculum inquiry*, entitled, "We don't want no *haole* buttholes in our stories: Local girls reading the *Babysitters Club* books in Hawaii," an article entitled "An experimental approach to integrating mathematics and literacy through theme studies in teacher education,' in *Action in teacher education*, and chapters on media literacy research in *Teaching popular culture: Beyond radical pedagogy*, edited by David Buckingham (1998), and in *Finding a place for pleasure in the primary classroom*, edited by Joseph Tobin (1997).

KAREN HAMBLEN is professor of art education in the department of Curriculum and Instruction of Louisiana State University. She is author of research that has been published in journals and books in the fields of art education, general education, anthropology, philosophy, and sociology. Professor Hamblen received the Mary Rouse Award and the June King McFee Award, both from the Women's Caucus of the National Art Education Association (NAEA), as well as the Manuel Barkan Award and the *Studies in Art Education* lectureship from the NAEA. She served as Senior Editor of *Studies in Art Education* and on the editorial boards of several journals in art education, early childhood education, and social theory. She was Vice President of the art committee for the National Board for Professional Teaching Standards, and served as Visiting Scholar at the J. Paul Getty Institute for Education in the Arts in 1996-1997.

MINETTE MANS is an associate professor of performing arts at the University of Namibia. Her university teaching encompasses the fields of ethnomusicology, dance, music education, and instrumental music. She sits on various national and international committees, and serves as Namibia's Chief Examiner for Integrated Performing Arts (in the secondary schools), as a Commissioner for Music in the Schools and Teacher Education, a program sponsored by the International Society for Music Education, and as a member of the editorial boards of three international journals. She is actively involved in field research on the musics and dance of Namibia, resulting in a growing archive of CD ROM and video documentations. Professor Mans' publications include a book on Namibian musical instruments, and articles in a number of international journals and anthologies. She is currently completing two books as part of a projected series on ethnomusicology and education. Dr. Mans frequently presents workshops at local and international conferences designed to bring the musical traditions practiced by older Namibian musicians to public attention.

BRUNO NETTL moved to the United States from his native Czechoslovakia when he was nine years old. He studied at Indiana University and the University of Michigan, and accepted a teaching position at the University of Illinois at Urbana-Champaign in 1964; he is now Professor Emeritus of Music and Anthropology at the University of Illinois and continues to teach part time. Professor Nettl served as a visiting professor at a number of institutions, including Harvard University, the University of Washington, the University of Chicago, Northwestern University, the University of Texas, the University of Minnesota, Carleton College and Colorado College. He holds honorary doctorates from the University of Illinois, Carleton College, and the University of Chicago, and is a fellow of the American Academy of Arts and Sciences. Active principally in the field of ethnomusicology, Professor Nettl has done field research with Native American peoples, in addition to work in Iran and southern India. Past president of the Society for Ethnomusicology, Professor Nettl currently serves as editor of its journal, *Ethnomusicology*. Among his several books, the best known include *Theory and method in ethnomusicology* (1964), *The study of ethnomusicology* (1983), and his more recent publications, *Blackfoot musical thought: Comparative perspectives* (1989), *The radif of Persian music* (revised edition, 1992), and *Heartland excursions: Ethnomusicological perspectives on schools of music* (1995). He is the editor of the 1978 publication, *Eight urban musical cultures*, and of a volume of studies on improvisation, *In the course of performance* (1998).

SHIFRA SCHONMANN is a senior lecturer at the Faculty of Education, University of Haifa where she currently serves as Head of the Development and Administration of Educational Systems Department and Head of the Laboratory for Research in Theatre/Drama Education. The continuing focus of her teaching and research is theatre/drama education, curriculum planning, and teacher education. She has published numerous articles on the issues, as well as a book (in Hebrew) entitled *Theatre of the classroom*, and another, *Behind closed doors: Teachers and the role of the teachers' lounge*, co-authored with M. Ben-Peretz, and recently published by SUNY Press. Professor Schonmann formerly served as Chief Inspector of Theatre Education at the kindergarten through university levels, on behalf of the Israeli Ministry of Education, and is now the Chair of the National Committee for Youth and Children's Theatre. Her current research involves theatre education, children's theatre festivals and workshops on war and peace, the Bible as theatrical text, and health education through theatre.

SUE STINSON is professor of dance at the University of North Carolina at Greensboro where she serves as department head and teaches undergraduate teacher preparation courses and graduate courses in research and curriculum. Her scholarly work has appeared in a number of journals, including *Bulletin of the council for research in music education, Choreography and dance, Dance research journal, Design for the arts in education, Drama/dance, Educational theory, Impulse: The international journal of dance science, medicine, and education, Journal of curriculum and supervision, Journal of curriculum theorizing, Journal of physical education, recreation, and dance, Visual arts research, Women in performance*, and *Young children*, and as chapters in edited books on dance and curriculum. Since the mid-1980s, Professor Stinson's research has focused on how young people interpret their experiences in dance education.

CHRISTINE MARME THOMPSON is an associate professor of art education in the School of Visual Arts at the Pennsylvania State University where she teaches graduate and undergraduate courses in child art and pedagogy. Her current research focuses on art and art education in the early childhood years, with particular emphasis on unsolicited drawings as an element of children's culture. From 1985-2001, Professor

Thompson taught at the University of Illinois at Urbana-Champaign, and served as chair of the art education program there from 1996 on. She has presented numerous papers at conferences of the National Art Education Association and other national and international organizations, and her writing has appeared in academic journals and as chapters in a number of anthologies. Professor Thompson edited *The visual arts in early childhood learning*, published by the National Art Education Association in 1995, and is the author of *Art Image early years*, a five volume curriculum guide published in 1994. Since 1999, she has been the senior editor of *Visual arts research*, and she currently serves on the editorial boards of the *International journal of education and the arts*, *Studies in art education*, and the *Journal of aesthetic education*. From 1998-2000, she was a member of the Early Childhood and Middle Childhood Standards Committee of the National Board of Professional Teaching Standards. Dr. Thompson received the Mary J. Rouse Award from the Women's Caucus of the National Art Education Association in 1995, and the Marilyn Zurmuehlen Award from the Seminar for Research in Art Education in 1994.

DANIEL K. THOMPSON is an assistant professor of curriculum and instruction at The Pennsylvania State University, University Park, where he teaches classes in social studies education and curriculum, and supervises students engaged in early field experiences. He taught in public schools in the Midwestern United States for fifteen years, and at the University of Illinois at Urbana-Champaign for six years. His research interests include the use of historical fiction in teaching history to children, reader response theory, whole language teaching, and the vernacular theories of preservice teachers.

JOSEPH TOBIN is the Nadine Mathis Basha Professor of Early Childhood Education at Arizona State University. His publications include *Preschool in three cultures: Japan, China and the United States*, *Re-made in Japan: Everyday life and consumer taste in a changing society*, and, most recently, *Good guys don't wear hats: Children's talk about the media*.

DANIEL J. WALSH is an associate professor in the College of Education at the University of Illinois at Urbana-Champaign. He has been involved with the schooling of young children since the late '60s. He was a prekindergarten and kindergarten teacher for a dozen years. He attended graduate school at the University of Wisconsin-Madison, and has been a teacher educator and researcher since the early '80s. His research activities have ranged widely, but all are informed by the conviction that beliefs strongly influence practice: More specifically, educators' beliefs--particularly those implicit, deeply embedded beliefs that Bruner calls "folk beliefs"--create critical, but often ignored, contexts for children's development. His writings have appeared in a wide range of journals. His most recent book (with M. Elizabeth Graue), *Studying children in context: Theories, methods, and ethics*, was published by Sage.

PETER R. WEBSTER is the John Beattie Professor of Music Education and Music Technology at Northwestern University where he serves as coordinator of the music education program and teaches courses in research and measurement, the psychology of musical behavior, creative thinking in music, music technology, and multimedia. His published work includes book chapters and articles on technology, perception, preference, and creative thinking in music. He recently completed the co-editing of a large section in the forthcoming second edition of the *Handbook of research in music teaching and learning* and wrote a major chapter in that volume on music technology research. The current president of the Association for Technology in Music Instruction, Professor Webster serves on several editorial boards and is a frequent speaker at state, national, and international conferences and seminars. Professor Webster is co-author, with David Williams, of *Experiencing music technology* (second edition, 1999), the standard textbook and CD used in introductory college courses in music technology in the United States.

GRAHAM WELCH is the University of London Chair of Music Education at the Institute of Education and Head of the Institute's School of Arts and Humanities. He holds visiting professorships at the University of Sidney, University of Limerick, and the University of Surrey Roehampton. He is currently co-chair of the Research Commission of the International Society for Music Education (ISME) and Chair for the Society for Research in the Psychology of Music and Music Education. Professor Welch serves as a consultant on voice education to the National Center for Voice and Speech in Iowa, the Australian National Voice Center in Sydney, and the Swedish Voice Center in Stockholm, His research and publications embrace varied aspects of musical development and music education, teacher education, the psychology of music, and voice science, with his current research focusing on issues of gender in cathedral choirs, the place of music in special education, and mapping Asian music in the United Kingdom.

BRENT WILSON is professor in charge of the graduate program in art education at The Pennsylvania State University. His research interests include cultural influences on children's artistic development, cross-cultural studies of graphic narratives, and the assessment of art education programs. He has evaluated arts education programs for the President's Committee on the Arts and the Humanities, the Getty Institute for Education in the Arts, and served as consultant for the first National Assessment of Educational Progress in Art from 1967 - 1982. In 1987 Professor Wilson conducted research for the National Endowment for the Arts and drafted *Toward civilization* (1988), a report to the President and the Congress on the state of arts education in the United States. A Fellow of the National Art Education Association, he has received the Manuel Barkan Award and the Lowenfeld Prize in recognition of his contributions ot research, and was designated National Art Education Association Art Educator of the Year in 1989.

Name Index